THE JOY·OF BRIDGE™

by Audrey Grant and Eric Rodwell

Introduction by Easley Blackwood

Prentice-Hall Canada Inc., Scarborough, Ontario

To Dodi, Jeffrey and Sarah — Eric
My first book to my first born, Joanna — Audrey

Canadian Cataloguing in Publication Data
Grant, Audrey
   The joy of bridge
ISBN 0-13-511494-2 (bound)   ISBN 0-13-511486-1 (pbk.)

1. Contract bridge.   I. Rodwell, Eric.   II. Title.

GV1282.3.G73 1984   795.41'5   C84-099149-5

Prentice-Hall, Inc., Englewood Cliffs, *New Jersey*
Prentice-Hall International, Inc., *London*
Prentice-Hall of Australia, Pty., Ltd., *Sydney*
Prentice-Hall of India Pvt., Ltd., *New Delhi*
Prentice-Hall of Japan, Inc., *Tokyo*
Prentice-Hall of Southeast Asia (Pte.) Ltd., *Singapore*
Editora Prentice-Hall do Brasil Ltda., *Rio de Janeiro*

ISBN 0-13 511486-1 (pbk.)
ISBN 0-13-511494-2 (bound)

Production Editor: *Neil Gallaiford*
Design: *Joe Chin*
Cover: *Michael van Elsen*
Production: *Alan Terakawa*
Typesetting: *ART-U Graphics Ltd.*

Printed and bound in Canada by Imprimerie Gagné Ltée
1 2 3 4 5 IG 88 87 86 85 84

Contents

A. BIDDING WITHOUT COMPETITION

C. MORE ON BIDDING

D.   PLAY OF THE HAND

E.   APPENDIXES

Introduction

There is a story about a foursome for Social Bridge who needed a substitute for one of the members who was unavailable. The hostess called a friend, whom we shall call June Smith, and asked her to fill in. June protested that she knew absolutely nothing about Bridge. The hostess suggested that June come thirty minutes early so that said hostess could teach June all about it.

This story may amuse those of us who, after many years of play and study, are still learning new things about bridge. While thirty minutes may not be enough time, this book will help a brand new player learn to play an acceptable game more quickly and with less pain than any other method I know of. Teachers who wish to teach new players quickly will do well to consider this as a text book.

The Easley Blackwood cup awarded to the leading player in the Central Indiana unit of the American Contract Bridge League has been awarded to Eric Rodwell nine of the last ten years. He has gone on to become national champion in a number of events and world champion in 1981. Audrey Grant of Toronto must be considered one of the great teachers of the game, if the size of her classes and the success of her pupils are any criteria. These two have put their talent together to write this amazing book.

While the book seems aimed at the brand new player, those of much more experience will also find new ideas. Just to take one example, Bridge theorists have long known that the distribution count proposed in the Forties for hand evaluation is not equal to the task in the Eighties; Rodwell and Grant have new ideas about this problem which have the virtue of simplicity and accuracy.

Eric Rodwell is a fine theoretician, and Audrey Grant is an excellent teacher; together they have produced a book that will make a considerable and lasting contribution to the game.

Easley Blackwood

Preface

Welcome to the wonderful world of Bridge. This may seem like a rather odd—or even presumptuous—thing to say, especially since the game has the reputation of being demanding, time-consuming and hard to learn. Many people come to the game with reservations—don't feel they have 'card sense', fear they aren't smart enough to learn Bridge, or dedicated enough to play it well. But it is *still* the most popular card game in the world and with the help of *The Joy of Bridge*, you'll soon understand why.

As a player, Eric has seen the difficulties people have in learning and understanding bridge. As a competitor and theorist, he knows how tough it is to design and use systems effectively. After years of trying all the available books and manuals with students, Audrey finally decided she needed a SIMPLE method that WORKS—one that keeps the fun in the game and still gets good results.

Eric developed the system and Audrey designed and tested the teaching methods on over three thousand students. Many re-writes and revisions later, we have achieved our goal: simple, successful Bridge that is fun!

Bridge is a truly marvellous game that can be enjoyed at any level...if you learn it well. We have played against thousands of beginners and more experienced players and know that a successful teaching and playing method needs three things:
- A simple, effective method that stresses only what you need to know
- Bright teaching ideas that make the concepts 'come alive'
- Ideas to develop your curiosity, observation and sense of fun in the game

We have incorporated these ideas into *The Joy of Bridge* with both the beginner and the more experienced player in mind. Beginners will be playing comfortably sooner than they ever thought they could, and experienced players will share insights previously understood only by the game's top players.

Come with us...discover the joy of Bridge!

Audrey Grant
Eric Rodwell

Acknowledgments

We are especially indebted to David Lindop for his tireless help with this project. His suggestions and ideas were invaluable.

We are most grateful to Evelynn Funston for introducing us to Janice Whitford whose continuous support throughout the whole project was so important.

Connie MacDonald deserves our appreciation for the many hours she spent testing the material.

We wish to thank Neil Gallaiford and Dick Hemingway for an excellent job of editing and Joe Chin for his splendid design.

Finally, but most importantly, our thanks go out to the thousands of students who helped us test, revise and refine *The Joy of Bridge*.

How to Use the Book

Learning is an individual process, and everyone has different ways of approaching the same material. This book has been structured to allow each reader to approach it in the manner with which he is most comfortable.

Here is the way the book has been laid out:
- A. Bidding Without Competition
- B. Competitive Bidding
- C. More on Bidding
- D. Play of the Hand
- E. Appendixes

If you are learning by yourself, get comfortable and read the first three sections in order, doing the exercises at the end of each chapter. Take your time. *The Joy of Bridge* is the kind of book you will enjoy re-reading.

Although Section D—Play of the Hand is at the end of the book, it can be read at any time. It is suggested that you read it as soon as you are starting to actually play, whether with a group of fellow students or with friends who already play the game.

In the appendixes are a glossary, answers to exercises and a scoring summary.

The Joy of Bridge isn't just a book, it's an evening's entertainment. Invite your friends and neighbors in and use the book to learn the game together. You can do it! The book is designed to get you playing and to have fun doing it.

Exercises

The exercises at the end of each chapter help you assimilate the material in that chapter. Even if you do not have time to complete all the exercises, it is recommended that you try a few at the end of each chapter. You might try doing the odd numbered exercises the first time through and the even numbered exercises when you review the material at a later date. The answers to the exercises are contained in Appendix 2.

For the Curious

At the end of many chapters is additional material labelled 'For the Curious'. This material is not necessary to the understanding and enjoyment of the game but does provide the interested reader with more detail on some of the concepts developed earlier in the chapter.

It is suggested that this material be skipped if you are just learning the game. You can return to it after you have played a little and some questions arise in your mind. If you have already played Bridge before reading this book, you will probably find the material useful in reconciling the ideas presented in this book with those you may have previously encountered.

Play of the Hand

While it is easy and natural to discuss the Bridge auction in a textbook, the play of the hand is a little harder to follow on paper. You have to become familiar with the "feel" of the cards.

If you have played other card games of a similar nature (Whist, Hearts, Euchre), this presents no problems. Also, if you are working with a group of four or more, you can practice together.

If you are learning by yourself, you should still try to simulate the play as much as possible. Use a deck of cards and follow the exercises wherever possible, dealing out hands and playing all four of them yourself. Read the section on the Play of the Hand carefully and deal yourself some practice hands.

Variations from other Methods

The Joy of Bridge has been developed by World Champion, Eric Rodwell, using the most currently accepted methods modified by teaching expert Audrey Grant. As such, it represents the simplest and soundest system available for learning the game.

Nonetheless, there are many other methods available. You will meet partners who ask questions such as "Do you play the Short Club?" or "Do you play 5-card Majors?". While there is some good theory behind these variations, they are not necessary to play and enjoy the game. Wherever possible, we have included discussions of other methods in the 'For the Curious' material.

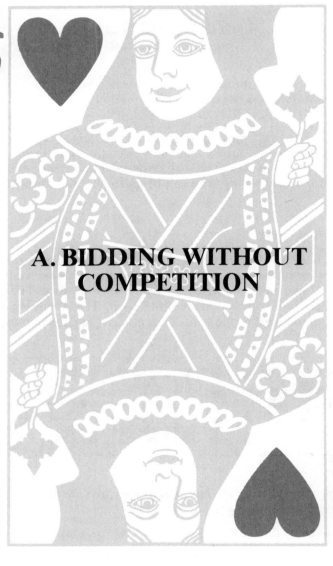

A. BIDDING WITHOUT COMPETITION

1

Getting Started

Bridge is one of world's most exciting games. It offers a way to meet new people, develop mental fitness and enjoy friendly competition. All you need are four people, a deck of playing cards, table and chairs, and a pencil and paper for scorekeeping. You can begin to play right now. Let's get started!

Choosing Partners

Bridge is a *partnership* game. The partnerships may be pre-arranged or chosen by a *cut* of the cards. To cut the cards, the cards are shuffled and spread face-down on the table. Each player draws one card. The result of the cut is determined by the *rank of the cards*. The Ace is the highest-ranking card, followed by the King, Queen, Jack, Ten down to the Two.

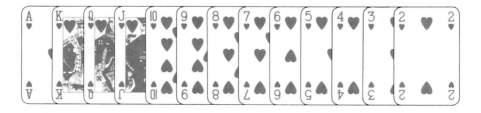

The two players drawing the *higher-ranking* cards are partners, playing against the players drawing the two *lower-ranking* cards.

A tie is broken by the *rank of the suits*:

     ♠   Spades...are highest
     ♥   Hearts
     ♦   Diamonds
     ♣   Clubs...are lowest

2

For example, suppose the following four cards are drawn:

The 'tie' between the two Kings is broken because Hearts rank higher than Diamonds. The player drawing the Ace of Spades plays with the player drawing the King of Hearts; the player drawing the King of Diamonds plays with the player drawing the Seven of Clubs.

Players sit around the table with the partners opposite one another.

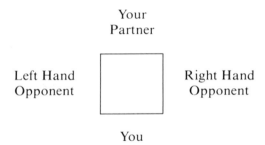

The players are often referred to by their geographic positions at the table: North, South, East and West. North and South are partners; East and West are partners.

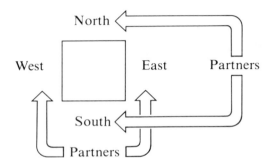

The Deal

Once partners are chosen and everyone is seated, the game is ready to begin. The player who drew the highest-ranking card in the cut is the *dealer* (if there was no cut for partners, cut for dealer). The cards are dealt face-down, one at a time, **clockwise** starting with the player on the dealer's left. When the dealer is finished, the *deal* is complete and all players will have thirteen cards.

Each player then picks up the cards in front of him, his *hand*, and sorts them into *suits*. It is convenient to alternate the red and black suits and to sort the cards in each suit by rank, with the highest cards on the left.

The Trick

The object of the *play* is to win as many tricks as possible. A *trick* consists of four cards, one contributed by each player. The cards are played one at a time moving clockwise around the table. The play to a trick looks like this:

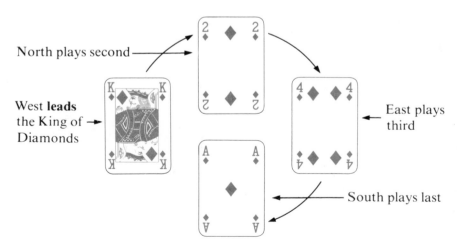

The play to each trick follows some rules:

- One of the players *leads* to the trick by placing any card he wishes face-up on the table.
- The other three players play a card, one at a time, in clockwise rotation.
- Players *follow suit* to the card led by playing a card in the same suit where possible.
- If a player cannot follow suit, he plays any card from another suit. This is called *discarding*.
- The trick is won by the highest card played in the suit that was led. The player winning the trick leads to the next trick.

In the above example, South wins the trick since the Ace of Diamonds is the highest card played. South leads to the next trick. Here is another example of a trick:

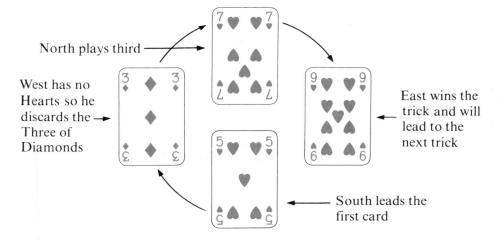

North plays third →

West has no Hearts so he discards the → Three of Diamonds

East wins the trick and will lead to the next trick

South leads the first card

Collecting Tricks

Traditionally, after a trick has been won, one of the players from the winning side collects the four cards, turns them face-down and stacks them in a neat pile at the edge of the table. It is easier to keep track of the number of tricks won or lost if only one player from each partnership collects tricks.

When the play of the hand is complete, there will have been thirteen tricks...some won by one partnership, some won by the other partnership.

The table will look something like this:

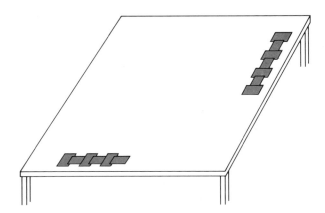

At the end of each hand, the cards are shuffled and the deal moves clockwise around the table.

In a learning environment, we recommend that the tricks be recorded in the same fashion used for Tournament Bridge. Instead of putting all four cards into a pile, each player keeps the card he played to the trick in front of him. After the winner of the trick has been determined, each player turns his card face-down, pointing in the direction of the side that won the trick. The table looks like this at the end of the hand:

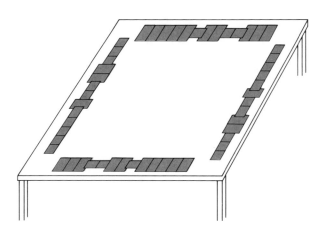

Playing the cards in this fashion allows each player to keep independent track of the tricks won and lost and has the advantage that each player can pick up the cards in front of him and re-construct his original hand. This is valuable if the players wish to discuss the hand afterward.

Trump and No Trump

A Bridge hand can be played either in No Trump or with a trump suit. In *No Trump* the highest card played in the suit led wins the trick. In a *trump suit*, one suit is 'wild' or trump. If a player cannot follow suit, a trump can be played. This is called *trumping* or *ruffing* the trick.

A trump beats any card in another suit. Sometimes more than one player will be unable to follow suit to the lead. If two or more players trump the trick, the highest trump played wins the trick. Here is an example of play to a trick when Spades are the trump suit:

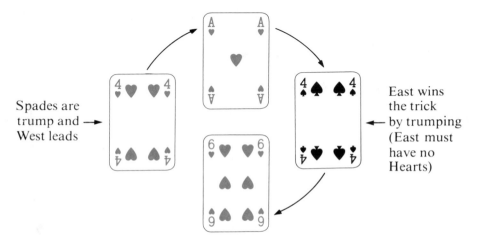

Spades are trump and West leads

East wins the trick by trumping (East must have no Hearts)

The Bidding

Before the play can commence, the trump suit must be determined. This is handled through a process called *bidding*. Bridge bidding is like an *auction*. The bidding starts with the dealer who suggests a trump suit, No Trump or refrains from bidding by saying "*Pass*".

At an auction, the bidding begins with a minimum dollar amount. To *open the bidding* in a Bridge auction, you must start with a commitment to take more than half the tricks. An *opening bid* is a commitment to take at least seven of the thirteen available tricks. The first player to open the bidding is called the *opening bidder* or *opener*.

The bidding usually starts at the *one-level*. But this one-level doesn't mean a commitment to take just one trick. The first six tricks are taken for granted. These six tricks are called the *book*. The one-level, then, is 6 + 1 = 7 tricks. If the bidding stopped at the three-level, it would be a commitment to try and win 6 + 3 = 9 tricks.

13	SEVEN-LEVEL
12	SIX-LEVEL
11	FIVE-LEVEL
10	FOUR-LEVEL
9	THREE-LEVEL
8	TWO-LEVEL
7	ONE-LEVEL

6
5
4
3
2
1

BOOK—the first six tricks

A player makes a *bid* by naming a *level* and a *denomination*, in that order:

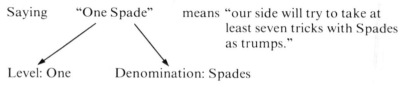

Saying   "One Spade"   means "our side will try to take at least seven tricks with Spades as trumps."

Level: One   Denomination: Spades

One-level: 6 + 1 = 7 tricks

Starting with the dealer, the bidding proceeds **clockwise** around the table. Everyone gets an opportunity to bid.

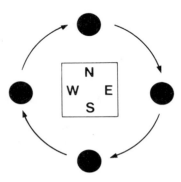

There will be ties. A player bids One Heart committing to seven tricks and wanting the trump suit to be Hearts; a member of the opposing pair is also willing to commit to seven tricks but wants to suggest that the trump suit be Spades. How can the tie be broken?

During the bidding, the suits are **ranked** just as they were during the cut. Clubs are the lowest, then Diamonds, Hearts and Spades. This means that a bid of One Spade outranks any other one-level bid in a suit. No Trump ranks higher than Spades. Thus, a bid of One No Trump is higher than any other one-level bid.

This is a good time to introduce you to the *bidding ladder* illustrated on the next page. You must always make a bid that is higher on the bidding ladder than the previous bid. For example, if a player has bid One Spade and you wish to change the trump suit to Clubs, you must bid Two Clubs since Spades rank higher than Clubs. This means you will have to commit to taking eight tricks.

The auction continues in a clockwise fashion with each player in turn making a bid that is higher than the previous bid or saying Pass. Players may bid more than once. An auction is finished when you hear "Going ...going...gone". In Bridge, when you hear "Pass...Pass...Pass", the auction is complete.

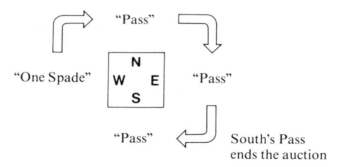

The last mentioned level and denomination becomes the final commitment, or *contract*. For example, if a player bids One Spade and this is followed by Pass, Pass, Pass, the contract is One Spade...a commitment to take 6 + 1 = 7 tricks, with Spades as the trump suit.

The Offense and the Defense

After the bidding is complete and the final contract has been determined, there will be two teams.

The *offense* will be the side that made the highest bid. They will have contracted to take a certain number of tricks. They will *make* their contract if they win at least the number of tricks contracted for.

The *defense* will try to prevent the offense from taking the promised number of tricks. If they do so, they will *defeat* or *set* the contract.

THE BIDDING LADDER

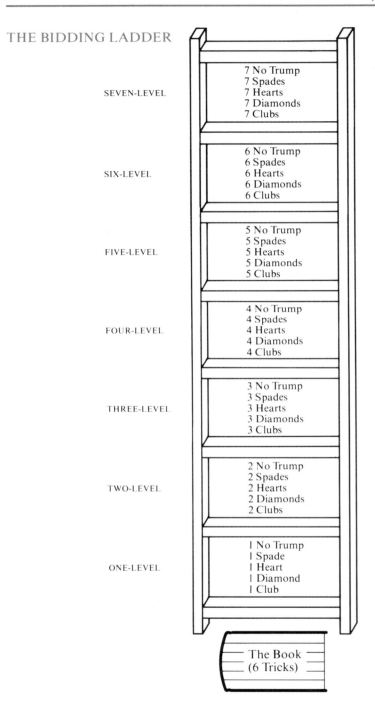

SEVEN-LEVEL

7 No Trump
7 Spades
7 Hearts
7 Diamonds
7 Clubs

SIX-LEVEL

6 No Trump
6 Spades
6 Hearts
6 Diamonds
6 Clubs

FIVE-LEVEL

5 No Trump
5 Spades
5 Hearts
5 Diamonds
5 Clubs

FOUR-LEVEL

4 No Trump
4 Spades
4 Hearts
4 Diamonds
4 Clubs

THREE-LEVEL

3 No Trump
3 Spades
3 Hearts
3 Diamonds
3 Clubs

TWO-LEVEL

2 No Trump
2 Spades
2 Hearts
2 Diamonds
2 Clubs

ONE-LEVEL

1 No Trump
1 Spade
1 Heart
1 Diamond
1 Club

The Book
(6 Tricks)

The Declarer and the Dummy

The player on the offensive team who first named the trump suit of the final contract is called the *declarer*. For example, if the final contract is Two Hearts, the player who bid Hearts first for the offensive team is the declarer. Here is an example of a complete auction:

WEST (Dealer)	NORTH	EAST	SOUTH
Pass	One Heart	One Spade	Two Hearts
Pass	Pass	Pass	

West is the dealer and says Pass. North opens the bidding One Heart, East bids One Spade and South bids Two Hearts. West, North and East each say Pass at their next opportunity. The auction is now complete. The final contract is Two Hearts and the declarer is North, the player who first bid Hearts for the offensive team. East and West will be the defense.

The declarer plays both the offensive team's hands...his and his partner's. The player on the declarer's left (defender) makes the *opening lead* by placing any card he wishes face-up on the table. Then declarer's partner puts his hand face-up on the table: this face-up hand is called the *dummy*. Declarer's partner is also referred to as the "dummy".

Declarer's partner (Dummy)

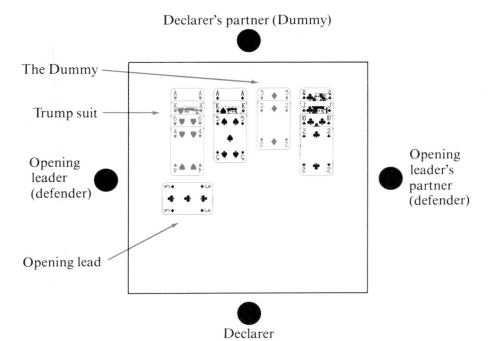

The Dummy

Trump suit

Opening leader (defender)

Opening leader's partner (defender)

Opening lead

Declarer

Some rules about the dummy hand:

- The dummy is put down **after** the opening lead has been made.
- The cards are put down in four rows, one row for each suit.
- If there is a trump suit, it goes on dummy's **right** (declarer's left).
- All plays from the dummy are made by the declarer (i.e. declarer plays both his and his partner's hand).
- When playing tournament style, declarer names the card to be played from the dummy (e.g. "Play the Ace of Spades") but his partner actually handles the dummy's cards.

A Play by Play Description

To illustrate how the play proceeds, let's look at an example. To make it easier to follow, we will assume that South is playing in a No Trump contract and eight tricks have already been played. There are only five cards left in each hand. South has won the previous trick and it is his turn to lead.

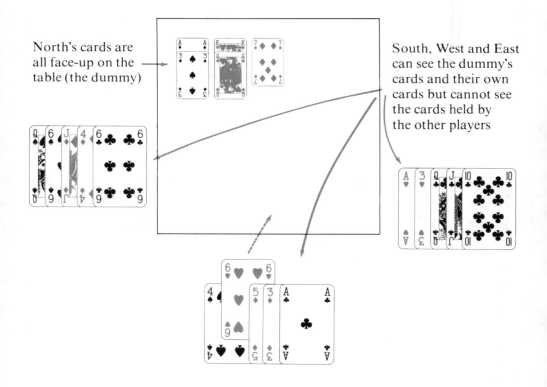

North's cards are all face-up on the table (the dummy)

South, West and East can see the dummy's cards and their own cards but cannot see the cards held by the other players

To follow the remaining play, it will help you to lay out the cards as illustrated and play them as described below.

South decides to lead the Six of Hearts. West, with no Hearts left, discards the Four of Diamonds. South tells North to play the Queen of Hearts from dummy and East wins the trick with the Ace of Hearts.

Having won the trick, it is East's turn to lead. East decides to lead the Queen of Clubs, South plays the Ace, West plays the Six and South tells North to discard dummy's Three of Spades. South has won the trick.

South now leads the Four of Spades, West plays the Six, the Ace is played from dummy and East discards the Three of Hearts. Dummy has won the trick.

South tells North to play dummy's King of Hearts. East discards the Ten of Clubs, South discards the Three of Diamonds and West has to decide whether to discard the Jack of Diamonds or the Queen of Spades. Since dummy is going to win the trick, West can see that dummy's remaining card, the Seven of Diamonds, must be led to the last trick. West discards the Queen of Spades.

On the last trick, dummy leads the Seven of Diamonds, East discards the Jack of Clubs, South plays the Four of Diamonds and West wins the trick with his carefully preserved Jack of Diamonds.

A few simple guidelines to help you get started are discussed in Chapter 24 — The Play of the Cards.

Summary

The four players divide themselves into two *partnerships*. The cards are dealt out clockwise and face-down. After each player has sorted his hand into suits, the *dealer* has the first chance to *bid* or *pass* and then, clockwise, each player in turn.

A bid must be higher on the *bidding ladder* than the bid that preceded it. The auction ends when a bid is followed by Pass, Pass, Pass. The partnership which made the highest bid becomes the *offense*. The offensive player who first mentioned the *denomination* of the final *contract* becomes the *declarer*. The other member of the offensive team is the *dummy*.

The player on the declarer's left makes an *opening lead* and the dummy puts his hand face-up on the table. Declarer plays both hands for the offense and tries to take enough *tricks* to make his contract. The *defense* works together to try and take enough tricks to defeat the contract.

Exercises (Answers to exercises are in Appendix 2)

For these exercises, you may find it helpful to use a deck of cards to follow along.

1) Four people sit down to play and cut the cards to determine partnerships. The cards drawn are the Four of Diamonds, the Ten of Hearts, the Queen of Hearts and the Ten of Clubs. Which players are partners? Which player is the dealer?

2) What is the highest-ranking card in the deck? What is the lowest-ranking card?

3) What is the maximum number of tricks that you and your partner could win in a single deal?

4) West leads the Five of Diamonds, North plays the Queen of Diamonds, East plays the Ace of Diamonds and South plays the Two of Diamonds. Who won the trick? Who will lead to the next trick?

5) In a No Trump contract, South leads the Jack of Hearts, West plays the Five of Hearts, North plays the Eight of Hearts and East plays the King of Spades. Who won the trick? Who will lead to the next trick?

6) In a contract with Spades as the trump suit, North leads the Six of Clubs, East plays the Five of Spades, South plays the Nine of Spades and West plays the Eight of Clubs. Who won the trick?

7) During an auction, you make a bid of Two Spades. How many tricks are you contracting to try and win? What would have to happen to make Two Spades the final contract?

8) Your opponents bid to a contract of Four Hearts. How many tricks will you have to take to defeat them?

9) The opponent on your right bids Three Spades. What is the lowest bid you can make to suggest Hearts as the trump suit?

10) You become the declarer in a contract of Three Clubs. Who will make the opening lead? Who will be the dummy? How many tricks will you have to take to make your contract?

2

Opening the Bidding
at the One-Level

How can you decide whether or not to open the bidding?

At an auction, you need to know how much money you have before you can start to bid. In Bridge, you have to know the value of your hand. The first step in bidding is to learn how to value your hand.

Hand Valuation

There are two factors which determine the trick-taking potential of a hand:

- **High cards** (Aces, Kings, Queens, Jacks)
- **Long suits** (A suit consisting of the Ace, King, Queen, Seven, Six and Three, for example, will often take five or six tricks.)

In the average hand, eight of the thirteen tricks are taken with the high cards and five tricks are taken with small cards. The *valuation* of a Bridge hand takes this into consideration. *Hand valuation* points are given for both *high cards* and for long suits.

HAND VALUE

HIGH CARD POINTS (HCPs)			LENGTH POINTS	
ACE	4 POINTS		5-CARD SUIT	1 POINT
KING	3 POINTS	+	6-CARD SUIT	2 POINTS
QUEEN	2 POINTS		7-CARD SUIT	3 POINTS
JACK	1 POINT		8-CARD SUIT	4 POINTS

The *high card points* (*HCPs*) are added to the *length points* to determine the total value, or *point count*, of the hand.

For example:

	High Card Points	Length Points
♠ A 7 3	4	0
♥ K 4	3	0
♦ J 9 8 6 3	1	1
♣ Q 7 3	2	0
	10 points +	1 point = 11 points

The value of this hand is 11 points. Another example:

	HCPs	Length Points
♠ 3	0	0
♥ K 9 7 6 5 2	3	2
♦ A Q 8 6 3	6	1
♣ A	4	0
	13 points +	3 points = 16 points

The value of this hand is 16 points.

Now let's see how we use hand value to determine whether or not to open the bidding.

Opening Bids Tell a Story

An opening bid tells your partner certain things about your hand:

Your *shape*—you open in No Trump or bid your longest suit

Your *strength*—opening bids show hands worth at least 13 points

The bidding is not just an auction, it is also an opportunity for you to describe your hand to your partner and for him to describe his hand to you. Through this "conversation" you decide what contract is best for you. The opening bid gives the partnership a good start in the bidding conversation. It is important to make the opening bid that best describes your hand.

First Priority—One No Trump

Some bids describe the hand in general terms while others are very specific. Whenever possible the bidder should try to describe the hand as precisely as possible. The most specific opening bid is **One No Trump**.

> ### RULE FOR A ONE NO TRUMP OPENING BID
>
> To open the bidding One No Trump you need:
> - A **balanced** hand and
> - 16, 17 or 18 Points

$$16 \mid 17 \mid 18$$

What is a *balanced hand*? It is a hand with no *voids* (zero cards in a suit), no *singletons* (one card in a suit) and no more than one *doubleton* (two cards in a suit). The following three hand patterns are balanced:

- A hand with one 4-card suit and three 3-card suits (this shape is described as '4-3-3-3'). For example:

♠ Q J 10 9   This hand has 17 points. The shape
♥ 8 7 6   is 4-3-3-3: four Spades, three Hearts,
♦ A K J   three Diamonds and three Clubs.
♣ A Q 7

- A hand with two 4-card suits, a 3-card suit and a doubleton (this shape is described as '4-4-3-2'). For example:

♠ 8 7   This hand has 18 points. The shape
♥ A K 8   is 4-4-3-2: four Clubs, four
♦ K Q J 4   Diamonds, three Hearts and
♣ A J 7 6   two Spades.

- A hand with one 5-card suit, two 3-card suits, and a doubleton (this shape is described as '5-3-3-2'). For example:

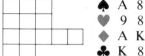

♠ A 8 7   This hand has 16 points. The shape
♥ 9 8 7   is 5-3-3-2: five Diamonds, three
♦ A K J 8 5   Spades, three Hearts and
♣ K 8   two Clubs.

Why do you want a balanced hand? With your opening bid of One No Trump, you are suggesting to partner that you would like to play the hand without a trump suit. You don't want to suggest this if you have one or two very long suits which would serve as trump suits or, conversely, if you are very short in one or more suits.

The following hands are examples of One No Trump opening bids:

5-3-3-2 shape   4-4-3-2 shape
18 points   16 points

Don't forget to open One No Trump if you have the right hand: 16 - 18 points and balanced *distribution*. Describing your hand accurately is one of the keys to good bidding.

Bids of One of a Suit

Most of the time, you will not have the hand for the specific One No Trump opening bid. Your second choice is to open *one of a suit*.

RULE FOR OPENING THE BIDDING WITH ONE OF A SUIT

With **13-21 points** (high card points plus length points), open the bidding with your **longest suit**.

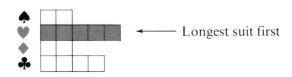

←——— Longest suit first

Why do you bid your *longest suit* first and not your strongest suit? The best trump suit for your side will usually be the suit in which your side has the most cards (and the opponents have the fewest). The best way to start the search for your side's longest suit is to tell partner which is your longest suit.

With less than 13 points, you do not open the bidding. Say Pass instead. Why do you need 13 points? This is part of the language of bidding, as we shall see. You are trying to exchange information with your partner to reach a contract that your side can make. For your partner to cooperate, he must have some idea of the minimum value of your hand when you open the bidding. This minimum is set at 13 points. Hands with 22 or more points will be discussed in the chapter on Powerhouse Hands.

Here are some examples. In each case, you have the first opportunity to open the bidding. What should you bid with each of these hands?

1) ♠ A K 8 7 6   2) ♠ 8 7   3) ♠ A K Q J   4) ♠ 8 7
   ♥ A 7 3   ♥ K J 9 8 7 6   ♥ 9 8 7 6 5 4   ♥ A K Q J
   ♦ Q 6   ♦ Q 8 7   ♦ A 5   ♦ Q J 9 8 7
   ♣ 9 8 3   ♣ 7 6   ♣ 8   ♣ A K

1) ONE SPADE. The hand contains 13 HCPs and 1 length point for the fifth Spade. The total point count is 14, enough to open the bidding. Although the hand is balanced, you do not have enough points to open the bidding One No Trump. Instead, choose the longest suit and open the bidding One Spade.

2) PASS. There are 6 HCPs and 2 length points for the 6-card Heart Suit, making a total of 8 points. This is not enough to open the bidding so you would say Pass.

3) ONE HEART. The hand contains 14 HCPs and 2 length points, enough to open the bidding. Although you have 16 points, you cannot bid One No Trump because your hand is not balanced. Choose the longest suit, even though it's weaker in high card strength, and open the bidding One Heart.

4) ONE DIAMOND. There are 20 HCPs and 1 point for length. This is a strong hand but it is still opened with one in a suit. You would open the bidding One Diamond.

Choosing Between Suits of Equal Length

Some hands have suits of the same length. There are some simple rules to guide you in choosing the appropriate suit with which to open the bidding. The reason for these rules is given in the "For the Curious" section at the end of the chapter.

RULE FOR OPENING THE BIDDING
WITH TWO 5- OR 6-CARD SUITS

With two 5-card or 6-card suits,
open the **higher-ranking** suit.

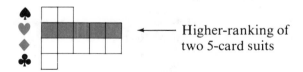

♠
♥ ←——— Higher-ranking of
♦   two 5-card suits
♣

For example:

1) ♠ 7   2) ♠ K 9 8 7 5
     ♥ Q 8 7 6 5   ♥ K 7
     ♦ A K Q 7 6   ♦ A K Q J 7
     ♣ J 8   ♣ 8

     1) ONE HEART. There are 12 HCPs and 2 length points, for a total of 14 points. You have two 5-card suits, so you should bid the higher-ranking suit. You would open the bidding One Heart.

     2) ONE SPADE. The hand contains 16 HCPs and 1 point for each of the 5-card suits, for a total of 18 points. With two 5-card suits, open with the higher-ranking suit...One Spade.

RULE FOR OPENING THE BIDDING WITH TWO 4-CARD SUITS

With two 4-card suits, open
the **lower-ranking** suit.

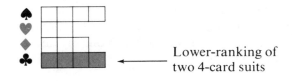

Lower-ranking of
two 4-card suits

RULE FOR OPENING THE BIDDING WITH THREE 4-CARD SUITS

With three 4-card suits, open
the **middle-ranking** suit.

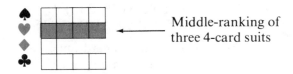

Middle-ranking of
three 4-card suits

Here are some more examples:

3) ♠ 9 8   4) ♠ K Q J 8
     ♥ A K Q 4   ♥ A 8 7 6
     ♦ K Q 9 8   ♦ J 7 6 4
     ♣ A J 6   ♣ A

3) ONE DIAMOND. There are 19 HCPs, enough to open the bidding. Although the hand is balanced, it has too many points to open the bidding One No Trump. With two 4-card suits, open the lower-ranking suit, Diamonds.

4) ONE HEART. With 15 points and three 4-card suits, bid the middle-ranking suit. Open the bidding One Heart.

Summary

The first step in the bidding process comes when you have an opportunity to *open the bidding*. To decide whether or not to open the bidding, *value* your hand.

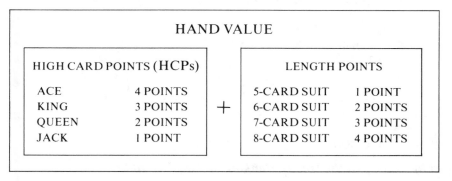

HAND VALUE

HIGH CARD POINTS (HCPs)			LENGTH POINTS	
ACE	4 POINTS	+	5-CARD SUIT	1 POINT
KING	3 POINTS		6-CARD SUIT	2 POINTS
QUEEN	2 POINTS		7-CARD SUIT	3 POINTS
JACK	1 POINT		8-CARD SUIT	4 POINTS

Add your *high card points (HCPs)* to your *length points* to determine the value of your hand and decide whether or not to open the bidding.

OPENING THE BIDDING AT THE ONE LEVEL

- With less than 13 points, Pass.
- With 13 to 21 points*:
  — Open the bidding One No Trump when you have 16 - 18 points and a balanced hand
  — Otherwise, open the bidding at the one-level in your longest suit.
- If you have a choice of suits:
  — Bid the higher-ranking of two 5-card (or 6-card) suits
  — Bid the lower-ranking of two 4-card suits
  — Bid the middle-ranking of three 4-card suits

---

* What to do with hands of 22 or more points is discussed in Chapter 21.

Exercises

1) You are the dealer and therefore have the opportunity to bid first. What would you bid with the following hands?

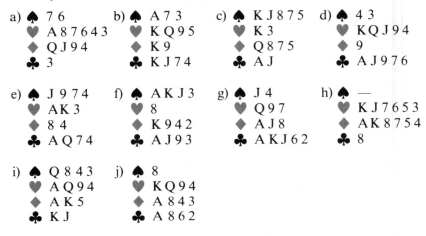

a) ♠ 7 6
   ♥ A 8 7 6 4 3
   ♦ Q J 9 4
   ♣ 3

b) ♠ A 7 3
   ♥ K Q 9 5
   ♦ K 9
   ♣ K J 7 4

c) ♠ K J 8 7 5
   ♥ K 3
   ♦ Q 8 7 5
   ♣ A J

d) ♠ 4 3
   ♥ K Q J 9 4
   ♦ 9
   ♣ A J 9 7 6

e) ♠ J 9 7 4
   ♥ A K 3
   ♦ 8 4
   ♣ A Q 7 4

f) ♠ A K J 3
   ♥ 8
   ♦ K 9 4 2
   ♣ A J 9 3

g) ♠ J 4
   ♥ Q 9 7
   ♦ A J 8
   ♣ A K J 6 2

h) ♠ —
   ♥ K J 7 6 5 3
   ♦ A K 8 7 5 4
   ♣ 8

i) ♠ Q 8 4 3
   ♥ A Q 9 4
   ♦ A K 5
   ♣ K J

j) ♠ 8
   ♥ K Q 9 4
   ♦ A 8 4 3
   ♣ A 8 6 2

For the Curious

Why You Open the Higher-Ranking of Two 5-Card Suits

As you will see in later chapters, the opening bid is just the start of the auction. As the auction progresses, opener describes his hand further so that the partnership can determine a suitable final contract. With two 5-card suits, opener will usually want to tell his partner about both of them during the auction so that his partner can choose an appropriate trump suit. Opener must consider the most economical way to do this.

Suppose opener has the following hand:

♠ A J 7 5 3
♥ A K 10 9 5
♦ 8 5
♣ 10

If he starts the auction with the lower-ranking suit, Hearts, the auction might continue:

OPENER	OPENER'S PARTNER
One Heart	One No Trump
Two Spades	?

At this point, opener's partner will often have to choose between Hearts and Spades as the trump suit. If he prefers Spades, he can say Pass and the final contract will be Two Spades…an eight trick contract. However, if he prefers Hearts, he will have to go to Three Hearts…a nine trick contract.

If, instead, opener starts with the higher-ranking suit, Spades, the auction might continue:

OPENER	OPENER'S PARTNER
One Spade	One No Trump
Two Hearts	?

If opener's partner prefers Hearts, he can say Pass and the final contract will be Two Hearts…an eight trick contract. If he prefers Spades, he can bid Two Spades…also an eight trick contract.

Thus, if opener bids the higher-ranking suit first, his partner can make the choice between trump suits at the two-level. If opener bids the lower-ranking suit first, his partner may have to go to the three-level to show which suit he prefers.

The above example is only one of the many ways in which the auction might continue. However, experience has shown that, in general, it is more economical to open the higher-ranking of two 5-card suits.

Why You Open the Lower-Ranking of Two 4-Card Suits

As you will see in later chapters, opener's partner bids a 4-card suit at the one-level provided that there is sufficient room (on the Bidding Ladder). By bidding the lower-ranking of your 4-card suits first, you give the partnership the best opportunity of finding a suitable trump suit. If your partner doesn't mention your second suit at the one-level, then you do not plan to make that suit trump. Instead, you will tend toward playing the hand in No Trump.

For example, suppose opener has the following hand:

♠ A K 10 7
♥ K 10 9 5
♦ K 8 5
♣ 10 2

If he starts the auction with the higher-ranking suit, Spades, the auction might continue:

OPENER	OPENER'S PARTNER
One Spade	One No Trump
?	

At this point, opener knows his partner doesn't like Spades but does not know if he likes Hearts. His partner may well have a Heart suit but, as you will see later, may not have enough points to bid it at the two-level. If opener now bids Two Hearts, he might find that his partner doesn't like either suit. Now the partnership might get too high on the Bidding Ladder while trying to find a suitable final contract.

If, instead, opener starts with the lower-ranking suit, Hearts, the auction might continue:

OPENER	OPENER'S PARTNER
One Heart	One No Trump
?	

Here opener knows that his partner doesn't like Hearts and also knows that his partner doesn't have four or more Spades since he didn't bid One Spade. Thus opener can be much more confident that One No Trump is a suitable final contract and can say Pass.

There are many possible sequences after opener starts the bidding with one of his two 4-card suits. However, experience has shown that the auction will continue much more smoothly if opener starts with the lower-ranking of his two 4-card suits. This will be clearer when you start to look at what opener's partner does after an opening bid of one in a suit (Chapter 7).

The reason for opening the middle-ranking of three 4-card suits is similar to the above argument. Opening the middle suit ensures that opener will always have a second suit available to bid if partner doesn't like the first suit he mentions. This will be clearer after you have read Chapters 8 and 9.

5-Card Majors and Better Minors

Suppose opener has the following hand:

> ♠ J 9 7 4
> ♥ A K 4 3
> ♦ A J 7
> ♣ 10 9

According to the guidelines laid out earlier in the chapter, the opening bid should be One Heart. As you will see later, this is perfectly acceptable since partner will not usually agree to play with Hearts as trumps unless he also has four of them.

Some systems suggest that you need at least **five** cards in a *Major* suit (Hearts or Spades) before you can open the bidding in that suit. How would you handle the above hand? Rather than opening a 4-card Major suit, you would open the best 3-card *Minor* suit (Clubs or Diamonds). On the above hand, you would open One Diamond. This is referred to as bidding the "Better Minor". While there are some sound reasons for doing this, there is no need for beginning players to use such methods.

Some players open such hands One Club...the "Short Club" or "Convenient Club". As you can see from the above hand, this distorts the picture of the hand that opener is trying to paint for his partner.

3

Objectives

The object of the game is to win as many tricks as you can because this is the way to score *points*. If you are the offensive team, you score points by taking enough tricks to make your contract. If you are the defensive team, you score points by taking enough tricks to defeat the opponents' contract.

The simplified Joy of Bridge method of scoring is discussed below. The traditional method of Rubber Bridge scoring is outlined at the end of the chapter in "For the Curious".

Scoring

Once you have cut the cards to determine the partnerships and the dealer, you are ready for a *round* of Bridge. A round of Bridge consists of four deals (or hands), each player dealing once in turn. The end of a round is the natural breaking point in the game of Bridge. The scores for both sides are totalled to determine the winner. Then you can play another round with the same partner, cut for new partners, stop for a snack or end the session.

Points won are recorded on a *score sheet* divided by a vertical line into two columns headed 'WE' and 'THEY'. Points won by you and your partner go under WE and points won by your opponents go under THEY.

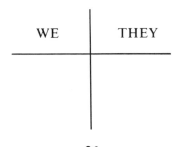

You get a *trick score* for the tricks you bid and make plus a *bonus* for making your contract. You get a bonus called a *penalty* for defeating the opponents' contract.

Trick Score

A partnership scores points for tricks bid and made (in excess of book) when it is the offensive team...the team that won the auction. Points are scored as follows:

TRICK SCORE

- 20 points per trick bid and made in Diamonds or Clubs...
  the *Minor suits*
- 30 points per trick bid and made in Spades or Hearts...
  the *Major suits*
- 40 points for the first trick bid and made in No Trump and
  30 points for each additional trick bid and made in No Trump

---

For example, your side bids to a contract of Two Hearts, committing to take eight tricks (6 + 2 = 8) with Hearts as the trump suit. If, when the hand is played, you win eight tricks, you receive a trick score of 30 points for each trick bid and made...30 + 30 = 60 points. You do not get any points for the first six tricks you made.

Similarly, if you bid and make a contract of Three No Trump, you receive a trick score of 100 points (40 + 30 + 30).

Game

If you bid and make a contract worth a trick score of 100 or more points, you are said to have won a *Game*. When you win a Game, you earn a large bonus in addition to your trick score. Your primary goal, therefore, should be to win Games. A Game can be *scored* by bidding and making the following contracts:

GAME CONTRACTS

Game in No Trump	=	Three No Trump (9 tricks)
		40 + 30 + 30 = 100
Game in a Major Suit	=	Four Hearts or Four Spades (10 tricks)
		30 + 30 + 30 + 30 = 120
Game in a Minor Suit	=	Five Clubs or Five Diamonds (11 tricks)
		20 + 20 + 20 + 20 + 20 = 100

Part-Game

A contract which is worth less than 100 points is called a *part-game* (*part-score*). You earn a small bonus for Part-Game. For example:

Contract	Trick Score
A Part-Game of Two No Trump:	40 + 30 = 70
A Part-Game of Two Diamonds:	20 + 20 = 40

Vulnerability

The exact size of bonuses for making or defeating contracts is affected by something called the *vulnerability*. If your side is **vulnerable**, the bonuses are higher than if your side is **not vulnerable**. Which side is vulnerable on any deal is determined as follows.

Neither side is vulnerable during the first hand of the round. Both sides are vulnerable during the last hand of the round. For the second and third hands, the dealer's side is vulnerable and the other side is not vulnerable.

VULNERABILITY DURING A ROUND OF BRIDGE

First hand — Neither side vulnerable
Second hand — Dealer's side vulnerable
Third hand — Dealer's side vulnerable
Fourth hand — Both sides vulnerable

For example, suppose North wins the cut to determine the dealer. Neither side is vulnerable for the first hand. East deals the second hand, making his side vulnerable and the North-South partnership not vulnerable. South deals the third hand and his side will be vulnerable and East-West will be not vulnerable. When West deals the last hand of the round, both sides are vulnerable.

Game and Part-Game Bonuses

All scores other than those for tricks bid and made are called *bonuses*. Bonuses are awarded for bidding and making contracts as follows:

- 500 points for bidding and making a vulnerable Game
- 300 points for bidding and making a not vulnerable Game
- 50 points for bidding and making a Part-Game vulnerable or not vulnerable

For example, if you deal and your side bids to a contract of Four Hearts on the first hand of the round and makes it, you receive the following score:

Trick Score (30 + 30 + 30 + 30)	120
+ Bonus for a not vulnerable Game	300
= Total score	420

On the second hand, if your opponents bid and make a contract of Three Clubs, they receive the following score:

Trick Score (20 + 20 + 20)	60
+ Bonus for a Part-Game	50
= Total score	110

On the third hand your partner deals, making your side vulnerable. If you bid and make a contract of Three No Trump, you receive the following score:

Trick Score (40 + 30 + 30)	100
+ Bonus for a vulnerable Game	500
= Total score	600

Overtricks

If you make more tricks than you contract for, the trick score for the extra tricks, the *overtricks*, is added to your score. For example, if you bid Two Spades and take ten tricks (make two overtricks), your score is as follows:

Trick Score (30 + 30)	60
+ Bonus for a Part-Game	50
+ Bonus for overtricks (30 + 30)	60
= Total score	170

Notice that you do **not** receive a Game bonus, only a Part-Game bonus, although you took enough tricks for a Game contract in Spades. The Game bonus is only awarded if you both **bid** and make a Game contract.

Since the bonus for Game is considerably bigger than that for Part-Game, you should **always try to bid to a Game contract if you think there is a reasonable chance to make it**. The next few chapters will focus on how you decide whether or not your side can make a Game contract.

Undertricks

What happens when you bid to a contract and don't take the required number of tricks? Then your contract has been defeated; you have *gone down* in your contract. The opponents get a bonus called a penalty for every trick (every *undertrick*) by which your contract is defeated. The penalty depends on the vulnerability (i.e. whether the defeated side was not vulnerable or vulnerable) as follows:

- Vulnerable: 100 points per undertrick
- Not vulnerable: 50 points per undertrick

For example, if you are not vulnerable and bid to a contract of Four Spades and only take seven tricks (you go down three), your opponents receive a score of 150 points (50 + 50 + 50). If you are vulnerable, they get 300 points (100 + 100 + 100).

Slam Bonuses

Other ways to get bonuses are:

- Bidding and making a *Small Slam* — a six-level contract (12 tricks)
- Bidding and making a *Grand Slam* — a seven-level contract
  (all 13 tricks)

Appendix 3 gives a summary of scoring if you need to know the value of a particular bonus.

Summary

The object of the game is to score more points than your opponents by:

1) Making the contracts you bid

TRICK SCORE

- 20 points per trick bid and made in Diamonds or Clubs...
  the *Minor suits*
- 30 points per trick bid and made in Spades or Hearts...
  the *Major suits*
- 40 points for the first trick bid and made in No Trump and
  30 points for each additional trick bid and made in No Trump

---

2) Getting a bonus for bidding and making a Part-Game, Game or Slam:
   (bonuses are discussed in Appendix 3)

GAME CONTRACTS

- Game in No Trump = Three No Trump (9 tricks)
- Game in a Major Suit = Four Hearts or Four Spades (10 tricks)
- Game in a Minor Suit = Five Clubs or Five Diamonds (11 tricks)

GAME AND PART-GAME BONUSES

- 500 points for bidding and making a *vulnerable* Game
- 300 points for bidding and making a not *vulnerable* Game
- 50 points for bidding and making a Part-Game vulnerable or not vulnerable

---

3) Defeating your opponents' contracts

PENALTIES

- Vulnerable: 100 points per trick
- Not vulnerable: 50 points per trick

Exercises

The exercises below deal with scoring. Some of the exercises are quite challenging, so don't worry about how many questions you get right.

1) The opponents deal first. On the first hand of the round no one is vulnerable. You bid and make a contract of Four Spades. What is your trick score? What is your bonus?

2) On the second hand, your opponents bid to a contract of Four Hearts and make it. Which side is vulnerable? How many points do they get?

3) On the third hand, you bid and make a contract of Two Diamonds. What is your trick score? Your bonus?

4) On the fourth hand, your opponents bid a contract of Four Spades and make only nine tricks. What is your bonus?

5) Draw up a score sheet showing the final result of the contracts bid and made in Exercises 1, 2, 3 and 4. Which side won the round?

6) If you want to make Spades the trump suit, what contract must you bid to score enough points for Game? Why might you want to bid higher? What danger is there in bidding higher?

7) Suppose your side could take exactly nine tricks either in a No Trump contract or in a contract with Clubs as trumps. Which contract would be preferable? Why?

8) Your opponents are vulnerable and bid to a contract of Two Spades. How many tricks must your side win to defeat the opponents' contract? What will happen if you defeat the contract by one trick?

9) On the first hand of a round, you bid to a contract of Two Hearts and make nine tricks. How many points do you score? What happens if you only make seven tricks?

10) You and your partner have bid and made a vulnerable Four Heart contract. How many tricks did you take? How many tricks did the opponents take? How many points did you score?

For the Curious

Rubber Bridge Scoring

The method of scoring described in this chapter is similar to that used in tournament play where each hand is scored individually. A more traditional form of scoring is often used in home-style play or "Rubber Bridge". It is substantially more complicated than Joy of Bridge scoring.

In Rubber Bridge, points are recorded on a score sheet which looks like a cross (see below). The vertical line still divides the sheet into a WE side and a THEY side. The horizontal line is appropriately called *the line*. Trick scores for contracts bid and made go *below the line*; bonuses go *above the line*.

The *rubber* (the counterpart of a round in Joy of Bridge scoring) continues until one side has won two Games. No bonus is awarded for making Part-Game or Game, only for winning the rubber. In addition to winning a Game by bidding to a contract worth 100 or more points, a Game can be won by bidding and making two or more Part-Game contracts that are each worth less than 100 points but whose total is 100 points or more. When one partnership wins a Game, a horizontal line is drawn beneath the scores of both sides indicating that a new Game is starting. Any previous Part-Games do not count toward the next Game.

Vulnerability in Rubber Bridge is determined as follows. When either side wins a Game, it is said to be vulnerable. Thus, when the rubber begins, neither side is vulnerable. When one side wins a Game, it becomes vulnerable while the other side is not vulnerable. If both sides win a Game, both sides are vulnerable. Whether or not a side is vulnerable affects the score for bonuses received above the line.

For example, the bonus for winning the rubber depends on whether or not the opponents have won a Game. If you win the rubber two Games to none, you get a bonus of 700 points. If you win the rubber two Games to one, you only get a bonus of 500. Here is an example of the scoring for a complete rubber:

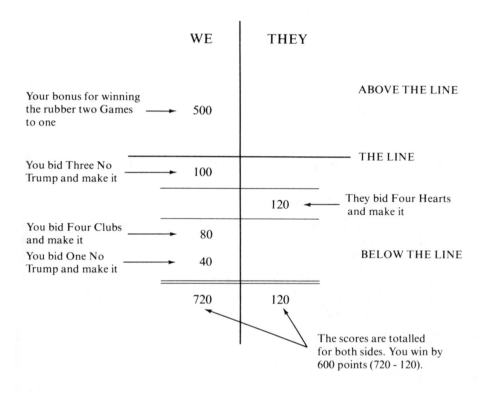

The scores are totalled for both sides. You win by 600 points (720 - 120).

4

The Captain

What do you do if your partner opens the bidding?

The Language of Bidding

Once either partner opens the bidding, the partnership, through the *language of bidding*, exchanges enough information to come to a consensus which solves two problems:

- HOW HIGH should the contract be (Part-Game, Game or Slam)?
- WHERE should the contract be played (Clubs, Diamonds, Hearts, Spades, No Trump)?

Every bid carries two messages:

- Level: the number of tricks the bidder is willing to try to take for the privilege of naming the denomination
- Denomination: the trump suit (or No Trump) the bidder wants to suggest

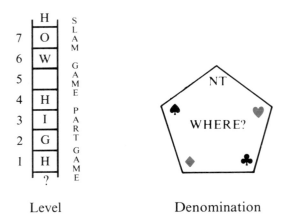

Level   Denomination

A bid at the one-level is a commitment to take 6 (Book) + 1 = 7 tricks. The dealer has the first opportunity to start the bidding. He can make an opening bid to suggest a denomination and level or he can Pass. If he Passes, then the privilege of opening the bidding goes to the player on the dealer's left. The bidding proceeds clockwise until someone can open the bidding.

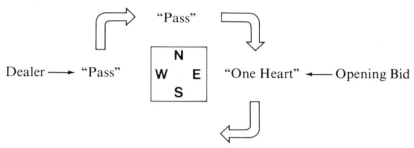

If all players say Pass, then the hand is *passed out* and another hand is dealt by the same dealer.

If someone opens the bidding, the auction continues clockwise around the table with each side bidding up the ladder for the privilege of playing the contract. The bidding ends when Pass, Pass, Pass is heard.

Let's assume for now that your side opens the bidding and that the opponents Pass throughout the auction. We will look at what happens when both sides are in the auction in the chapters on competitive bidding.

Suppose your partner opens the bidding and the opponent on your right Passes. Your partner's opening bid tells you something about his strength and shape. What now?

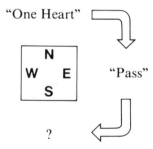

The Responder

The partner of the opening bidder is called the *responder*...he *responds* to his partner's opening bid. The responder works with the opening bidder to get to a final contract.

Opening Bidder

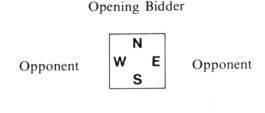

Opponent   Opponent

Responder

The Captain

Bridge is a partnership game. Throughout the auction you and your partner work together, through your bidding, to exchange information so that you can settle on a reasonable final contract. To work together successfully, the crew of a ship needs a captain; so does a Bridge partnership. The *captain* is in charge of directing the partnership to its final contract. He chooses the level and denomination of the contract.

Which player should be the captain? In a Bridge game, captaincy changes with each hand. The player who knows more about both hands, his own hand and his partner's, becomes the captain because he will be better able to 'add up' the assets of the *combined hands* to determine the best contract.

Which player knows more... opener or responder? After the opening bid has been made, the responder knows more about the combined hands. For example, consider the situation when opener bids One No Trump:

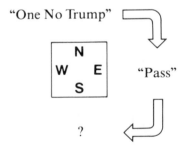

A One No Trump opening bid is very descriptive... a balanced hand with 16, 17, or 18 points:

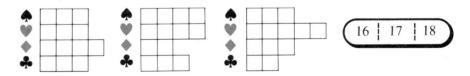

Which player knows more about the combined partnership assets?

ONE NO TRUMP OPENER...
- knows what is in his own hand
- knows nothing about partner's hand

PARTNER OF THE ONE NO TRUMP OPENER...
- knows what is in his own hand
- knows that partner has a balanced hand with 16, 17, or 18 points

The partner of the opener knows more about the combined partnership assets and this qualifies him as the captain. Thus:

RESPONDER IS CAPTAIN

Responder is in charge of directing the partnership to its final contract.

The Describer

Opener has a job also. As *describer* he describes his hand to responder, the captain. Thus:

OPENER IS DESCRIBER

The opening bid is the first step in this process. With later bids, opener can finish his 'story'.

The Captain's Two Decisions

The captain determines the final contract. A contract has two parts:

1. The **level** — the number of tricks the partnership contracts to take; this decision is called:

HOW HIGH — How high should we bid?

7	H O	S L A M
6	W	
5		G A M E
4	H	
3	I	P A R T
2	G	G A M E
1	H	
	?	E

Level

2. The **denomination** — No Trump or the trump suit that the partner-ship chooses; this decision is called:

WHERE — Where should we play the hand?

How does the captain make these decisions?

The First Decision: HOW HIGH

There are seven levels... one through seven. Some levels are more attractive than others. There are big bonuses for Game, Slam, and Grand Slam contracts.

The seven levels can be put into four different groups: Grand Slam, Slam, Game and Part-Game. These bonus levels are shown on the Bidding Ladder at the end of the chapter.

Although Slam bidding is one of the most interesting and exciting aspects of Bridge, we will leave it for a later chapter. For now, we'll consider only the two most common choices: Game and Part-Game.

Should you bid Part-Game or Game?

It is now time to tie hand value into trick-taking potential. You need to know how many points in the combined partnership hands are needed in order to take nine tricks in No Trump, ten tricks in Hearts or Spades, or eleven tricks in Clubs or Diamonds. These are the contracts that make up the Game bonus level.

If you and your partner hold all the high card points (40), you would expect to take all thirteen tricks. How many points would you need to take nine tricks in No Trump or ten or eleven tricks with a trump suit?

Experience has demonstrated that:

---

26 COMBINED POINTS OFFER A REASONABLE PLAY
FOR A GAME CONTRACT
IN HEARTS OR SPADES (the Major suits) OR IN NO TRUMP

29 COMBINED POINTS OFFER A REASONABLE PLAY
FOR A GAME CONTRACT
IN DIAMONDS OR CLUBS (the Minor suits)

Therefore, any time the captain realizes that there are at least 26 combined points, he directs the partnership to a Game contract in the Major suits or in No Trump. Only when the captain knows that there are 29 or more combined points does he consider directing the partnership to a Game contract in the Minor suits.

If you ignore the rare cases when the captain is interested in directing the partnership to a Game contract in a Minor suit, you can decide between Game and Part-Game by asking the following question:

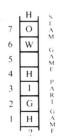

THE KEY QUESTION FOR DECIDING HOW HIGH

Do we have 26 combined points?

If the answer is YES: Play in a Game contract.
If the answer is NO: Play in a Part-Game contract.

The captain answers HOW HIGH by adding his points to the points that opener has promised. Here is an example:

Partner opens the bidding with One No Trump (16 - 18 points, balanced). As responder, HOW HIGH would you bid with the following hand?

♠ A 8 7
♥ K 6 5
♦ Q 7 6 5
♣ J 5 4

You have 10 points. How many combined points do you have?... Add your points to opener's promised points:

Your points	10	10
+ Partner's points	16 (at least)	18 (at most)
= Combined points	26 (at least)	28 (at most)

Your thought process should be something like this: "We have at least 26 points between us...enough for Game. HOW HIGH is answered...we will play the hand in a Game contract. When I decide WHERE to play the hand, I'll know what the final contract should be." Another example:

Partner opens One No Trump. HOW HIGH would you bid with the following hand?

♠ A 8
♥ J 7 6 4
♦ 8 6 5
♣ J 9 8 7

You have 6 points in your hand. How many combined points are there? Are there enough for Game?

6 + 16 = 22 (the **least** you can have between you)

6 + 18 = 24 (the **most** you can have between you...still not enough).

There are 22 - 24 combined points...not enough for Game.

Your thoughts should be: "We have at most 24 points between us...not enough for Game. HOW HIGH is answered...we will play the hand in a Part-Game contract. If I can decide WHERE, I'll be finished."

Now we are ready to look at the decision...WHERE

The Second Decision: WHERE

There are five possible denominations...Clubs, Diamonds, Hearts, Spades or No Trump. How can the captain choose among them to decide WHERE?

There are thirteen cards in every suit. If you pick a suit as trump, you want to have more trumps than your opponents:

YOUR SIDE

□ □ □ □ □ □

If you have 6 (or fewer) combined trumps,

OPPONENTS

□ □ □ □ □ □ □

they have 7 trumps...more than you do!

□ □ □ □ □ □ □

If you have 7 combined trumps,

□ □ □ □ □ □

they have 6 trumps...a slight advantage for your side.

□ □ □ □ □ □ □ □

If you have 8 (or more) combined trumps,

□ □ □ □ □

they have 5 (or fewer) trumps... a clear advantage for your side!

We can summarize these ideas in the following table:

NUMBER OF COMBINED TRUMPS	'QUALITY' OF TRUMP FIT
6 or fewer	Unacceptable
7	Acceptable
8 or more	MAGIC!

A trump suit with eight or more cards in the combined hands is called a *Magic Fit*. How does the captain determine whether or not there are eight or more combined trumps? Opener, as describer, tells responder, through the language of bidding, something about his shape as well as his strength. For example, suppose opener starts the bidding with One Heart. Opener always bids his longest suit first, so responder knows that opener must have at least four Hearts. If responder also has four Hearts, he knows that the partnership has at least eight Hearts in the combined hands.

OPENER'S HEARTS + RESPONDER'S HEARTS = MAGIC FIT

Playing a contract with eight or more combined trumps is like magic. Experience has shown that it will usually produce one more trick than a No Trump contract with the same cards. Sometimes a Magic Fit will produce two, three, or even more extra tricks than No Trump. In No Trump, the opponents have the first opportunity to lead and will select the best suit for their side. Sometimes a long suit will be played and you won't be able to stop them from taking several tricks. If there is a trump suit, however, you can trump tricks in the opponents' long suits which would otherwise be lost.

Let's take this idea... Magic Fits usually produce at least one more trick than No Trump... and use it to decide which is better: Game in No Trump or Game in a Magic Fit? Let's first review the possible Game contracts:

GAME CONTRACTS

Game in No Trump   = Three No Trump (nine tricks)
Game in a Major Suit = Four Hearts or Four Spades (ten tricks)
Game in a Minor Suit = Five Clubs or Five Diamonds (eleven tricks)

Playing the Contract in Game

Major Suit Game vs. Three No Trump

Suppose the partnership has a Magic Fit in Hearts and 26 points... enough to bid Game. Though Four Hearts is a ten-trick contract and Three No Trump is a nine-trick contract, Four Hearts should be safer. You know that a Magic Fit will usually produce one more trick than No Trump. In that case, it doesn't matter which contract you play. However, on many hands the Magic Fit produces two extra tricks...a difference that is often important. Therefore:

> ANY TIME YOU HAVE AT LEAST EIGHT CARDS IN
> A MAJOR SUIT, A MAGIC FIT, PLAY THE HAND
> WITH THAT SUIT AS TRUMP.

Minor Suit Game vs. Three No Trump

Suppose you have a Magic Fit in Diamonds and 26 points. Minor suit Games require about 29 combined points which indicates that you should choose Three No Trump as the Game contract when you only have 26 to 28 points. In addition, the suit Game is an eleven-trick contract...two tricks more than Three No Trump requires. Since a Magic Fit usually produces only one more trick than No Trump, a Five Diamond contract would fail on many hands where Three No Trump would succeed.

Thus, some Game contracts are more attractive than others.

> THE KEY QUESTION FOR DECIDING WHERE
> WHEN BIDDING TO A GAME CONTRACT
> **Do we have a MAGIC MAJOR SUIT FIT?**
> If the answer is YES: Play in Four Hearts or Four Spades.
> If the answer is NO: Play in Three No Trump.

Playing the Contract in Part-Game

What if there are less than 26 combined points? In that case, the captain should place the contract in Part-Game. He needs to decide which is better: Part-Game in No Trump or Part-Game in a Magic Fit.

Major and Minor Suit Part-Games vs. No Trump

Suppose you have a Magic Fit and 20 combined points...not enough to bid Game. Thus, you can choose any trump suit at a comfortably low level. Any suit contract at the two-level should play at least as well as One No Trump, if not better, as long as there is a Magic Fit. So, if the captain decides to play in Part-Game:

THE KEY QUESTION FOR DECIDING WHERE WHEN BIDDING TO A PART-GAME CONTRACT

Do we have any MAGIC FIT?

If the answer is YES: Play Part-Game in that suit.
If the answer is NO: Play Part-Game in No Trump.

Summary

During the auction, the partnership works together using the *language of bidding* to determine the best final contract. The opener acts as the *describer* and describes his strength and shape. The decision on the final contract is the responsibility of the *captain, responder*, who makes two decisions:

- HOW HIGH should the contract be played? (Part-Game, Game or Slam)
- WHERE should the contract be played? (Clubs, Diamonds, Hearts, Spades or No Trump)

HOW HIGH?

Game...If there are at least 26 combined points
Part-Game...If there are less than 26 combined points

WHERE?

Game: Four Hearts or Four Spades...If there is a Magic Major Suit Fit
Three No Trump...If there is no Magic Major Suit Fit

Part-Game: In a suit...If there is a Magic Fit
In No Trump...If there is no Magic Fit

This may seem like a lot to learn, but you will find it gets much easier with practice. The next chapter gives plenty of practice being captain, deciding HOW HIGH and WHERE, and placing the final contract. The bidding ladder on the next page has the bonus levels indicated.

THE BIDDING LADDER

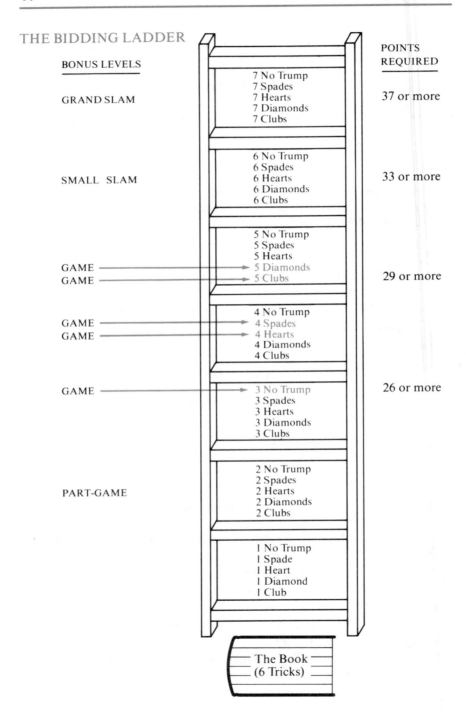

POINTS
REQUIRED

BONUS LEVELS

GRAND SLAM

7 No Trump
7 Spades
7 Hearts
7 Diamonds
7 Clubs

37 or more

SMALL SLAM

6 No Trump
6 Spades
6 Hearts
6 Diamonds
6 Clubs

33 or more

5 No Trump
5 Spades
5 Hearts
GAME ──────→ 5 Diamonds
GAME ──────→ 5 Clubs

29 or more

4 No Trump
GAME ──────→ 4 Spades
GAME ──────→ 4 Hearts
4 Diamonds
4 Clubs

GAME ──────→ 3 No Trump
3 Spades
3 Hearts
3 Diamonds
3 Clubs

26 or more

PART-GAME

2 No Trump
2 Spades
2 Hearts
2 Diamonds
2 Clubs

1 No Trump
1 Spade
1 Heart
1 Diamond
1 Club

The Book
(6 Tricks)

CAPTAIN'S CHOICES FOR THE FINAL CONTRACT

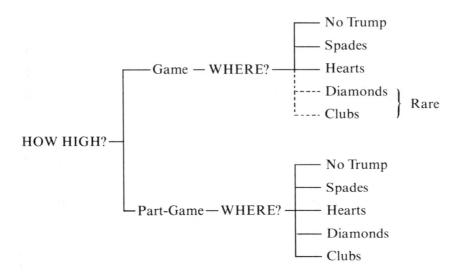

Exercises

1) Suppose your partner opens the bidding One No Trump and the opponent on your right says Pass. Which one of you is responder? Which one of you is captain?

2) Your partner opens One No Trump. Approximately how many combined points do you and your partner have when you hold each of the following hands? HOW HIGH should the final contract be played... Part-Game or Game?

a) ♠ J 7 3
♥ 9 6 4
♦ K 8 3
♣ J 9 8 5

b) ♠ K 9 6
♥ A J 4
♦ K J 7 6
♣ 6 3 2

c) ♠ J 9 6 5 4 2
♥ J 4
♦ 7 6
♣ K 3 2

d) ♠ K 6 3
♥ A J 10 7 6 4
♦ J 8 4
♣ 2

3) Your partner opens One Spade and you hold the following hand:

♠ 10 9 6
♥ Q J 4
♦ J 7 6 5
♣ 7 4 3

What is the minimum number of combined points you and your partner hold? What is the maximum number? HOW HIGH should the final contract be played... Part-Game or Game?

4)   Your partner opens One Heart and you hold the following hand:

♠ J 9 6
♥ A J 9 4
♦ K J 7 6
♣ K 6

What is the minimum number of Hearts in the combined hands?
WHERE should the final contract be played... Hearts or No-Trump?
HOW HIGH should the final contract be played... Part-Game or
Game?

5)   If your partner opens the bidding One Spade, what is the minimum
number of Spades you must hold to be certain that you have a Magic
Fit?

6)   If your partner opens the bidding One No Trump, what is the minimum number of Hearts you must hold to be certain that you have a
Magic Fit?

7)   Suppose you determine that your side has 26 or more points and an
8-card Diamond Suit fit but no other 8-card fit. What should the final
contract be?

5

Responding to a
One No Trump Opening

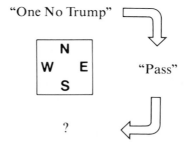

"One No Trump"

"Pass"

?

The One No Trump opening is a highly limited bid since it shows a narrow point range and balanced distribution. It should be easy for responder to add up the combined hands to determine **HOW HIGH** to play the hand, **WHERE** to play the hand and what the final contract should be.

Review of the One No Trump Opening

Let's start by reviewing the requirements for a One No Trump opening bid:

RULE FOR A ONE NO TRUMP OPENING BID

To open the bidding One No Trump you need:

- A balanced hand
- 16, 17 or 18 points

Responder's Decisions

Let's also review responder's decisions:

HOW HIGH

Game...If there are at least 26 combined points

Part-Game...If there are less than 26 combined points

WHERE

Game: Four Hearts or Four Spades...If there is a Magic
               Major Suit Fit
               Three No Trump...If there is no Magic Major Suit Fit

Part-Game: In a suit...If there is a Magic Fit
               In No Trump...If there is no Magic Fit

Deciding HOW HIGH

Using this information, let's see how you, as responder, determine HOW
HIGH after your partner opens One No Trump. Suppose you hold the
following hand:

♠ A 4 3
♥ J 5 3
♦ 8 6 4 2
♣ 9 6 4

Are there enough combined points for Game? Adding opener's promised
points to your 5 points:

	Your points	5	5
+	Partner's points	+ 16	+ 18
=	Combined points	21 (at least)	23 (at most)

Even if opener has his maximum point count of 18, there are not the
required 26 points for Game. HOW HIGH ... Part-Game.

As another example, your partner opens One No Trump and your hand is:

♠ A 4 3
♥ J 6 4
♦ K 7 5 4
♣ Q 10 7

Are there enough points for Game? Adding opener's points to your 10 points:

Your points	10	10
+ Partner's points	+ 16	+ 18
= Combined points	26 (at least)	28 (at most)

Even if opener has his minimum of 16, there are enough points for Game. HOW HIGH...Game.

Deciding WHERE

Deciding WHERE to play the hand is also a matter of addition. The key question is "Do we have a Magic Fit?". Responder can usually determine this by adding the number of cards in his longest suit to the length opener has promised. Remember that opener's hand is balanced...4-3-3-3, 4-4-3-2, or 5-3-3-2. Therefore, in any suit opener has:

- at least two cards
- probably three or four cards
- maybe five cards

The following table shows us whether or not responder can expect a Magic Fit when partner opens One No Trump:

CARDS IN RESPONDER'S SUIT	MAGIC FIT?
6 or more	Yes
5	Probably
4	Sometimes
3 or fewer	Unlikely

Using this information to shape your thinking about the possibility of a Magic Fit, let's see how you could decide WHERE if your partner opens One No Trump and your hand is:

♠ J 3
♥ K J 8 4 3 2
♦ A 8 7
♣ 4 2

Do you have a Magic Fit in Hearts? Opener has promised at least two Hearts, so the Magic Fit has been found.

Putting It Together: Placing the Contract

If responder can decide both HOW HIGH and WHERE to play the hand, he places the final contract. For example, partner opens One No Trump and you are the responder. Your hand is:

♠ A 6 2
♥ K 9 8
♦ Q 9 7 4 2
♣ J 5

Your hand has 11 points... 10 HCPs plus 1 point for the fifth Diamond. You know the combined point total to be between 27 and 29 points. Thus, you can answer HOW HIGH... Game.

You have fewer than four cards in each Major, so there is unlikely to be a Magic Major Suit Fit. Thus you can answer WHERE... No Trump. Remember, you either play Game in a Magic Major Suit Fit or in No Trump. You can forget about playing in a Minor suit Game contract... you would need too many tricks.

Once you know what the final contract should be, you bid it. In this example, you know that the final contract should be Three No Trump, so that is what you bid. This is how it looks:

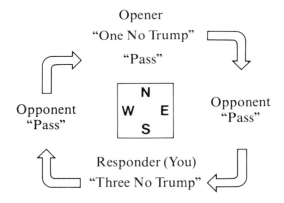

Opener
"One No Trump"
"Pass"

Opponent
"Pass"

Opponent
"Pass"

Responder (You)
"Three No Trump"

Since responder is the captain, it is up to responder to place the contract. In our example, you placed the final contract by bidding Three No Trump. Opener must respect your captaincy and Pass the Three No Trump bid. This makes Three No Trump the final contract. The auction after your Three No Trump bid will finish off with Pass, Pass, Pass.

Here's another example. Partner opens One No Trump. What is your bid with the following hand?

♠ K 3
♥ Q J 9 7 4 3
♦ A 8 7
♣ 8 5

You have 12 points... 10 HCPs plus 2 points for the length in Hearts. You know there are 28 - 30 combined points. HOW HIGH... Game.

You have six Hearts and partner has at least two, so a Magic Fit is assured. Play in a Major any time there is a Magic Fit. That settles WHERE... Hearts.

Your situation is almost identical to the first example. You know HOW HIGH and WHERE, and want to play a specific Game contract. This time, though, you want to play Four Hearts, a message you convey by bidding Four Hearts. It looks like this:

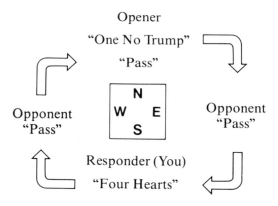

Opener

"One No Trump"

"Pass"

N
W   E
S

Opponent
"Pass"

Opponent
"Pass"

Responder (You)

"Four Hearts"

The Easy Approach to Responses

In practice, responder does best to consider HOW HIGH first when responding to One No Trump. The easy way for him to do this is to use his point count to put his hand into one of three groups:

1. Part-Game ...... Responder has 0 - 7 points
2. Maybe Game .... Responder has 8 - 9 points
3. Game .... Responder has 10 - 14 points

We will temporarily ignore the infrequent case where responder has more than 14 points until we take up the material on Slam bidding. For now, let's take a look at each of the above cases in turn.

Part-Game...Responder Has 0 - 7 Points

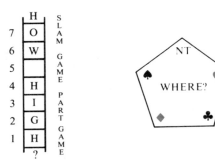

When responder knows there are not enough combined points for Game, he wants to direct the partnership to the best Part-Game contract. Since the bidding is already at One No Trump, a glance at the Bidding Ladder will show that the lowest available Part-Games are:

> Two Spades
> Two Hearts
> Two Diamonds
> Two Clubs
> One No Trump

How can responder choose the best Part-Game? If the partnership has a Magic Fit, he wants to play Part-Game with that suit as trump. Otherwise, he wants to play the Part-Game in No Trump. Responder uses the following chart to help him decide whether or not there is a Magic Fit:

- With a 6-card suit or longer, there **must** be a Magic Fit (6 + 2 = 8)
- With a 5-card suit, there is **probably** a Magic Fit (i.e. if opener has three or four cards in the suit):

Responder's Length	*Opener's Length*	*Fit*

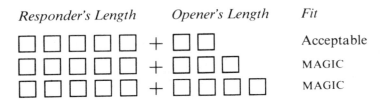

- With a 4-card suit, there is **probably not** a Magic Fit (i.e. if opener has two or three cards in the suit)

Thus, if responder has a 5-card suit or longer, he can "play the odds" and assume that there is a Magic Fit. Note that if responder has five cards and opener has only two, the trump fit is still acceptable (seven cards). A 7-card fit is often a better Part-Game denomination than One No Trump... the long trump suit provides protection from your opponents' long suits.

If responder does not have a 5-card suit or longer, he can assume there is not a Magic Fit and can play Part-Game in No Trump by saying Pass. One No Trump is the final contract.

There is one exception. A response of Two Clubs to an opening bid of One No Trump has a special meaning. We will discuss this response in the chapter on the Stayman Convention. For now, avoid responding Two Clubs to partner's One No Trump opening. If you have a 5-card or longer Club suit, choose One No Trump as your Part-Game by saying Pass. To summarize:

RESPONDING TO ONE NO TRUMP WITH 0 - 7 POINTS

- Pass with no 5-card or longer suit (other than Clubs)
- Bid Two Diamonds, Two Hearts or Two Spades with a 5-card or longer suit

---

Remember that responder is captain. If he chooses to Pass or bid Two Diamonds, Two Hearts or Two Spades, all of which show a weak hand, opener must not bid again. Responder is simply deciding on the best Part-Game. Such a response, one that says "Please Pass, partner", is called a *sign-off bid*. Here are some examples:

Your partner opens the bidding One No Trump. What would you respond with each of the following hands?

1) ♠ A 7	2) ♠ 4 2	3) ♠ J 8 7 5 3	4) ♠ 3
♥ Q 8 4 2	♥ K 8 7 5 3 2	♥ A 9 7	♥ 6 4 2
♦ 8 7 3	♦ 5 4 2	♦ 5 4 3 2	♦ 7 6 5 4 3 2
♣ 10 7 4 3	♣ Q 4	♣ 7	♣ 8 4 2

1) PASS. With 6 points, there is no hope of Game. You have no 5-card suit, so you would Pass. The final contract will be One No Trump.

2) TWO HEARTS. With 7 points...5 HCPs plus 2 for the 6-card suit... there is not quite enough to hope for Game. You know there is a Magic Fit in Hearts, so bid Two Hearts. Your partner will accept your captaincy and Pass.

3) TWO SPADES. Your 6 points offers no chance for Game. Bid to the likely best Part-Game for your side, Two Spades. You are the captain so opener will say Pass.

4) TWO DIAMONDS. Don't be tempted to Pass just because you have a weak hand. The weaker your hand is, the worse your partner will do playing in a contract of One No Trump. With Diamonds as trump, your hand will be worth a couple of tricks at least. Sign-off in Two Diamonds.

Maybe Game...Responder has 8 or 9 Points

When responder has 8 or 9 points he doesn't yet have the answer to HOW HIGH. He needs to know if opener has enough points for Game.

Responder wants to make a bid that:

- Announces interest in Game
- Asks opener to:
  — bid Game with a maximum hand (18 points)
  — settle for Part-Game with a minimum hand (16 - 17 points)

Responder can convey this message with one bid, Two No Trump. This Two No Trump response is an *invitational bid*. Opener is invited to continue to Three No Trump but he is allowed to Pass.

The Two No Trump bid says:

- I have 8 or 9 points and want to play No Trump
- I want you to:
  — bid Three No Trump with 18 points
  — Pass with 16 - 17 points.

In summary:

RESPONDING TO ONE NO TRUMP WITH 8 - 9 POINTS

- Bid Two No Trump

If responder isn't sure that he wants to play the hand in No Trump, the only bid available is the specialized Two Club response. You will see later how the Two Club response solves this problem. Some examples:

Each of the following hands should respond Two No Trump to a One No Trump opening bid:

1) ♠ K 3 2   2) ♠ Q J 7   3) ♠ K 7   4) ♠ 6 4 3
   ♥ J 7 6   ♥ 7 6   ♥ J 5   ♥ Q
   ♦ K J 8 4   ♦ Q 4 3   ♦ 9 6 2   ♦ A J 8 5 3 2
   ♣ 10 9 7   ♣ K 8 5 4 3   ♣ Q 10 7 5 3 2   ♣ 10 7 4
   8 points   9 points   8 points   9 points

Game...Responder has 10 - 14 Points

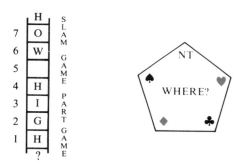

When responder knows there are enough combined points for Game, the only decision is WHERE. If there is a Magic Major Suit Fit, Game should be played in the Major suit; otherwise, the final contract should be Three No Trump:

- Bid Four Hearts or Four Spades with a Magic Major Suit Fit (i.e. when you have a 6-card or longer Major suit)
- Bid Three No Trump with no possible Magic Major Suit Fit (i.e. when you lack 4 or more cards in either Major suit)

If responder has a 5-card Major, he doesn't know if there is a Magic Major Suit Fit. He will have to get some help from his partner. He knows there is a Magic Fit unless opener has only two cards in the suit. He wants to make a bid that:

- Announces a 5-card Major and enough points for Game
- Requests opener to choose the best Game contract:
   —Four of the Major, with three or more trumps **or**
   —Three No Trump, with only two trumps

Responder conveys this message in one bid, Three of a Major suit. For example:

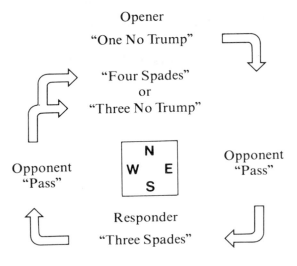

Opener

"One No Trump"

"Four Spades"
or
"Three No Trump"

Opponent
"Pass"

Opponent
"Pass"

Responder

"Three Spades"

Responder's Three Spade bid says:

- I have exactly five Spades and at least 10 points
- I want you to bid:
  — Four Spades, with three or more Spades
  — Three No Trump, with only two Spades

Three Spades is called a *forcing bid* because it forces a response from partner. The One No Trump opening bidder is being asked to bid Four Spades or to bid Three No Trump. The opener is not being asked to consider a Pass.

In summary:

RESPONDING TO ONE NO TRUMP WITH 10 - 14 POINTS

- Bid Four Hearts or Four Spades with a 6-card or longer Major suit
- Bid Three Hearts or Three Spades with a 5-card Major suit
- Bid Three No Trump with no possible Magic Major Suit Fit

If responder has a 4-card Major, he wants to make a bid that asks Opener to bid any 4-card Major suit that he holds. Responder can do exactly that by using the special Two Club response described in Chapter 20.

Try these examples. Partner opens One No Trump. What is your response with the following hands?

1) ♠ K J 3	2) ♠ A 4 3	3) ♠ K Q 9 7 5	4) ♠ 3
♥ A J 8 5 3 2	♥ 5 3	♥ A 9	♥ A K 10 7 4
♦ —	♦ Q 5 2	♦ A 6 2	♦ Q 8 7 5
♣ 8 6 5 3	♣ K 9 7 5 3	♣ 10 9 7	♣ 8 5 4

1) FOUR HEARTS. You have 11 points, enough for Game. There is a Magic Fit in Hearts, so you should respond Four Hearts.

2) THREE NO TRUMP. You have 10 points, enough for Game and there is no Magic Major Suit Fit, so bid Three No Trump.

3) THREE SPADES. Here you have 14 points, enough for Game. There is probably a Magic Fit in Spades. Respond Three Spades announcing exactly five Spades and ask opener to choose the best Game.

4) THREE HEARTS. You have 10 points, enough for Game. Bid Three Hearts to show exactly five Hearts and ask opener to choose the best Game.

Summary

When your partner opens the bidding One No Trump, you are the captain and must determine HOW HIGH and WHERE to place the final contract.

RESPONSES TO AN OPENING BID OF ONE NO TRUMP

- With 0 - 7 points: Bid Two Diamonds or Two Hearts or Two Spades with a 5-card or longer suit. Otherwise, Pass.

- With 8 - 9 points: Bid Two No Trump with no Magic Major Suit Fit. (Otherwise, bid Two Clubs*.)

- With 10 - 14 points: Bid Four Hearts or Four Spades with a 6-card or longer Major suit. Bid Three Hearts or Three Spades with a 5-card Major suit. (Bid Two Clubs with a 4-card Major suit*.) Otherwise, bid Three No Trump.

---

* The Two Club response will be discussed in Chapter 20.

Until you learn how to use the special Two Club response, bid to the appropriate level in No Trump:

- Two No Trump with 8 or 9 points
- Three No Trump with 10 to 14 points

Exercises

1) Partner opens One No Trump. Ask yourself HOW HIGH and put your hand in one of the three groups: Game, Part-Game or Maybe Game. Then ask yourself WHERE and pick the best response.

a) ♠ K 3
   ♥ A 7 3
   ♦ J 8 7 4 3
   ♣ 10 4 3

b) ♠ 6 4
   ♥ K 10 9 8 5
   ♦ 10 5 4 3
   ♣ 8 2

c) ♠ A J 10 7 5
   ♥ K 5 2
   ♦ J
   ♣ K 9 8 6

d) ♠ Q J 9
   ♥ A K J 6 3 2
   ♦ 4
   ♣ 9 6 5

e) ♠ A 4
   ♥ K J 10
   ♦ Q 7 6 5 3
   ♣ 6 5 2

f) ♠ 10 9 7 5 3
   ♥ A 10
   ♦ K 6 4 3
   ♣ K 8

g) ♠ K J 9 7 6 3
   ♥ 5 2
   ♦ K 3
   ♣ Q 8 6

h) ♠ Q 9 7 5 3
   ♥ 3 2
   ♦ Q 6 4 3 2
   ♣ 10

i) ♠ Q J 3
   ♥ 3
   ♦ A Q 8 6
   ♣ Q 9 7 4 2

j) ♠ J 8
   ♥ K 8 5
   ♦ 7 5
   ♣ J 8 7 5 3 2

6

The Messages of Bidding

In the previous chapter, we mentioned three types of bids:

- Sign-off bids
- Invitational bids
- Forcing bids

Each bid made during the bidding conversation sends a message to your partner. As in any conversation, it is important to have your message understood. This chapter discusses the *bidding messages* that partners exchange throughout the auction.

The Sign-off Bid

A sign-off bid is like the warning on a stop sign...STOP. When a player makes a sign-off bid, partner is expected to Pass; HOW HIGH and WHERE have been determined and there's no need to search further. For example, when responding to an opening bid of One No Trump, the following are sign-off bids:

	Four Spades	HOW HIGH	Game
Captain		WHERE	Spades
signs-off	Four Hearts	HOW HIGH	Game
in Game		WHERE	Hearts
	Three No Trump	HOW HIGH	Game
		WHERE	No Trump

Captain signs-off in Part-Game	Two Spades	HOW HIGH WHERE	Part-Game Spades
	Two Hearts	HOW HIGH WHERE	Part-Game Hearts
	Two Diamonds	HOW HIGH WHERE	Part-Game Diamonds

You will recognize sign-off bids in the text because they will be accompanied by a red stop sign

When you, or your partner, make a sign-off bid, the message is clear... STOP! (Pass).

The Invitational Bid

An invitational bid can be symbolized by a triangular sign which says... PROCEED WITH CAUTION. When a player makes an invitational bid, partner may Pass if he is satisfied with the contract or may bid again if he has the values to warrant bidding on. For example, when responding to an opening bid of One No Trump, the following response is invitational:

Two No Trump	HOW HIGH	Not sure; Game or Part-game
	WHERE	No Trump

Opener is invited to make the final decision. He can Pass with a minimum hand (16 or 17 points) or bid Three No Trump with a maximum hand (18 points).

The opening bid of One No Trump is itself an invitational bid: partner may Pass or bid on to a different final contract. Opening bids of One Club, One Diamond, One Heart and One Spade are also invitational. You will recognize invitational bids in the text because they will be accompanied by a triangle

The Forcing Bid

A forcing bid is like the green signal on a traffic light...GO. When the captain needs more information, he makes a forcing bid. Partner must bid again. After an opening bid of One No Trump, these bids are forcing:

Three Hearts	HOW HIGH	Game
	WHERE	Not sure; Hearts or No Trump
Three Spades	HOW HIGH	Game
	WHERE	Not sure; Spades or No Trump

Opener must make the final decision. He bids Game in the Major with three or more trumps (responder is showing exactly five) or he bids Three No Trump. He cannot Pass. You will recognize forcing bids in the text because they will be accompanied by a (GO) symbol.

The Marathon Bid

While a forcing bid tells partner that he must bid again at his next turn, it has no further implication. After partner bids, he is under no obligation to bid again unless he hears another forcing bid. This can sometimes make the auction awkward as you have to continually be concerned about whether a bid is forcing or not at each turn.

To make the bidding simpler, certain bids are **forcing to Game**. If one partner makes a bid that is forcing to Game, both partners must continue to bid until the Game level is reached. Such bids are called *marathon bids* because the partnership must continue the auction until it 'crosses the finish line' (i.e. until Game is reached).

After a marathon bid, HOW HIGH has been determined...Game...and the partnership can focus its attention on WHERE. Marathon bids allow the captain to explore which Game to play without fear of the bidding stopping too soon.

For example, the responses of Three Hearts and Three Spades to an opening bid of One No Trump are not only forcing bids but are also marathon bids. Opener must continue to bid until Game is reached. This is a simple case since opener's next bid will put the partnership in Game but you will encounter further examples later in the text.

The marathon bids in the text will be indicated by a sunburst sign GO. This indicates that the bid is forcing all the way to Game.

Bidding Messages

How do you know whether a bid is a sign-off, invitational, forcing or marathon? It's like hearing a chord on the piano in harmony or discord. It takes a little practice, but you get to know the sounds. In most cases, your intuition will be enough to guide you.

As we discuss the bidding from here on, we'll use the symbols: sign-off is a stop sign STOP ; invitational is a triangle ▼ ; forcing is a go sign GO ; marathon is a sunburst go sign GO . After a while, you will start to see the pattern.

Summary

Each bid carries one of four messages:
- Sign-off: STOP partner must pass
- Invitational: ▼ partner may bid or pass
- Forcing: GO partner must bid again
- Marathon: GO the partnership keeps bidding until at least game is reached

Exercises

1) Is an opening one bid a sign-off, invitational or forcing? Why?

2) Your partner opens One No Trump. What types of bids are the following responses: Two Diamonds, Two Hearts, Two Spades, Three No Trump, Four Hearts and Four Spades?

3) What is the invitational bid in response to a One No Trump opening bid?

4) Why do we say Three Hearts and Three Spades are forcing responses after a One No Trump opening?

5) You open One No Trump. Your partner responds Two Hearts. What do you do when it is your next turn to bid? Why?

6) You open One No Trump with the following hand:

      ♠ A Q 7
      ♥ K J 9 6
      ♦ K 7
      ♣ Q J 8 5

Partner responds Two No Trump. What do you say next? Why?

7) You open One No Trump with the following hand:

      ♠ K Q 8 4
      ♥ A Q 6
      ♦ K Q 3
      ♣ Q 9 4

Partner responds Two No Trump. What do you bid now? Why?

8) Partner opens One No Trump and you have:

      ♠ Q 7
      ♥ K J 9 8 7 6
      ♦ A 3
      ♣ J 7 4

What do you respond? What will your partner do next? Why?

9) You open One No Trump with the following hand:

      ♠ K J
      ♥ A Q 6
      ♦ K J 9 7 3
      ♣ Q 10 3

Partner responds Three No Trump. What do you say next? Why?

10) You open One No Trump with the following hand:

      ♠ A J 7
      ♥ A 5
      ♦ K J 7 3
      ♣ K 9 8 5

Partner responds Three Spades. What do you say next? Why? What would you have done if partner had responded Three Hearts?

7

Responding to Opening Bids of One in a Suit

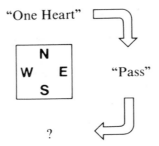

"One Heart"

N
W   E
S

"Pass"

?

One-level opening bids in a suit...One Club, One Diamond, One Heart and One Spade...are very common. Let's compare them to an opening bid of One No Trump.

OPENING BID	POINT RANGE	DISTRIBUTION
One No Trump	16 - 18	Balanced
One Spade One Heart One Diamond One Club	13 —— 21	Balanced or Unbalanced

An opening one bid in a suit is much less specific than One No Trump, both in point range and possible hand distributions. Responder cannot answer HOW HIGH and WHERE right away. Responder needs more information about opener's hand. How does he get more information? Through the bidding conversation. He starts by making a bid that tells opener something about his hand. Opener then describes his hand further to allow responder, in most cases, to determine the final contract. The aim of the bidding conversation is the same: to discover whether the partnership has at least 26 points...enough for Game...and to uncover a Magic

Major Suit Fit. If Game isn't possible then the partnership wants to uncover any Magic Fit for the best Part-Game.

How does responder decide what to bid first? *Responder's Four Questions*, through the order in which they are asked, guide responder to the best bid.

RESPONDER'S FOUR QUESTIONS

1. CAN I RAISE PARTNER'S MAJOR?
2. DO I HAVE A WEAK HAND (0 - 5 POINTS)?
3. CAN I BID A NEW SUIT AT THE ONE-LEVEL?
4. DO I HAVE A MINIMUM HAND (6 - 10 POINTS)?

Let's look at how responder uses each of the four questions.

Question One

Responder's first priority is to try and uncover a Magic Major Suit Fit. So the first question is:

---

1. CAN I RAISE PARTNER'S MAJOR?

Since partner must have at least a 4-card suit to open One Heart or One Spade, you can *support* partner's Major if you have at least **4-card support** (4 + 4 = 8). You've uncovered a Magic Major Suit Fit. This solves the problem of WHERE. You can agree with partner to play with the Major suit as trump. You do this by *raising* partner's suit to an appropriate level.

Raises of partner's suit sound like this:

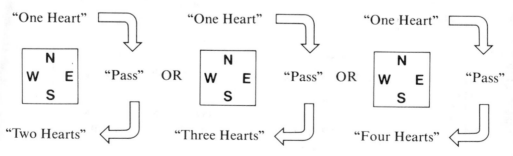

Having decided to raise partner's suit, you need to determine HOW HIGH.

Once you've found a Magic Fit, your hand becomes more powerful. Two heads are better than one, two hands are better than one. When you and your partner can agree on a trump suit, you can value your hand in a slightly different manner than when you are opening the bidding. Since you will be supporting partner's suit and therefore will be putting your hand down as dummy at the end of the auction (partner bid the suit first), these are called *dummy points*.

To illustrate the idea of dummy points, let's look at an example:

♠ —
♥ 7 4 3 2
♦ 9 7 3 2
♣ A 9 8 6 4

This hand is more valuable if partner opened One Heart than if partner opened One Spade. Dummy points take this into consideration. If the opening bid is One Spade, you would value the hand in the normal way: 4 points for the Ace of Clubs and 1 point for the fifth Club, a total of 5 points. If the opening bid is One Heart, you have found a Magic Fit... partner has at least four Hearts and you have four Hearts.

Now the Spade void (no cards in the suit) is more valuable than the Ace of Spades. Why? If the opponents lead the Spade Ace, you'll use a small Heart to trump it and win the trick. When you are dummy and Hearts are trump, your hand should be able to take several tricks because you can win tricks with your trumps whenever Spades are led.

When you have found a fit, a void has more power than an Ace and is worth 5 points. Similarly, other short suits (singletons, doubletons) are valuable after you have found a fit. Thus:

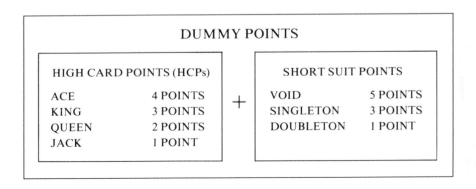

WHEN YOU ARE RAISING PARTNER'S MAJOR SUIT, REVALUE YOUR HAND USING DUMMY POINTS

DUMMY POINTS

HIGH CARD POINTS (HCPs)			SHORT SUIT POINTS	
ACE	4 POINTS	+	VOID	5 POINTS
KING	3 POINTS		SINGLETON	3 POINTS
QUEEN	2 POINTS		DOUBLETON	1 POINT
JACK	1 POINT			

The high card points (HCPs) are added to the short suit points to determine the total value of your hand. **The short suit points take the place of length points once you have found a Magic Major Suit Fit.**

Returning to our earlier example, partner opens the bidding One Heart and you have the following hand:

> ♠ —
> ♥ 7 4 3 2
> ♦ 9 7 3 2
> ♣ A 9 8 6 4

Since you have 4-card support for partner's Major suit, you want to raise partner's suit to the appropriate level. Value your hand using dummy points:

> 4 High Card Points + 5 Short Suit Points = 9 Dummy Points

If partner had opened One Club, One Diamond, One Spade or One No Trump, you wouldn't value your hand using dummy points since you haven't yet found a Magic Major Suit Fit. Instead, you would value your hand in the normal fashion: 4 High Card Points + 1 Length Point = 5 Points.

Having identified a Magic Major Suit Fit and valued your hand using dummy points, you can determine HOW HIGH to bid using the following scale:

RAISING OPENER'S MAJOR

DUMMY POINTS	BID		
0 - 5	Pass	STOP	Game is very unlikely, so stop at the lowest Part-Game.
6 - 10	Raise to the ♥ two-level		Game is possible if opener has 16 - 21 points.
11 - 12	Raise to the ♥ three-level		Game is very likely and this bid strongly invites opener to go on to Game.
13 - 16	Raise to the ♥ four-level		Game should definitely be bid as there are at least 26 combined points.

(We'll consider hands with more than 16 points when we take up the chapters on Powerhouse Hands and Slam Bidding.)

Having answered yes to the question "Can I raise partner's Major?", responder evaluates his hand using dummy points and raises to the appropriate level. Let's look at some examples:

Your partner opens the bidding One Spade. What would you respond with each of the following hands?

1) ♠ J 8 6 4   2) ♠ K 10 7 5   3) ♠ Q 7 6 3   4) ♠ Q J 8 6 4
    ♥ 10 3   ♥ 8 7 4   ♥ A 7 3   ♥ 5
    ♦ Q 7 5 4   ♦ 5 3   ♦ —   ♦ A K 10 6
    ♣ 10 4 3   ♣ K Q 7 4   ♣ J 9 6 4 3 2   ♣ 8 4 2

5) ♠ J 7
    ♥ A 7 6 4 2
    ♦ K Q 10 5
    ♣ J 3

1) PASS. You can support partner's Major but have only 4 dummy points...3 HCPs and 1 for the doubleton Heart. Your response would be Pass (0 - 5 dummy points) since Game is very unlikely.

2) TWO SPADES. Can you raise partner's Major? Yes, you have 4-card support. Valuing with dummy points, you have 9 points...8 HCPs plus 1 for the doubleton Diamond. Raise to the appropriate level, Two Spades (6 - 10 dummy points).

3) THREE SPADES. With four Spades, you can raise partner's Major. You have 12 dummy points...7 HCPs plus 5 for the Diamond void. You would raise to the three-level, Three Spades.

4) FOUR SPADES. You have five Spades, more than enough to raise partner's Major. You have 13 dummy points...10 HCPs and 3 for the singleton Heart. You would raise to the appropriate level, Four Spades (13 - 16 dummy points).

5) You only have two Spades, not enough to support your partner's Major. It's time to move on to the next question.

Question Two

The second question is designed to keep the partnership from getting too high in its search for the best denomination:

> ### 2. DO I HAVE A WEAK HAND (0 - 5 POINTS)?

If the answer is yes, **Pass**. (STOP) . With 0 - 5 points, Game is very unlikely.

Why isn't this the first question? A hand originally valued as weak might be strong enough for a response when you count dummy points. You wouldn't be able to discover this unless you first asked 'Can I raise partner's Major?'.

Let's look at some examples combining the first two questions:

Partner opens the bidding One Heart. What would you respond with the following hands?

1) ♠ K 8 7   2) ♠ A 6 5 4
  ♥ 6 5   ♥ K 10 7 5
  ♦ J 10 5 4   ♦ J 8 6 3
  ♣ 9 6 4 3   ♣ 7

1) PASS. Here you can't raise partner's Major so you ask yourself the second question: "Do I have a weak hand (0 - 5 points)?". Since the answer is yes (you only have 4 points), you would Pass.

2) THREE HEARTS. Can you raise partner's Major? Yes. Valuing with dummy points, you have 11 points...8 HCPs and 3 points for the singleton Club. You would raise to Three Hearts.

Partner opens the bidding One Club. What would you respond with the following hands?

3) ♠ 8 7   4) ♠ A J 8 7
  ♥ 10 6 5 4   ♥ K 9 7 6
  ♦ J 8 6 5 4 ♦ 9 8
  ♣ 9 7   ♣ J 8 6

3) PASS. You can't raise partner's Major because he didn't bid one. Do you have a weak hand? Yes, you only have 2 points...1 HCP and 1 point for the fifth Diamond. With a weak hand (0 - 5 points), Pass and keep the bidding at the lowest possible contract.

4) Your answer is no to the first two questions. You can't raise partner's Major (he didn't bid one) and you don't have a weak hand...you have 9 HCPs. You must bid something, but what? It's time to move on to the third question.

Question Three

The third question is designed to guide you to the best denomination. It encourages you to bid up the Bidding Ladder without missing a suit at the one-level:

> ### 3. CAN I BID A NEW SUIT AT THE ONE-LEVEL?

If you can, **bid that suit** (GO) .

If you have reached this question, you could not raise partner's Major suit...either he didn't bid one or you have less than 4-card support...but you do have 6 or more points. You are still looking for a Magic Fit and it is best to start looking at the lowest level. The best way to continue to look for a Magic Fit is for you to bid a 4-card or longer suit of your own... perhaps partner has support for your suit.

A new suit at the one-level is a forcing bid (GO) . It is part of the bidding conversation, not a final bid. **Responder could have as few as 6 points or as many as 20 points or even more.** Opener must bid again because there may be enough combined points for Game. On the other hand, if responder's hand is weak there is still time to stop at a low Part-Game contract on the next round of bidding.

You may find the Bidding Ladder helpful in deciding which suits can be bid at the one-level after partner has opened the bidding.

OPENING BID	SUITS RESPONDER CAN BID AT THE ONE-LEVEL
One Spade	NONE. Spades is the highest-ranking suit.
One Heart	SPADES. Minor suits are lower-ranking.
One Diamond	HEARTS or SPADES. Clubs, being lower-ranking than Diamonds, can't be bid at the one-level.
One Club	DIAMONDS, HEARTS or SPADES. All suits are higher-ranking than Clubs.

If you have only one suit that can be bid at the one-level, bid that suit. Occasionally you have a choice of two or three suits that can be bid at the one-level; use the same rules for an opening bid:

- Bid your longest suit first
- Bid the higher-ranking of two 5-card or 6-card suits
- Bid the lower-ranking of two 4-card suits
- Bid the middle-ranking of three 4-card suits

These rules are used only to break ties among those suits that could be bid at the one-level. For example, partner opens the bidding One Diamond and you have the following hand:

♠ J 8 7
♥ Q 7 4 2
♦ 6
♣ K J 7 5 3

Respond One Heart. Even though your longest suit is Clubs, you only consider those suits you can bid at the one-level when answering the third question.

Let's look at some examples combining the first three questions:

Partner opens the bidding One Diamond. What would you respond with the following hands?

1) ♠ 7 5 4 3   2) ♠ Q 6 4 3 2   3) ♠ K 9 4 3   4) ♠ K Q J 3
   ♥ A 4 2   ♥ K J 8 6 4   ♥ J 8 6 3   ♥ 10 7 6 5 2
   ♦ J 8   ♦ K 8   ♦ —   ♦ 9 2
   ♣ K Q 6 5   ♣ 8   ♣ A J 10 7 4   ♣ A 10

5) ♠ K 8 7
   ♥ Q J 7
   ♦ J 3 2
   ♣ Q 10 9 3

1) ONE SPADE. Can you raise partner's Major? No, he didn't bid a Major suit. Do you have a weak hand? No, you have 10 HCPs. Can you bid a new suit at the one-level? Yes, you have a 4-card Spade suit. You also have a 4-card Club suit but you can't bid it at the one-level. Thus, you should respond One Spade. The quality of the suit is not important; you're looking for the Magic Major Suit Fit.

2) ONE SPADE. You can't raise partner's Major and don't have a weak hand. You have 11 points...9 HCPs and one for each of the 5-card suits. You have two suits, both of which can be bid at the one-level. Since they are both 5-card suits, bid the higher-ranking first and respond One Spade.

3) ONE HEART. Partner hasn't bid a Major and you don't have a weak hand...you have 10 points. Can you bid a new suit at the one-level? Yes, you can bid One Heart, the lower-ranking of your two 4-card suits. Even though you have a longer Club suit, you bid One Heart because you only consider the suits you can bid at the one-level when answering the third question.

4) ONE HEART. Having answered no to the first two questions, you have two suits you could bid at the one-level. With five Hearts and only four Spades, bid the longer suit and respond One Heart.

5) You can't support partner's Major and you don't have a weak hand. You have 9 points, all in high cards. Since Clubs are lower-ranking than Diamonds, you don't have a suit you can bid at the one-level. It's time to look at the fourth question.

Question Four

By the time you reach the fourth question, you have answered no to the first three questions.

- You cannot raise partner's Major suit (Question One)
- You do not have a weak hand of 0 - 5 points (Question Two)
- You cannot bid a new suit at the one-level (Question Three)

The fourth question is designed to keep you from bidding too high in your search for the best denomination:

> ## 4. DO I HAVE A MINIMUM HAND (6 - 10 POINTS)?

Let's look first at what happens if you answer yes. With only 6 - 10 points, the strength of your hand is very limited and you have to make a response that keeps the auction going (in case opener has a lot of points) but keeps the partnership from getting too high on the Bidding Ladder (in case opener does not have a lot of points). Since you can't support partner's Major and don't have a suit you can bid at the one-level, you are left with only two choices:

- Raising opener's Minor suit to the two-level
- Responding One No Trump

Raising Opener's Minor Suit to the Two-level

Raising opener's Minor suit to the two-level tells opener that you have a minimum hand (6 - 10 points) and at least 4-card support. Raising opener's Minor is similar to raising opener's Major but has lower priority. You want to avoid Minor suit Games (preferring No Trump contracts) so **don't count dummy points when raising partner's Minor**. Short suits won't help in No Trump.

Responding One No Trump

If you don't have enough support to raise opener's Minor, you are left with the response of One No Trump. This tells opener that you have 6 - 10 points and can't bid anything else. The One No Trump response by responder is a sort of "catch-all". It has nothing to do with the kind of hand required to open the bidding One No Trump.

Let's look at some examples:

Your partner opens the bidding One Diamond. What do you respond with the following hands?

1) ♠ A 9	2) ♠ Q	3) ♠ 9 7 5	4) ♠ Q 8
♥ J 6 4	♥ 10 4	♥ K 10 4	♥ A 9 3
♦ K 9 8 6 4	♦ 10 3 2	♦ Q 7 5	♦ 5 3 2
♣ 9 6 4	♣ K J 9 7 6 3 2	♣ K 9 6 3	♣ A Q J 10 7

1) TWO DIAMONDS. Can you support partner's Major? No, he didn't bid one. Do you have a weak hand (0 - 5 points)? No, you have 9 points...8 HCPs plus 1 for the fifth Diamond. Can you bid a new suit at the one-level? No. Do you have a minimum hand (6 - 10 points)? Yes. Since you have support for opener's Minor suit, you can raise to Two Diamonds. Note that you don't value your hand using dummy points when raising partner's Minor suit.

2) ONE NO TRUMP. You can't support partner's Major and you don't have a weak hand. You can't bid a new suit at the one-level since your only suit is Clubs. You do have a minimum hand. You have 9 points...6 HCPs and 3 points for the 7-card Club suit. Since you don't have enough Diamonds to raise partner's Minor, you're left with the "catch-all" response of One No Trump. Note that this response does not tell opener that you have a balanced hand, only that you have a minimum hand (6 - 10 points) and nothing else to respond.

3) ONE NO TRUMP. You can't support opener's Major, don't have a weak hand, can't bid a new suit at the one-level but do have a minimum hand...you have 8 points. Since you can't support opener's Minor, you would respond One No Trump.

4) Partner didn't bid a Major, you don't have a weak hand and you can't bid a new suit at the one-level. Do you have a minimum hand (6 - 10 points)? No, you have 14 points...13 HCPs plus 1 for the fifth Club. It's time to take a look at what happens when you answer no to all four questions.

The Final Choice

If you answer no to all four questions, you must have at least 11 points. If your hand has 11 or more points, there is a very good chance that the partnership can make a Game since the opening bid showed at least 13 points. You have enough points to move to the two-level or higher. Since you can't support partner's Major and don't have a suit you can bid at the one-level, you are left with these choices:

- Raising opener's Minor suit — to the three-level
                                    — to Game (Three No Trump)
- Bidding a new suit at the two-level

Raising Opener's Minor Suit to the Three-level

Raising an opening Minor suit bid to the three-level shows:

- 4-card or longer support for opener's Minor suit
- 11 - 12 points

This response tells opener you are limited to 11 or 12 points. This is similar to raising opener's Major except you don't count dummy points since the Game, if there is one, is likely to be in No Trump. The range is very narrow and so it is an invitational bid ▼. If opener has a minimum hand of 13 or 14 points, he will know that there are probably not enough points for Game and will Pass.

Raising Opener's Minor Suit to Game (Three No Trump)

To make this response, you must have:

- 4-card or longer support for opener's Minor suit
- 13 - 16 points

This response is invitational ▼. Three No Trump is the most likely Game when you don't have a Magic Major Suit Fit, so opener will Pass unless he has a very unbalanced hand or is interested in Slam.

Bidding a New Suit at the Two-level (GO)

A response in a new suit at the two-level shows:

- A 4-card or longer suit
- 11 or more points

A response in a new suit at the two-level is a forcing bid (GO). Opener knows that you have at least 11 points but does not know how many more you have. He cannot say Pass when it is his turn to bid as there may be enough points for Game.

Let's look at some examples:

Your partner opens the bidding One Diamond. What do you respond with the following hands?

1) ♠ K 4 2	2) ♠ A 4 3	3) ♠ K 10
♥ 3 2	♥ K	♥ 9 7
♦ A J 8 4 3	♦ K J 9 8 3 2	♦ K 10 4
♣ Q 10 3	♣ Q 10 3	♣ K Q 7 5 4 3

   1) THREE DIAMONDS. You can't raise partner's Major, you do not have a weak hand, you can't bid a new suit at the one-level and you do not have a minimum hand, you have 11 points (10 HCPs and 1 for the fifth Diamond). With five Diamonds, you have more than enough to raise partner's Minor. Respond Three Diamonds telling opener that you have 11 or 12 points and four or more Diamonds.

2) THREE NO TRUMP. Again, you can't support partner's Major, don't have a weak hand, can't bid a new suit at the one-level and don't have a minimum hand. You have 15 points...13 HCPs and 2 points for the 6-card Diamond suit. You have too many points to raise opener's Minor suit to the three-level. Instead, your response is Three No Trump, telling opener you have 13 - 16 points and four or more Diamonds.

3) TWO CLUBS. Your answer is no to all four questions. Since you have 13 points...11 HCPs and 2 points for the 6-card Club suit...but do not have support for opener's Minor suit, you would bid a new suit at the two-level, Two Clubs.

If you have more than one suit that could be bid at the two-level, you choose the suit in the familiar way:

- Bid the longest suit first
- Bid the higher-ranking of two 5-card or 6-card suits
- Bid the lower-ranking of two 4-card suits
- Bid the middle-ranking of three 4-card suits

Here are some examples. Partner opens the bidding One Spade and for each of the following hands your answer is no to all four questions. What would you respond?

1) ♠ K 2
   ♥ J 10 7 3 2
   ♦ A K 4 3
   ♣ Q 10

2) ♠ 3
   ♥ A 3
   ♦ K J 9 6 2
   ♣ Q 10 7 6 3

3) ♠ K 10
   ♥ A 9 2
   ♦ K 10 6 4
   ♣ Q 7 5 2

4) ♠ 9
   ♥ A 10 8 3
   ♦ J 7 5 3
   ♣ A Q 9 8

1) TWO HEARTS. With a 5-card suit and a 4-card suit which could be bid at the two-level, bid the longer suit. Respond Two Hearts to the opening bid of One Spade.

2) TWO DIAMONDS. With two 5-card suits, bid the higher-ranking, Diamonds.

3) TWO CLUBS. Here the choice is between two 4-card suits. Bid the lower-ranking suit, Clubs.

4) TWO DIAMONDS. With a choice of three 4-card suits, bid the middle-ranking. Respond Two Diamonds to partner's opening bid.

Summary

When your partner opens the bidding with one of a suit, you can determine the appropriate response by asking yourself Responder's Four Questions:

Question One: CAN I RAISE PARTNER'S MAJOR?

If the answer is YES: Revalue your hand using dummy points (instead of length points) and raise to the appropriate level.

DUMMY POINTS					
Ace	4 points		Void	5 points	
King	3 points	+	Singleton	3 points	
Queen	2 points		Doubleton	1 points	
Jack	1 point				

APPROPRIATE LEVEL	
0 - 5 points	Pass
6 - 10 points	Raise to the two-level
11 - 12 points	Raise to the three-level
13 - 16 points	Raise to the four-level

If the answer is NO: Go on to the next question.

Question Two: DO I HAVE A WEAK HAND (0 - 5 POINTS)?

If the answer is YES: Pass.
If the answer is NO: Go on to the next question.

Question Three: CAN I BID A NEW SUIT AT THE ONE-LEVEL?

If the answer is YES: Bid the appropriate suit.
If the answer is NO: Go on to the next question.

Question Four: DO I HAVE A MINIMUM HAND (6 - 10 POINTS)?

If the answer is YES:
• Raise opener's Minor suit to the two-level with 4-card support
• Bid One No Trump.

If the answer is NO:
• Raise opener's Minor suit to the three-level with 11 - 12 Points.
• Raise opener's Minor to Game (Three No Trump) with 13 - 16 Points.
• Bid a new suit at the two-level.

Another View of Responses to Opening Bids

You have different choices as responder depending on the strength of your hand. The possible responses are listed here by order of preference within each point range:

POINT RANGE	POSSIBLE RESPONSES
0 - 5	• Pass
6 - 10	• Two-level Major suit raise • New suit at the one-level • Two-level Minor suit raise • One No Trump
11 - 12	• Three-level Major suit raise • New suit at the one-level • Three-level Minor suit raise • New suit at the two-level
13 - 16	• Four-level Major suit raise • New suit at the one-level • Three No Trump (Minor suit raise) • New suit at the two-level

Exercises

Partner opens the bidding One Heart. Use Responder's Four Questions to determine the correct response.

1) ♠ 8 7 3
   ♥ K 4 3 2
   ♦ Q 4 3 2
   ♣ Q 4

2) ♠ J 8 3
   ♥ 9 7 5
   ♦ K 7 4
   ♣ 10 9 7 5

3) ♠ K 9 7 3
   ♥ Q 3
   ♦ 10 8 6 4 2
   ♣ Q 7

4) ♠ K J 5
   ♥ J 5
   ♦ Q 9 7 5 3
   ♣ J 8 3

5) ♠ K Q 5
   ♥ J 5
   ♦ K J 8 7 3 2
   ♣ A J

Partner opens the bidding One Diamond. Use Responder's Four Questions to determine appropriate response.

6) ♠ A J 7 3
   ♥ K 9 8 2
   ♦ Q 7 3
   ♣ A 4

7) ♠ 8 3
   ♥ K 7 5
   ♦ K 3
   ♣ A Q 9 6 3 2

8) ♠ K 8
   ♥ Q J 3
   ♦ 10 8 6 4 3 2
   ♣ 8 7

9) ♠ 3 2
   ♥ A 9 7
   ♦ K Q 9 7 5
   ♣ J 8 3

10) ♠ K 5
    ♥ 7 5
    ♦ A K J 8 7 3
    ♣ Q 6 3

For the Curious

What Does Responder Do With 17 or More Points?

In this chapter, no mention was made of how responder deals with very powerful hands of 17 or more points. When responder holds this many points, Game should always be bid and there is the possibility of bidding higher, to a Slam contract. Slam bidding is discussed in more detail in Chapter 22.

Responder can use the Four Questions with hands of 17 or more points but there are a couple of modifications that should be considered.

As you will see in the chapter on Slam bidding, approximately 33 combined points are needed for a Small Slam and 37 for a Grand Slam. If responder has 17 or more points and answers yes to the question "Can I raise partner's Major?", he can raise to the appropriate level as follows:

17 - 19 points	Raise to the five-level
20 - 23 points	Raise to the six-level (Small Slam)
24 + points	Raise to the seven-level (Grand Slam)

For example, suppose opener bids One Heart and you have the following hand:

♠ K 9 3
♥ A Q 7 6 5
♦ A K 10 4 3
♣ —

With 21 points... 16 in high cards plus 5 for the Club void... raise to Six Hearts.

The Jump Shift

In some systems, there is another way to show opener that responder has a very powerful hand. If responder has 17 or more points and answers yes to the question "Can I bid a new suit at the one-level?", instead of bidding the suit at the one-level he can bid it at the two-level, one level higher than necessary. Such a response is called a *Jump Shift* and alerts opener to the possibility of slam. A Jump Shift is a marathon bid 〔GO〕 since it forces the partnership to at least the Game level.

For example, partner opens the bidding One Club and you hold the following hand:

♠ A K J 10 8 7 6
♥ A 5
♦ 8
♣ K J 7

You could respond One Spade but, with 19 points, you can show the power of your hand by making a Jump Shift to Two Spades.

Similarly, if you were about to bid a new suit at the two-level but held 17 or more points, you could jump to the three-level to show your extra strength. However, a Jump Shift takes away some of your bidding room on the Bidding Ladder and is not used much anymore since a new suit by responder is forcing **GO**

Why Does Responder Bid the Lower-Ranking of Two 4-card Suits?

Suppose opener bids One Club and responder has the following hand:

♠ A J 8 7
♥ K 10 7
♦ Q 8 5 4
♣ 8 6

Responder has a choice of 4-card suits to bid at the one-level. Why should he bid One Diamond, the lower-ranking suit, rather than One Spade, the Major suit? There are two reasons:

- It is possible that you should be in a Diamond contract at the Part-Game level. For example, opener might have a 13 point hand with four Clubs and four Diamonds or five Clubs and four Diamonds.
- If opener also has a 4-card Spade suit, he will bid it after your One Diamond response. Thus there is no danger that the Magic Fit in Spades will get lost.

Do You Ever Play a Game Contract in Five Clubs or Five Diamonds?

The guidelines presented so far indicate that you always play in Three No Trump rather than Five Clubs or Five Diamonds. There are certainly hands that will make Game in a Minor suit but not Three No Trump. However, they are rare. Much more common are hands that make Three No Trump but not Game in a Minor suit.

In later chapters there will be situations introduced where you end up in Game in a Minor suit. For example:

- In competitive auctions, the auction may get beyond the Three No Trump level, making Game in a Minor suit the best alternative.
- When trying for a Slam contract, there may not be sufficient combined strength and the auction ends at the five-level in a Minor suit.

Other than in such exceptional cases, you will do much better in the long run if you play in Three No Trump rather than Game in a Minor suit when there is no Magic Major Suit Fit.

8

Opener's Rebid After a One-Level Response

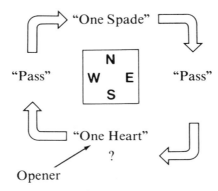

Having looked at responses to opening bids, we now go back across the table to consider what the opener does after hearing responder's bid.

Opener's Rebid

Opener acts as the **describer**. He describes his hand to the responder who, as captain, uses the information to decide HOW HIGH and WHERE to place the contract. Opener's original bid started the description. After hearing responder's bid, opener can make a second bid which tells responder more about the strength and shape of his hand. Opener's second bid is called *opener's rebid*.

When making his rebid, opener must not only look at his own strength and shape but also keep in mind the message transmitted by responder's bid. Responder's bid will fall into one of the following categories:

- A response at the one-level
- A response at the two-level
- A raise of opener's suit

In this chapter, we shall look at the first case, a one-level response. The other cases will be discussed in the following chapters.

Let's start by reviewing the signal that responder is sending with a one-level response.

Responder's Message

There are two types of one-level response:

NEW SUIT
- Forcing
- 6 or more points
- Opener has to bid again

ONE NO TRUMP
- Invitational
- 6 - 10 Points
- Opener can Pass or bid again

Classifying Opener's Strength

To help opener determine his best rebid, he classifies the strength of his hand into:

MINIMUM HAND: 13 - 16 Points | 13 | 14 | 15 | 16 | 17 | 18 | 19 | 20 | 21 |

MEDIUM HAND: 17 - 18 Points | 13 | 14 | 15 | 16 | 17 | 18 | 19 | 20 | 21 |

MAXIMUM HAND: 19 - 21 Points | 13 | 14 | 15 | 16 | 17 | 18 | 19 | 20 | 21 |

How does opener determine which rebid to make? Opener's Four Questions through the order in which they are asked, will guide opener to the best rebid.

OPENER'S FOUR QUESTIONS

1. CAN I RAISE PARTNER'S MAJOR?
2. CAN I BID A NEW SUIT AT THE ONE-LEVEL?
3. IS MY HAND BALANCED?
4. SHOULD I BID A NEW SUIT AT THE TWO-LEVEL?

The questions are very similar to those used by responder.

Question One

The search is still on for a Magic Major Suit Fit. So the first question is:

> ### 1. CAN I RAISE PARTNER'S MAJOR?

Opener thinks about raises much the same way that responder did:

- Raise with 4-card support (4 + 4 = 8)
- Revalue the hand using dummy points (opener will be dummy)
- Raise to the appropriate level

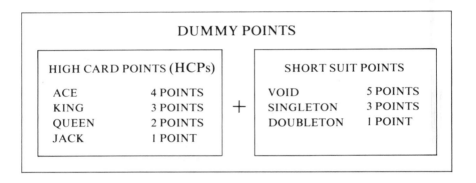

DUMMY POINTS			
HIGH CARD POINTS (HCPs)		**SHORT SUIT POINTS**	
ACE	4 POINTS	VOID	5 POINTS
KING	3 POINTS	SINGLETON	3 POINTS
QUEEN	2 POINTS	DOUBLETON	1 POINT
JACK	1 POINT		

For example:

♠ A J 9 3
♥ 3
♦ A K 8 6 3 2
♣ J 3

You would originally value the hand as 15 points (13 HCPs plus 2 points for the Diamond length)...a minimum hand...and open the bidding One Diamond. If partner responds One Spade, you are going to be the dummy because you plan to raise Spades. How many dummy points are there? Your hand is worth 17 points (13 HCPs plus 3 points for the singleton and 1 point for the doubleton)...a medium strength hand.

Having identified a Magic Major Suit Fit and revalued your hand using dummy points, you determine HOW HIGH to raise responder's Major.

RAISING RESPONDER'S MAJOR SUIT RESPONSE

OPENER'S DUMMY POINTS	OPENER'S REBID
13 - 16 points (minimum hand)	Raise to the two-level ♥. Responder could have as few as 6 points and this will be high enough. If responder has a strong hand, he will be able to carry on to a Game contract.
17 - 18 points (medium hand)	Raise to the three-level ♥. This is a strong invitation to responder to carry on to a Game contract but lets the partnership stop in Part-Game if responder only has 6 to 8 points.
19 - 21 points (maximum hand)	Raise to the four-level ♥. Even if responder only has 6 to 8 points, there should be enough combined points to make a Game contract.

Let's look at some examples:

You open the bidding One Club and your partner responds One Heart. What do you rebid with each of the following hands?

1) ♠ K 5	2) ♠ A J 6 4	3) ♠ 4	4) ♠ K J 7 5
♥ A 8 7 4	♥ J 9 6 3	♥ A J 7 3	♥ 9 2
♦ 5 3	♦ —	♦ A 5 4	♦ K Q 4
♣ K Q 7 4 2	♣ A K 8 4 3	♣ A K J 10 9	♣ A J 8 3

1) TWO HEARTS. Can you raise partner's Major? Yes, you have 4-card support. Revaluing with dummy points, you have 14 points...12 HCPs plus 1 for each doubleton. Raise to the two-level to show a minimum hand (13 - 16 points). Responder will decide what to do next.

2) THREE HEARTS. You have four Hearts, enough to raise responder's Major, and 18 dummy points...13 HCPs plus 5 for the Diamond void. Raise to the appropriate level, Three Hearts, to show a medium hand (17 - 18 points). This is a strong invitation, but not a demand, for responder to continue to Game.

3) FOUR HEARTS. You can raise responder's Major and have 20 dummy points... 17 in high cards and 3 for the singleton Spade. Raise responder to Game. Even if responder has only 6 points, there will be enough combined points for a Game contract.

4) You only have two Hearts, not enough to raise partner's Major. It's time to move on to the next question.

Question Two

If you can't raise responder's Major, the second question is designed to continue the search for a Magic Fit:

---

2. CAN I BID A NEW SUIT AT THE ONE-LEVEL?

If you have a 4-card suit or longer that you can still bid at the one-level, you bid that suit with 13 - 18 points (minimum or medium hand) ▼ .

If you have 19 - 21 points (maximum hand), you want to describe this strength to responder, the captain. Responder has at least 6 points so you know there should be enough combined strength for Game. You can show a maximum hand by bidding your suit with a jump to the two-level, one level higher than necessary. Since you are 'jumping' a level on the Bidding Ladder and are 'shifting' to a new suit, this is called a *Jump Shift* 〈GO〉 . For example:

OPENER	RESPONDER
One Club	One Heart
Two Spades	

Opener's Jump Shift is a marathon bid 〈GO〉 . HOW HIGH has been determined... Game. Now the partnership can focus attention on WHERE knowing that the bidding must continue until a Game is reached.

OPENER'S REBID WITH A NEW SUIT THAT CAN BE BID AT THE ONE-LEVEL

OPENER'S POINTS	OPENER'S REBID
13 - 16 points (minimum hand)	
`13` `14` `15` `16` 17 18 19 20 21	Bid the new suit at the one-level ▼ . The search is still on for the Magic Major
17 - 18 points (medium hand)	Suit Fit.
13 14 15 16 `17` `18` 19 20 21	
19 - 21 points (maximum hand)	Bid the new suit at the two-level 〈GO〉 . The Jump Shift is a marathon bid.
13 14 15 16 17 18 `19` `20` `21`	

Let's look at some examples combining the first two questions:

You open the bidding One Diamond and your partner responds One Heart. What do you rebid with each of the following hands?

1) ♠ A K 2
   ♥ A 8 7 4
   ♦ Q 7 5 3
   ♣ 4 2

2) ♠ K J 6 4
   ♥ Q 3
   ♦ A J 8 5
   ♣ K 8 3

3) ♠ A Q 6 4
   ♥ A 7 3
   ♦ A K Q 5 4
   ♣ 8

4) ♠ K J 5
   ♥ 9 2
   ♦ K Q 7 6 4
   ♣ A 7 5

1) TWO HEARTS. Can you raise partner's Major? Yes, you have 4-card support. Revaluing with dummy points, you have 14 points … 13 HCPs plus 1 for the doubleton. Raise to Two Hearts, to show a minimum hand (13 - 16 points).

2) ONE SPADE. Here you can't raise your partner's Major - you don't have 4-card support. So you ask yourself the second question: "Can I bid a new suit at the one-level?" Since the answer is yes and you have a minimum hand (14 points), rebid One Spade.

3) TWO SPADES. Again, you can't raise responder's Major but you can bid a new suit at the one-level. However, to show your maximum hand (20 points) Jump Shift and rebid Two Spades. This will tell responder to keep the auction going until Game (at least) is reached.

4) You can't support responder's Major with only two cards and you don't have another suit you can bid at the one-level. It's time to go on to the third question.

Question Three

If you have answered no to the first two questions, the next question is designed to allow you to describe both your strength and distribution to responder:

> ### 3. IS MY HAND BALANCED?

With a balanced hand, describe your strength to responder as follows:

OPENER'S REBID WITH A BALANCED HAND

OPENER'S POINTS	OPENER'S REBID

13 - 15* points (minimum hand)

| 13 | 14 | 15 | 16 | 17 | 18 | 19 | 20 | 21 |

Rebid No Trump at the cheapest level (One No Trump) ▼. This tells responder that you have a balanced hand **too weak** to open One No Trump.

If responder has already bid One No Trump, Pass ⬣. Since responder has only 6 - 10 points, there cannot be enough combined points for Game.

16* - 18 points (medium hand)

| 13 | 14 | 15 | 16 | 17 | 18 | 19 | 20 | 21 |

There is no rebid to show a balanced hand with this strength. This type of hand would have been opened One No Trump.

19 - 21 points (maximum hand)

| 13 | 14 | 15 | 16 | 17 | 18 | 19 | 20 | 21 |

Jump in No Trump ✺GO✺. This tells responder that you have a balanced hand **too strong** to open One No Trump. Like the Jump Shift, this rebid is a marathon bid, forcing to Game.

* The adjustment here is due to the range of the One No Trump opening bid (16 - 18 points).

Let's look at some examples combining the first three questions:

You open the bidding One Club and your partner responds One Heart. What do you rebid with each of the following hands?

1) ♠ K 8 3 2) ♠ A J 6 4 3) ♠ A Q 8 4) ♠ K J 8
♥ 7 4 ♥ 6 3 ♥ J 7 3 ♥ 2
♦ A 5 3 ♦ A 8 6 ♦ A J 4 ♦ K Q 4
♣ K Q 7 4 2 ♣ A J 9 2 ♣ A K J 9 ♣ A J 8 7 6 3

1) ONE NO TRUMP. Can you raise partner's Major? No, you don't have 4-card support. Can you bid a new suit at the one-level? No, you don't have a 4-card Spade suit. Is your hand balanced? Yes, your shape is 3-2-3-5. With 13 points, rebid One No Trump to tell responder that you have a balanced hand too weak to open One No Trump. If responder had bid One No Trump instead of One Heart, you would Pass.

2) ONE SPADE. You can't raise partner's Major but you do have a suit you can bid at the one-level. Rebid One Spade.

3) TWO NO TRUMP. You can't raise responder's Major and you don't have a suit you can bid at the one-level. Your hand is balanced. With 20 points, rebid Two No Trump to show a hand too strong to open One No Trump. This rebid is forcing to Game. If responder had bid One No Trump rather than One Heart, you would jump to Three No Trump.

4) You can't raise partner's Major and you can't bid a new suit at the one-level. You also don't have a balanced hand. It's time to look at the fourth question.

Question Four

The fourth question is to help you decide whether you should introduce a new suit into the auction:

> ### 4. SHOULD I BID A NEW SUIT AT THE TWO-LEVEL?

If you have a second suit of at least four cards, you will usually, but not always, bid it at the two-level.

Why would you **not** bid a new suit at the two-level? You have to be careful not to push the bidding too high with a minimum hand (13 - 16 points). To see how this could happen, you might find it helpful to look at the Bidding Ladder while studying the following examples:

1) OPENER	RESPONDER	2) OPENER	RESPONDER
One Heart	One Spade	One Club	One Spade
Two Clubs		Two Hearts	

In both examples, opener is showing both a Heart suit and a Club suit. Suppose responder, as captain, wants to choose a Part-Game contract in one of these suits at his next bid. In the first example, he can make the choice at the two-level. He can Pass if he wants to play Part-Game in Clubs or he can bid Two Hearts if he wants to play Part-Game in Hearts. In the second example, responder could Pass if he wants to play Part-Game in Hearts but would have to go to the three-level...Three Clubs...if he wants to play Part-Game in opener's first suit. If both opener and responder have minimum hands, the three-level may be too high.

When opener has a minimum hand (13 - 16 points), he does not want to push responder to the three-level if he can avoid it. In the first example, opener's second suit, Clubs, is lower-ranking than his first suit, Hearts. In the second example, opener's second suit, Hearts, is higher-ranking than his first suit, Clubs. **If opener has a minimum hand, he should not bid a new suit at the two-level if it is higher-ranking than his first suit**.

If opener has a medium hand (17 - 18 points), he can bid a new suit at the two-level whether or not it is higher-ranking than his first suit. If he pushes the bidding to the three-level, there should be enough combined strength to make the contract. As in answering the second question, if opener has a maximum hand (19 - 21 points), he should jump a level when bidding a new suit (Jump Shift) to describe his strength to responder.

OPENER'S REBID WITH A NEW SUIT THAT CAN BE BID AT THE TWO-LEVEL

OPENER'S POINTS	OPENER'S REBID
13 - 16 points (minimum hand) 	If your second suit is **lower-ranking** than your first suit, bid your second suit at the two-level ▼.
17 - 18 points (medium hand) 	Bid your second suit at the two-level even if this pushes the bidding to the three-level ▼.
19 - 21 points (maximum hand)	Jump in your second suit 🔘. This is a Jump Shift and is a marathon bid (forcing to Game).

Let's look at some examples:

You open the bidding One Diamond and your partner responds One Spade. You can't raise partner's Major, can't bid a new suit at the one-level and your hand isn't balanced. You arrive at the fourth question. What do you rebid with the following hands?

1) ♠ 3	2) ♠ K J 8	3) ♠ A Q 8	4) ♠ 4
♥ K 4	♥ A Q 7 4	♥ 3	♥ A 8 6 3
♦ A J 9 5 3	♦ A K 7 5 4	♦ A K Q J 4	♦ A K J 10 6
♣ K Q 7 4 2	♣ 3	♣ A 9 7 4	♣ Q 8 4

1) TWO CLUBS. Your hand is worth 15 points...13 HCPs plus 1 for each of your 5-card suits. With a minimum hand (13 - 16 points) and a second suit that is lower-ranking than your first suit, bid your second suit. Rebid Two Clubs.

2) TWO HEARTS. You have 18 points which puts your hand in the medium category (17 - 18 points). With this strength bid your second suit at the two-level, Two Hearts.

3) THREE CLUBS. Your hand is worth 21 points. Even if responder has as few as 6 points, you should have enough combined points for Game. Jump Shift to Three Clubs. This is a marathon bid which tells responder that he must keep the bidding going until Game (at least) is reached.

4) You have a minimum hand...15 points...and your second suit is higher-ranking than your first suit. If you bid Two Hearts you may get the partnership too high when responder also has a minimum hand. It's time to look at what happens when you answer no to all four questions.

The Final Choice

If partner made a response at the one-level and you answered no to all four questions then:

- You can't raise partner's Major
- You can't bid a new suit at the one-level
- Your hand isn't balanced
- You can't bid a new suit at the two-level.

This leaves two possibilities:

- Rebidding your first suit
- Raising partner's Minor if you have 4-card support.

The level at which you rebid is determined according to your strength:

OPENER'S REBID IN HIS FIRST SUIT OR WHEN RAISING RESPONDER'S MINOR

OPENER'S POINTS	OPENER'S REBID
13 - 16 points (minimum hand) `13 14 15 16` 17 18 19 20 21	Rebid your first suit or raise partner's Minor to the two-level ▼.
17 - 18 points (medium hand) 13 14 15 16 `17 18` 19 20 21	Jump rebid your first suit or jump raise partner's Minor to the three-level ▼.
19 - 21 points (maximum hand) 13 14 15 16 17 18 `19 20 21`	Jump to Game in your Major suit or to Three No Trump with a Minor suit ▼.

Let's look at some examples:

You open the bidding One Diamond and your partner responds One Spade. What do you rebid with the following hands?

1) ♠ 3	2) ♠ Q 9 8	3) ♠ J 8	4) ♠ 4
♥ A J 9	♥ A K	♥ K J 10	♥ A Q 9 3
♦ K Q 8 7 5 3	♦ A Q J 8 7 4	♦ A Q J 9 6 3	♦ K J 10 7 5
♣ Q 8 7	♣ 3 2	♣ A Q	♣ Q 7 2

1) TWO DIAMONDS. Can you raise partner's Major? No. Can you bid a new suit suit at the one-level? No. Is your hand balanced? No. Should you bid a new suit at the two-level? You don't have one. Your hand is worth 14 points...12 HCPs plus 2 for your 6-card suit. With a minimum hand (13 - 16 points) rebid your suit at the two-level...Two Diamonds.

2) THREE DIAMONDS. You can't raise partner's Major. You can't bid a new suit at the one-level and your hand is not balanced. You have 18 points which puts your hand in the medium category (17 - 18 points). With no second suit you are strong enough to make a jump rebid of Three Diamonds.

3) THREE NO TRUMP. You can't raise partner's Major or bid a new suit at the one-level and your hand isn't balanced. In addition, you don't have a second suit to consider bidding at the two-level. This time you have 20 points. Describe your hand with a rebid of Three No Trump. Partner will know you have a maximum hand (19 - 21 points) and a long Diamond suit.

4) TWO DIAMONDS. You can't raise partner, can't bid a new suit at the one-level and your hand isn't balanced. Should you bid your second suit? No. Your second suit is higher-ranking than your first suit and you have a minimum hand...13 points. You should rebid your first suit at the two-level...Two Diamonds.

Summary

After you open the bidding and your partner responds at the one-level, you have the opportunity to make a second bid. As opener, you are the describer and your second bid is called *opener's rebid*. You can determine the appropriate rebid by asking yourself Opener's Four Questions:

Question One: *CAN I RAISE PARTNER'S MAJOR?*

If the answer is YES: Revalue your hand using dummy points and raise to the appropriate level:

13 - 16 points	Raise to the two-level
17 - 18 points	Raise to the three-level
19 - 21 points	Raise to the four-level (Game)

If the answer is NO: Go on to the next question.

Question Two: *CAN I BID A NEW SUIT AT THE ONE-LEVEL?*

If the answer is YES: Bid the new suit at the appropriate level:

13 - 18 points	Bid at the one-level
19 - 21 points	Bid at the two-level (Jump Shift)

If the answer is NO: Go on to the next question.

Question Three: *IS MY HAND BALANCED?*

If the answer is YES: Rebid No Trump at the appropriate level:

13 - 15 points	Stay at the same level
19 - 21 points	Jump a level

If the answer is NO: Go on to the next question.

Question Four: *SHOULD I BID A NEW SUIT AT THE TWO-LEVEL?*

If the answer is YES: Bid the new suit at the appropriate level:

13 - 16 points	Bid at the two-level*
17 - 18 points	Bid at the two-level
19 - 21 points	Bid at the three-level (Jump Shift)

If the answer is NO: Rebid your first suit (or raise partner's Minor) at the appropriate level:

13 - 16 points	Bid at the two-level
17 - 18 points	Bid at the three-level
19 - 21 points	Bid at the four-level (Major) or bid Three No Trump

* Only bid a new suit if it is lower-ranking than your first suit.

Another Way of Looking at Opener's Rebid

If your hand is minimum (13 - 16 points), do something that sounds minimum:

- Support partner at the cheapest level
- Rebid your suit at the cheapest level
- Bid No Trump at the cheapest level
- Introduce a new suit:
  — if it is at the one-level or
    — if it is at the two-level and doesn't push your partner to the three-level should he want to play with your first suit as trump.

If your hand is medium (17 - 18 points), do something that sounds medium:

- Support partner with a jump
- Rebid your suit with a jump
- Introduce a new suit even if it may push your partner to the three-level

If your hand is maximum (19 - 21 points), do something that sounds maximum:

- Support partner with a jump to Game
- Rebid your suit with a jump to Game
- Bid No Trump with a jump
- Jump in a new suit (Jump Shift)

Exercises

1) You open the bidding One Club. Your partner responds One Diamond. What is your rebid with each of the following hands?

a) ♠ A J 9 4 b) ♠ Q J 6 c) ♠ A 7 2 d) ♠ 4
   ♥ K J 3   ♥ K 8 2   ♥ 9 7   ♥ K 9 3
   ♦ 9 4   ♦ 7 3   ♦ Q 3   ♦ A 8 6 3
   ♣ A 9 6 2   ♣ A Q J 8 3 ♣ K Q 10 8 7 3 ♣ K Q 8 3 2

2) You open the bidding One Club and your partner responds One Heart. What do you do next with the following hands?

a) ♠ A 3   b) ♠ A 9 8 5 c) ♠ 10 3 2 d) ♠ 9 3
   ♥ K Q 4 2   ♥ 6 5   ♥ 2   ♥ A 7
   ♦ Q 8   ♦ 3   ♦ A Q 5 4   ♦ K 8
   ♣ Q 10 7 6 2 ♣ A K 8 6 5 3 ♣ K Q J 6 3 ♣ A Q J 8 5 3 2

3) You open the bidding One Heart and your partner bids One Spade. What do you do with the following hands?

a)♠ 9 7 4 2   b)♠ J 4   c)♠ A 2   d)♠ K 3 2
   ♥ K Q 7 3   ♥ A Q 7 5 3 ♥ A K Q 7 5 3 2 ♥ A K Q 6 3
   ♦ 8   ♦ 8 3   ♦ K 8 3   ♦ A K 6 3
   ♣ A K Q 2   ♣ A K 5 3   ♣ 3   ♣ 8

4) You open the bidding One Diamond and your partner responds One No Trump. What do you do now with the following hands?

a)♠ Q 4   b)♠ A K 8 2 c)♠ 5   d)♠ A Q
   ♥ A 10 6 3 ♥ 5   ♥ 10 9   ♥ K 10 3
   ♦ K J 9 4   ♦ A K J 8 7 3 ♦ A J 10 7 4 3 ♦ A Q 7 6 3 2
   ♣ A 9 7   ♣ J 3   ♣ K Q J 3 ♣ K 2

5) You open the bidding One Diamond and your partner bids One Spade. What do you rebid with the following hands?

a)♠ A 7 4 2 b)♠ J 10   c)♠ A 2   d)♠ A K
   ♥ A 8   ♥ 4   ♥ K Q 9 3 ♥ J
   ♦ K Q 8 4 ♦ K Q J 8 3 ♦ A Q 6 3 ♦ A Q 10 4 3
   ♣ A Q 2   ♣ A J 10 3 2 ♣ K Q 10 ♣ K J 9 7 6

For the Curious

Why Does Opener Jump to Two No Trump With a Maximum Hand?

If opener has a balanced hand of 19 - 21 points and responder bids a new suit at the one-level, the third question (Is my hand balanced?) indicates that opener should jump to Two No Trump. Since opener knows that responder has at least 6 points, why doesn't opener just jump right to Game, Three No Trump?

Remember that opener is only **describing** his hand, not trying to place the final contract...that is the captain's job. By rebidding Two No Trump, a marathon bid, there is room left for responder to explore other possible Game contracts (or Slam contracts).

For example, suppose these are the combined hands:

OPENER	RESPONDER
♠ K 7 6	♠ Q J 9 8 3
♥ A 9	♥ 10 3
♦ K J 5	♦ Q 10 3
♣ A K J 8 5	♣ Q 9 3

Opener would start the auction off with One Club. Responder would bid One Spade. If opener now jumped to Three No Trump, responder would have to guess whether to leave the contract in Three No Trump or bid Four Spades and hope that there was a Magic Major Suit Fit...opener might only have two Spades. If, instead, opener bids Two No Trump, responder can explore in a more scientific fashion:

OPENER	RESPONDER
One Club	One Spade
Two No Trump	Three Spades
Four Spades	Pass

When opener rebids Two No Trump, responder knows that this is a marathon bid, forcing to the Game level. He can concentrate on WHERE. He knows that opener doesn't have four Spades since opener did not raise his response. By bidding Three Spades, responder gives opener a second chance to show support. Opener, having already denied holding four Spades, can now raise responder's suit and the Magic Fit is found.

Another reason that opener jumps to Two No Trump with a maximum balanced hand rather than Three No Trump is that the jump to Three No Trump is used to show a maximum hand with support for responder's Minor suit.

The auction after opener's rebid will be explained more fully in later chapters.

9

Opener's Rebid After a Two-Level Response

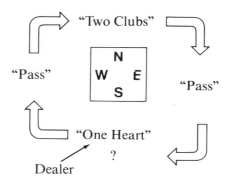

"Two Clubs"

"Pass"

"Pass"

"One Heart"

?

Dealer

Opener's rebid after the response of a new suit at the two-level is similar to the rebid after a new suit at the one-level.

Opener is the describer. Responder's bid of a new suit at the two-level is forcing:

NEW SUIT
- Forcing
- 11 or more points

Opener must bid again to tell responder enough about his strength and distribution that responder will be in a position to decide HOW HIGH and WHERE to place the contract.

Opener uses the same approach as after a one-level response. He classifies the strength of his hand as:

MINIMUM HAND: 13 - 16 Points | 13 | 14 | 15 | 16 | 17 | 18 | 19 | 20 | 21 |

MEDIUM HAND: 17 - 18 Points | 13 | 14 | 15 | 16 | 17 | 18 | 19 | 20 | 21 |

MAXIMUM HAND: 19 - 21 Points | 13 | 14 | 15 | 16 | 17 | 18 | 19 | 20 | 21 |

Opener then uses Opener's Four Questions to guide him to the best rebid.

OPENER'S FOUR QUESTIONS

1. CAN I RAISE PARTNER'S MAJOR?
2. CAN I BID A NEW SUIT AT THE ONE-LEVEL?
3. IS MY HAND BALANCED?
4. SHOULD I BID A NEW SUIT AT THE TWO-LEVEL?

What's Changed?

A response of a new suit at the two-level shows at least 11 points. Game is close since there must be a minimum of 24 combined points (13 + 11 = 24). The effect on opener's rebid is illustrated in the following chart:

OPENER'S POINTS		RESPONDER'S MINIMUM POINTS		MINIMUM COMBINED POINTS		
13	+	11	=	24	Part-Game	
14	+	11	=	25		Opener's MINIMUM
15	+	11	=	26	Game	rebids are FORCING
16	+	11	=	27		
17	+	11	=	28	Game	Opener's MEDIUM
18	+	11	=	29		rebids are MARATHON
19	+	11	=	30		
20	+	11	=	31	Game	Opener's MAXIMUM
21	+	11	=	32		rebids are MARATHON

After a response at the one-level, opener's rebids with minimum hands (13 - 16 points) or medium hands (17 - 18 points) are invitational ▼ . However, after a response at the two-level, opener's rebids which show minimum hands are forcing **(GO)** because Game is still possible...even if responder has only 11 points. Similarly, opener's rebids which show medium hands are marathon (forcing to Game) because there are always enough combined points for Game.

Let's see how opener uses the point ranges and Opener's Four Questions after the response of a new suit at the two-level.

Question One

---

1. CAN I RAISE PARTNER'S MAJOR?

If you have 4-card support, revalue your hand using dummy points and raise to the appropriate level based on your strength.

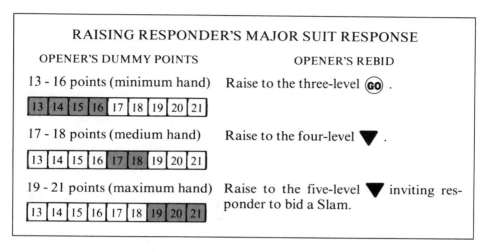

RAISING RESPONDER'S MAJOR SUIT RESPONSE

OPENER'S DUMMY POINTS · · · · · · · · · · · OPENER'S REBID

13 - 16 points (minimum hand) · · · · Raise to the three-level **GO** .

| 13 | 14 | 15 | 16 | 17 | 18 | 19 | 20 | 21 |

17 - 18 points (medium hand) · · · · Raise to the four-level ▼ .

| 13 | 14 | 15 | 16 | 17 | 18 | 19 | 20 | 21 |

19 - 21 points (maximum hand) · · Raise to the five-level ▼ inviting responder to bid a Slam.

| 13 | 14 | 15 | 16 | 17 | 18 | 19 | 20 | 21 |

Let's look at some examples: You open the bidding One Spade and your partner responds Two Hearts. What would your rebid be with each of the following hands?

1) ♠ A J 8 7 3
   ♥ 9 7 5 4
   ♦ A 9
   ♣ K 8

2) ♠ A K 9 7 2
   ♥ A Q 7 5
   ♦ 8
   ♣ Q 8 3

3) ♠ A Q J 9 8 2
   ♥ A Q 7 6
   ♦ A 9
   ♣ 7

4) ♠ K J 9 7 3
   ♥ 8 3
   ♦ A Q 9
   ♣ K 6 4

1) THREE HEARTS. Can you raise partner's Major? Yes. Valuing with dummy points, you have 14 points...12 HCPs and 1 for each doubleton. With a minimum hand (13 - 16 points) raise to Three Hearts. The bidding is now on 'automatic pilot'. Since Three Hearts is forcing, responder will bid Four Hearts (unless he is interested in Slam).

2) FOUR HEARTS. You can support partner's Major and your hand revalues to 18 points ...15 in high cards and 3 for the singleton. Four Hearts shows a medium hand (17 - 18 points).

3) FIVE HEARTS. Again you can support partner's Major. This time you have 21 points...17 in high cards, 3 for the singleton and 1 for the doubleton. Five Hearts tells responder you have a maximum hand (19 - 21 points) and invites partner to continue to Slam. We will discuss Slam bidding in more detail in Chapter 22.

4) You only have two Hearts, not enough to support partner's Major. It's time to move on to the next question.

Question Two

2. CAN I BID A NEW SUIT AT THE ONE-LEVEL?

Since the bidding is already at the two-level, opener always moves past Question Two and on to Question Three.

Question Three

3. IS MY HAND BALANCED?

With a balanced hand, describe your strength to responder as follows:

OPENER'S REBID WITH A BALANCED HAND

OPENER'S POINTS	OPENER'S REBID
13 - 15 points (minimum hand) 13 14 15 16 17 18 19 20 21	Rebid No Trump at the cheapest level (Two No Trump) **GO** . This tells responder that you have a balanced hand **too weak** to open One No Trump.
16 - 18 points (medium hand) 13 14 15 16 17 18 19 20 21	There is no rebid to show a balanced hand with this strength. This type of hand would have been opened One No Trump.
19 - 21 points (maximum hand) 13 14 15 16 17 18 19 20 21	Rebid No Trump with a jump ▼ . This tells responder that you have a balanced hand **too strong** to open One No Trump.

Let's look at some examples:

You open the bidding One Heart and your partner responds Two Clubs. What would you do now with each of the following hands?

1) ♠ K 7 4	2) ♠ A K J 7	3) ♠ Q 8 2
♥ A 9 7 5 4	♥ A Q 7 5	♥ A Q J 7 6
♦ Q J 5	♦ K 8 3	♦ K 9 4 2
♣ K 8	♣ Q 2	♣ 3

1) TWO NO TRUMP. Can you raise partner's Major? No, he hasn't bid one. Is your hand balanced? Yes, your shape is 5-3-3-2. With 14 points, rebid Two No Trump to tell responder you have a balanced hand too weak to open One No Trump.

2) THREE NO TRUMP. Partner hasn't bid a Major so you can't support it. Rebid Three No Trump to show partner a hand that was too strong to open One No Trump originally.

3) You can't raise partner's Major and you don't have a balanced hand. Time to move on to the last question.

Question Four

> **4. SHOULD I BID A NEW SUIT AT THE TWO-LEVEL?**

As with the rebid after a one-level response, the answer to this question depends on whether or not you have a second suit at least 4 cards in length and on your strength.

If you have a second suit, bid as follows:

OPENER'S REBID WITH A NEW SUIT THAT CAN BE BID AT THE TWO-LEVEL

OPENER'S POINTS	OPENER'S REBID
13 - 16 points (minimum hand) `13` `14` `15` `16` `17` `18` `19` `20` `21`	If your second suit is **lower ranking** than your first suit **and can be bid at the two-level**, bid your second suit **GO** .
17 - 18 points (medium hand) `13` `14` `15` `16` `17` `18` `19` `20` `21`	Bid your second suit **GO** .
19 - 21 points (maximum hand) `13` `14` `15` `16` `17` `18` `19` `20` `21`	Jump in your second suit *GO* . This is a **Jump Shift** and is a marathon bid (forcing to Game).

From this chart you can see that there are only two cases where opener should not bid a new suit after partner has responded at the two-level:

- If opener has a minimum hand (13 - 16 points) and his second suit is **higher-ranking** than his first. Bidding a higher-ranking suit describes a medium hand (17 - 18 points).

- If opener has a minimum hand (13 - 16 points) and his second suit is **lower-ranking** than his first but can't be bid at the two-level. For example:

OPENER	RESPONDER
One Spade	Two Hearts
Three Clubs	

This sequence would describe a medium hand.

Let's look at some examples:

You open the bidding One Spade and your partner responds Two Diamonds. What would your rebid be with each of the following hands?

1) ♠ A Q 9 7 4	2) ♠ A K 9 7 5	3) ♠ A Q J 9 8	4) ♠ K Q 9 8 2
♥ K 10 5 4	♥ A 5	♥ A K J 3	♥ 9 3
♦ A J	♦ 10	♦ 10 9	♦ Q 5
♣ 9 3	♣ K Q 8 3 2	♣ A 10	♣ A J 7 4

1) TWO HEARTS. You have 15 points...14 in high cards and 1 for your fifth Spade. With a minimum hand (13 - 16 points) you can bid a new suit if it is lower-ranking than your first suit and there is still room to bid it at the two-level. Rebid Two Hearts.

2) THREE CLUBS. Your hand is worth 18 points...16 in high cards and 1 for each of your 5-card suits. With a medium hand (17 - 18 points) you can bid your second suit even though you have to go to the three-level.

3) THREE HEARTS. This time you have 20 points...19 in high cards and 1 for your 5-card suit. With a maximum hand (19 - 21 points) jump in your second suit, Three Hearts. This is a Jump Shift and shows a maximum hand.

4) You have 13 points...a minimum hand. Even though you have a lower-ranking suit, you would have to bid it at the three-level. It's time to find out what happens when you answer no to all the questions.

The Final Choice

If partner responded at the two-level and you answered no to all four questions then:

- You can't support partner's Major (if he bid one)

- You can't bid a new suit at the one-level
- Your hand isn't balanced
- You can't bid a new suit at the two-level or higher

This leaves two possibilities:

- Rebidding your first suit
- Raising partner's Minor if you have 4-card support

The level at which you rebid is determined according to your strength as follows:

OPENER'S REBID IN HIS FIRST SUIT OR WHEN RAISING RESPONDER'S MINOR

OPENER'S POINTS	OPENER'S REBID
13 - 16 points (minimum hand)	Rebid your first suit at the two-level or raise partner's Minor to the three-level **GO** .
13 14 15 16 17 18 19 20 21	
17 - 18 points (medium hand)	Jump rebid your first suit at the three-level or jump raise partner's Minor to the four-level **GO** .
13 14 15 16 17 18 19 20 21	
19 - 21 points (maximum hand)	Jump to Game in your first suit or raise partner's Minor to Game ▼ .
13 14 15 16 17 18 19 20 21	

Note that you by-pass Three No Trump with medium and maximum Minor suit hands because you are interested in Slam when partner responds at the two-level and you have a strong hand. Since all Slam contracts are played at the same level, there is no longer the over-riding concern to play in No Trump rather than a Minor suit. If you don't have enough for Slam, you can be comfortable in a Minor suit Game because you almost certainly have 29 combined points.

Let's look at some examples:

You open the bidding One Heart and your partner responds Two Diamonds. What do you rebid with the following hands?

1) ♠ 3	2) ♠ J 8	3) ♠ A 5	4) ♠ 4
♥ A J 9 7 2	♥ A K J 9 6 3	♥ K Q J 9 7 4 3	♥ A Q 9 5 3
♦ Q 8	♦ A 4	♦ 3	♦ K J 10 5
♣ A 10 9 8 7	♣ K 4 2	♣ A K 5	♣ Q 7 2

1) TWO HEARTS. With a minimum hand (13 - 16 points) you can only bid a new suit if it is lower-ranking than your first suit and if you can bid it at the two-level. Rebid your first suit at the two-level, Two Hearts, to tell responder that you have a minimum hand.

2) THREE HEARTS. You have 18 points which puts your hand in the medium category (17 - 18 points). With no second suit, make a jump rebid of Three Hearts.

3) FOUR HEARTS. This time you have 20 points. You can show partner that you have a maximum hand (19 - 21 points) by jumping to Game, Four Hearts.

4) THREE DIAMONDS. With a minimum hand of 13 points and 4-card support for partner's Minor, raise to Three Diamonds. Note that you don't revalue your hand using dummy points when raising partner's **Minor**.

Summary

When you open the bidding and your partner responds in a new suit at the two-level, you can determine your rebid by asking the following questions:

Question One: CAN I RAISE PARTNER'S MAJOR?

If the answer is YES: Revalue your hand using dummy points and raise to the appropriate level:

13 - 16 points	Raise to the three-level
17 - 18 points	Raise to the four-level
19 - 21 points	Raise to the five-level

If the answer is NO: Go on to the next question.

Question Two: CAN I BID A NEW SUIT AT THE ONE-LEVEL?

The answer is always NO: Go on to the next question.

Question Three: IS MY HAND BALANCED?

If the answer is YES: Rebid No Trump at the appropriate level:

| 13 - 15 points | Stay at the same level (Two No Trump) |
| 19 - 21 points | Jump a level (Three No Trump) |

If the answer is NO: Go on to the next question.

Question Four: SHOULD I BID A NEW SUIT AT THE TWO-LEVEL?

If the answer is YES: Bid the new suit at the appropriate level:
13 - 16 points	Bid your second suit*
17 - 18 points	Bid your second suit
19 - 21 points	Jump in your second suit (Jump Shift)

If the answer is NO: Rebid your first suit (or raise partner's Minor) at the appropriate level:
13 - 16 points	Bid at the two-level or raise to the three-level
17 - 18 points	Bid at the three-level or raise to the four-level
19 - 21 points	Bid Game in your suit or raise to the five-level

* Only bid a new suit if it is lower-ranking than your first suit and you can bid it at the two-level.

Exercises

1) You open the bidding One Spade. Your partner responds Two Hearts. What is your rebid with each of the following hands?

a) ♠ A J 9 4 3	b) ♠ A Q J 6 3	c) ♠ A J 9 8 7 2	d) ♠ K Q 7 5 4
♥ K J 3 2	♥ 8 2	♥ 9	♥ A Q 9 3
♦ 9 4	♦ K 7 3	♦ Q 3	♦ A 6 3
♣ A 2	♣ Q J 3	♣ K Q 7 3	♣ 6

2) You open the bidding One Spade and your partner responds Two Diamonds. What do you do next with the following hands?

a) ♠ K J 9 5 3	b) ♠ A Q 9 8 5	c) ♠ K Q 10 3 2	d) ♠ A K J 9 3
♥ K Q 4 2	♥ A 5	♥ J 2	♥ A 7
♦ Q 8	♦ K Q 3	♦ A 4	♦ 9 8
♣ Q 10	♣ K J 3	♣ Q J 6 3	♣ A J 9 8

3) You open the bidding One Heart and your partner bids Two Clubs. What do you do with the following hands?

a) ♠ A 7 4 2	b) ♠ J 4	c) ♠ A Q J 2	d) ♠ K 2
♥ K Q 7 3	♥ A Q 7 5 3	♥ A K 5 3 2	♥ A K Q 9 7 6 3
♦ K 9 8	♦ 8 3	♦ K 8 3	♦ K Q
♣ Q 2	♣ A K 5 3	♣ 3	♣ 8 3

4) You open the bidding One Diamond and your partner responds Two
Clubs. What do you do now with the following hands?

a) ♠ A Q 4
  ♥ 9 6 3
  ♦ K J 10 4
  ♣ A 9 7

b) ♠ 10 3
  ♥ A 5
  ♦ K J 8 7 6 2
  ♣ Q J 3

c) ♠ A 10 3
  ♥ K 9
  ♦ A Q J 8 7 3
  ♣ Q 3

d) ♠ A Q 3 2
  ♥ K 9 2
  ♦ A K Q 2
  ♣ J 10

e) ♠ A 2
  ♥ A 10 9 8
  ♦ K Q 8 4 2
  ♣ 10 2

f) ♠ A 10
  ♥ 6 4
  ♦ K J 9 8 3
  ♣ A J 10 2

g) ♠ A 2
  ♥ 9 3
  ♦ A Q J 6 3
  ♣ K Q 9 3

h) ♠ A J 10 2
  ♥ K 5
  ♦ A Q 10 8 7
  ♣ K 3

10

Opener's Rebid
After a Raise

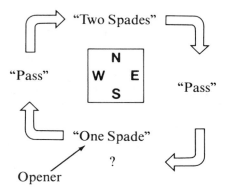

Raises are the easiest responses to deal with because responder is announcing that a Magic Fit has been found. There is no need to search further for an acceptable denomination in which to place the final contract ...responder has told opener WHERE to play the hand. The only question that remains is HOW HIGH.

After a Raise: WHERE

If responder raises opener's Major suit:

> WHERE — The agreed Major suit for a Part-Game or Game
> contract

If responder raises opener's Minor suit:

> WHERE — The agreed Minor suit for a Part-Game contract
> — Three No Trump for a Game contract

After a Raise: HOW HIGH

Responder's raise has conveyed additional information to opener...the strength of responder's hand:

- A raise to the two-level (*single raise*) shows 6 - 10 points
- A raise to the three-level (*jump raise*) shows 11 - 12 points
- A raise to the Game level (*Game raise*) shows 13 - 16 points

Opener takes on the role of captain and adds his points to those promised by responder to determine HOW HIGH to place the contract.

Opener's Rebid After a Single Raise

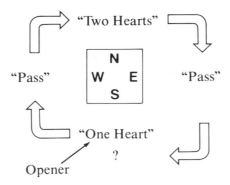

Responder's single raise shows 6 to 10 points. Opener classifies his hand as minimum, medium or maximum to determine HOW HIGH to bid.

With a minimum hand, opener knows HOW HIGH...Part-Game. With a maximum hand, opener also knows HOW HIGH...Game. With a medium hand (17 - 18 points), opener isn't sure if there are enough points for Game. He wants to be in Game if responder is at the top of his range...9 or 10 points...but not if responder is at the bottom of his range...6,7 or 8 points. For example, if opener has 17 points:

OPENER'S POINTS		RESPONDER'S POINTS		COMBINED POINTS	
17	+	6	=	23	Part-Game
17	+	7	=	24	Part-Game
17	+	8	=	25	Part-Game
17	+	9	=	26	Game
17	+	10	=	27	Game

```
        OPENER'S REBID AFTER
          A SINGLE RAISE

   13 - 16 points      Pass      [STOP]    Game is unlikely so settle
   (minimum hand)                          for Part-Game.

   17 - 18 points      Raise to the  ▼     There may be enough
   (medium hand)       three-level         combined points for Game.

   19 - 21 points      Raise to the [STOP] There should be enough
   (maximum hand)      Game level          combined points for Game.
```

When opener doesn't have enough information to determine **HOW HIGH**, he makes an invitational bid by raising to the three-level. Responder will then make the final decision about **HOW HIGH**. Note that it is not possible to be totally accurate. If opener has 16 points, responder could have 10 (unlikely). Similarly, if opener has 19, he will have to hope that responder doesn't have exactly 6 points.

Here are some examples.

You open the bidding One Heart and your partner responds Two Hearts. You now have to decide what rebid to make. You know **WHERE** because partner has supported your Major. You have only to determine **HOW HIGH**. What would you rebid with each of the following hands?

1)	♠ 10 8 5	2)	♠ A 7	3)	♠ A 10 7
	♥ A 8 7 6 3		♥ K J 8 6 5 2		♥ A Q J 8 7 6
	◆ K 7 3		◆ A Q 5		◆ A K
	♣ A Q		♣ J 5		♣ 6 4

1) PASS. You have only 14 points and responder has a maximum of 10 points. There are not enough combined points for Game. You should Pass.

2) THREE HEARTS. Here you have 17 points. If responder has only 6, 7 or 8 points, there will not be enough combined points for Game. However, if responder has 9 or 10 points, there will be enough for Game. Bid Three Hearts to encourage responder to continue on to Game if he has the upper range of his promised points.

3) FOUR HEARTS. With 20 points, there should be enough for Game even if responder has only 6 points.

Some more examples:

You open the bidding One Club and your partner raises to Two Clubs. What would you rebid with each of the following hands?

4) ♠ 10 9   5) ♠ A 8   6) ♠ A 10
   ♥ A 8 3   ♥ 7 2   ♥ K 9 8 5
   ♦ A K 10 3   ♦ K Q 5   ♦ A Q
   ♣ Q 9 6 3   ♣ A Q 7 6 5 3   ♣ A K 10 6 4

4) PASS. You have only 13 points and responder has a maximum of 10 points. There are not enough combined points for Game.

5) THREE CLUBS. Here you have 17 points. If responder has the bottom of his range, there will not be enough combined points for Game. However, if responder has the top of his range, there will be enough for Game. Bid Three Clubs to invite responder to continue on to Game (Three No Trump) when he has 9 or 10 points.

6) THREE NO TRUMP. With 21 points, there should be enough for Game even if responder has only 6 points. You should raise to the Game level. Since you don't have a Magic Major Suit Fit, you should bid Game in No Trump.

Opener's Rebid After a Jump Raise

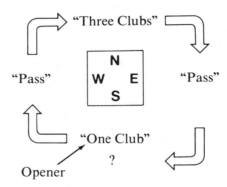

This is a very encouraging response by your partner, showing 11 or 12 points. Opener should carry on to Game with all but the weakest of hands:

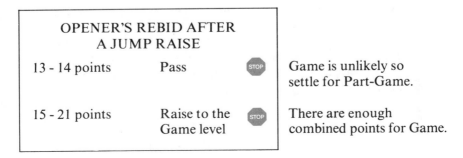

OPENER'S REBID AFTER A JUMP RAISE		
13 - 14 points	Pass STOP	Game is unlikely so settle for Part-Game.
15 - 21 points	Raise to the Game level STOP	There are enough combined points for Game.

For example, you open the bidding One Club and your partner raises to Three Clubs. What rebid would you make with each of the following hands?

1) ♠ A K Q 3 2) ♠ Q 7
   ♥ 10 9 2   ♥ K 8
   ♦ 10 3   ♦ A Q 8 5
   ♣ K J 7 5   ♣ K J 10 7 4

1) PASS. You have only 13 points and responder has at most 12 points. There are not enough combined points for Game. You should Pass.

2) THREE NO TRUMP. Here you have 16 points. Even if responder has only 11 points, there will be enough combined points for Game. Bid Three No Trump.

You open the bidding One Spade and your partner responds Three Spades. What rebid would you make with each of the following hands?

3) ♠ 9 8 5 4 3 4) ♠ A J 9 8 7
   ♥ A J 6   ♥ A 8 6 5 2
   ♦ K 7 3   ♦ A 5
   ♣ K J   ♣ 6

3) PASS. You have only 13 points and responder has a maximum of 12 points and could have only 11. There can not be enough combined points for Game.

4) FOUR SPADES. You have 15 points. Even if responder has only 11 points, there will be enough combined points for Game.

Opener's Rebid After a Game Raise

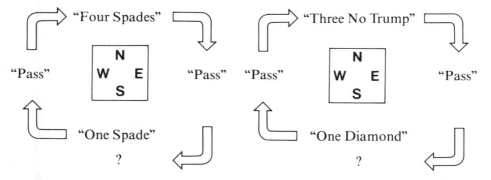

This is a strong response by your partner, showing 13 to 16 points. Since you are already in a Game contract, you can Pass with most hands.

However, if you have a very strong hand, there is the possibility of making a Slam contract and receiving a very large bonus. Slam bidding is discussed in more detail in a later chapter. For now, you can use the following guide:

OPENER'S REBID AFTER A GAME RAISE			
13 - 16 points (minimum hand)	Pass	STOP	Slam is unlikely so settle for Game.
17 - 18 points (medium hand)	Raise to the next level		There may be enough combined points for Slam.
19 - 21 points (maximum hand)	Raise to the six-level	STOP	There should be enough combined points for Slam.

For example, you open the bidding One Spade and your partner responds Four Spades. What would you do next with each of the following hands?

```
1) ♠ A Q 8 5      2) ♠ K J 9 7 4 2    3) ♠ K Q J 8 7 6
   ♥ K J 6           ♥ A 10              ♥ A 10 9
   ♦ 7 3 2           ♦ A 9 6             ♦ A 7
   ♣ K J 6           ♣ A 7               ♣ A 4
```

1) PASS. You have 14 points and responder has between 13 and 16 points. You have found out WHERE to play the contract...Spades. You have also determined HOW HIGH to play the contract ...Game. Since your side is already in the best contract, Pass.

2) FIVE SPADES. Here you have 18 points. There may be enough points in the combined hands to make a Slam contract. Rebid Five Spades to encourage responder to continue on to Slam if he has the upper range of his promised points.

3) SIX SPADES. With 20 points, there should be enough for Slam even if responder has only 13 points. Rebid Six Spades. Slam bidding will be discussed in more detail later.

Some more examples:

You open the bidding One Diamond and your partner responds Three No Trump. What would you do next with each of the following hands?

```
4) ♠ A Q         5) ♠ A Q 7 3       6) ♠ A 10 9
   ♥ K J 6 3        ♥ K 2              ♥ K J 6
   ♦ K J 7 3        ♦ A Q J 9 6        ♦ A Q 10 8 7 3
   ♣ 10 8 6         ♣ J 7              ♣ A
```

4) PASS. You have 14 points and responder has between 13 and 16 points. Even though you have a Magic Fit in Diamonds, it should be easier to take nine tricks in No Trump than eleven tricks with Diamonds as trump. Since your side is already in the best contract, Pass.

5) FOUR NO TRUMP. Here you have 18 points. There may be enough points in the combined hands to make a Slam contract. Rebid Four No Trump to encourage responder to continue on to Slam (Six Diamonds) if he has the upper range of his promised points.

6) SIX DIAMONDS. With 20 points, there should be enough for Slam even if responder has only 13 points. Rebid Six Diamonds. At the Slam level, it will usually be safer to play in your known Diamond fit than in No Trump. Slam bidding will be discussed in more detail later.

Summary

If responder has raised your suit, you need look no further to determine WHERE to play the hand. In addition, responder has conveyed information about his strength through the level to which he raised your suit. Combining this information with the strength of your hand allows you to determine HOW HIGH to rebid.

OPENER'S REBID AFTER A RAISE

- After a Single Raise: 13 - 16 points   Pass
            17 - 18 points   Raise to the three-level
            19 - 21 points   Raise to the Game level

- After a Jump Raise: 13 - 14 points   Pass
            15 - 21 points   Raise to the Game level

- After a Game Raise: 13 - 16 points   Pass
            17 - 18 points   Raise to the next level
            19 - 21 points   Raise to the six-level
                   in your agreed trump suit

Exercises

1) You open the bidding One Spade. Your partner responds Two Spades. What is your rebid with each of the following hands?

a) ♠ A J 9 4   b) ♠ J 9 6 4 2   c) ♠ K 8 5 3 2
   ♥ A K 3   ♥ 3   ♥ A 7
   ♦ K Q 2   ♦ A 7 5 3   ♦ A 3
   ♣ A 6 2   ♣ A Q J   ♣ K Q 7 3

2) You open the bidding One Heart and your partner responds Three Hearts. What do you do next with the following hands?

a) ♠ A 3
   ♥ K Q 7 4 2
   ♦ K Q 8
   ♣ 7 6 2

b) ♠ A 8 5
   ♥ A 9 8 6 5
   ♦ J 8 3
   ♣ K 3

c) ♠ K 9
   ♥ A Q 9 5 2
   ♦ Q
   ♣ K Q 8 6 3

3) You open the bidding One Spade and your partner raises to Four Spades. What do you do with the following hands?

a) ♠ Q 9 7 4 2
   ♥ K 3
   ♦ K Q 8
   ♣ K 6 2

b) ♠ A K J 5 2
   ♥ A
   ♦ A 10 9 8 3
   ♣ K 3

c) ♠ A J 9 5 2
   ♥ K 9
   ♦ A 8
   ♣ A J 10 3

4) You open the bidding One Club and your partner responds Two Clubs. What do you do now with the following hands?

a) ♠ K Q
   ♥ A 3
   ♦ K J 9 8
   ♣ A 9 7 6 2

b) ♠ A 9 8 2
   ♥ A J 5
   ♦ J 8
   ♣ K J 4 3

c) ♠ A Q 7 5
   ♥ K 9
   ♦ A Q
   ♣ K J 8 6 3

5) You open the bidding One Diamond and your partner bids Three Diamonds. What do you rebid with the following hands?

a) ♠ A 7 4 2
   ♥ 5
   ♦ J 9 8 4
   ♣ A K J 2

b) ♠ K J 10
   ♥ A J 5
   ♦ K Q J 8 3
   ♣ K 6

c) ♠ A 9 5 2
   ♥ Q 9
   ♦ A Q 6 3 2
   ♣ K 3

11

Responder's Rebid After Opener's Minimum Rebid

Some auctions end swiftly. For example, opener bids One Heart, responder raises to Two Hearts and opener, with a minimum hand, says Pass. In many auctions, however, the final contract will not have been determined by opener's rebid:

OPENER	RESPONDER
One Heart	One Spade
Two Spades	?

Responder's bid at this point is called *responder's rebid*.

Responder's Rebid — HOW HIGH and WHERE

By the time responder comes to make his second bid (rebid), he has heard two bids from opener. In the two bids, opener has usually described his hand so that responder is in position similar to that when the opening bid was One No Trump...opener has described both his strength and shape within a narrow range.

After an opening bid of One Heart, responder knows only that opener's strength lies between 13 and 21 points, a large range. Opener's rebid limits his hand to a much narrower range. Depending on the bid he makes, opener will describe one of the following hands:

MINIMUM HAND:
13 - 16 points

13	14	15	16	17	18	19	20	21

MEDIUM HAND:
17 - 18 points

13	14	15	16	17	18	19	20	21

MAXIMUM HAND:
19 - 21 points

13	14	15	16	17	18	19	20	21

After an opening bid of One Heart, responder knows only that opener has at least four Hearts. After opener's rebid, responder has a much better idea of opener's shape. For example:

OPENER	RESPONDER	
One Heart	One Spade	Opener's bids show a balanced
One No Trump		hand with 13 - 15 points

OPENER	RESPONDER	
One Heart	One Spade	Opener's bids show an unbalanced
Three Hearts		hand with 17 - 18 points

Thus, when it comes time to make his rebid, responder is in the role of captain and can use two familiar tools to place the final contract:

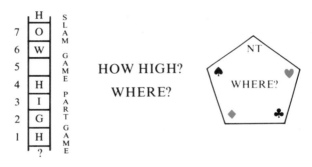

HOW HIGH?

WHERE?

Since responder's decision as to HOW HIGH to place the final contract is dependent on the strength that opener has shown, let's look at four cases:

- Opener has shown a minimum hand (13 - 16 points)
- Opener has shown a minimum or medium hand (13 - 18 points)
- Opener has shown a medium hand (17 - 18 points)
- Opener has shown a maximum hand (19 - 21 points)

In this chapter we will look at the first two cases. In the next chapter we will examine the cases where opener has shown a medium or maximum hand.

After Opener Shows a Minimum Hand

The following rebids by opener describe a minimum hand:

	OPENER	RESPONDER
• A minimum raise of responder's Major	One Diamond **Two Spades**	One Spade
• A minimum rebid in No Trump	One Heart **One No Trump**	One Spade
• A minimum rebid of opener's suit	One Heart **Two Hearts**	Two Clubs
• A minimum raise of responder's Minor	One Club **Two Diamonds**	One Diamond

If opener has shown a minimum hand, responder knows that opener has 13 - 16 points. Since 26 combined points are needed for Game, there are three possibilities:

- Part-Game if the combined strength is less than 26 points. This will be the case when responder has a minimum hand of 6 - 10 points. (The only exception would be if responder held exactly 10 points and opener held exactly 16 points...too infrequent to worry about.)
- Maybe Game. This will be the case when responder has a medium hand of 11 - 12 points. If opener only has 13 or 14 points there is probably not enough combined strength for Game but if opener has 15 or 16 points there will be enough strength for Game.
- Game if the minimum combined strength is 26 points. This will be the case when responder has a maximum hand of 13 or more points.

Let's look at how responder handles each case.

Responder's Rebid with 6 to 10 Points

When opener has shown a minimum hand (13 - 16 points) and responder has 6 to 10 points, responder knows that the partnership is not close to making a Game contract and should settle for the best Part-Game. He needs to make a bid that is *discouraging*. Opener will then almost always Pass. There are two rebids by responder that convey this message:

- Pass

- An **old suit** at the two-level

An *old suit* is a suit previously bid by opener or responder.

Responder chooses whichever of the above bids is the safest Part-Game.

For example:

OPENER	RESPONDER	
One Diamond	One Spade	♠ K 9 6 3
Two Spades	?	♥ J 8 3
		♦ A 6
		♣ 10 9 7 2

HOW HIGH: Part-Game. With only 8 points responder is certain that there is not enough combined strength for Game since opener has shown a minimum hand (13 -16 points).

WHERE: Spades. Opener has raised responder's Major, showing 4-card support. Since responder knows that there is a Magic Major Suit Fit, he has the answer to WHERE. The contract is already a Spade Part-Game so responder puts an end to the auction by saying Pass.

Another example:

OPENER	RESPONDER	
One Heart	One Spade	♠ J 10 9 6 3 2
One No Trump	?	♥ A 8 3
		♦ 8 6
		♣ 10 2

HOW HIGH: Part-Game. With 7 points responder knows that Game is unlikely since opener has shown a minimum hand.

WHERE: Spades. Since opener has shown a balanced hand, he must have at least two Spades. Knowing there is a Magic Major Suit Fit responder would choose Two Spades, an old suit at the two-level, as his discouraging rebid.

Here are more examples. You are responder and the auction starts off:

OPENER	RESPONDER
One Diamond	One Heart
One No Trump	?

Ask yourself HOW HIGH and WHERE to decide your rebid with the following hands:

1) ♠ Q 9 8 7	2) ♠ J 3	3) ♠ 10 6 5	4) ♠ 10 3
♥ A 8 7 3	♥ K 9 8 7 2	♥ K Q 9 6 5 3	♥ Q J 9 2
♦ 9 7 4	♦ K 10 9 8	♦ J	♦ 9 2
♣ 8 4	♣ 10 7	♣ J 6 5	♣ Q J 7 5 2

1) HOW HIGH: Part-Game. Opener is showing a minimum hand and you have only 6 points. You want to stop in the best Part-Game.

WHERE: No Trump. Partner did not raise Hearts so there is no Magic Fit in Hearts. Could there be a Magic Fit in Spades? No. If opener had a 4-card Spade suit, he would have rebid One Spade rather than One No Trump. You are already in the best Part-Game contract so you should PASS.

2) HOW HIGH: Part-Game. With 8 points you want to stop in the best Part-Game.

WHERE: Diamonds. Your choice is to Pass or to bid an old suit at the two-level...Two Diamonds or Two Hearts. From the opening bid you know that opener has at least four Diamonds. When playing Part-Game, any Magic Fit is acceptable so you should play in Diamonds. Rebid TWO DIAMONDS. Opener will Pass.

3) HOW HIGH: Part-Game. With 9 points you want to settle for the best Part-Game.

WHERE: Hearts. Since opener must have at least two Hearts, you should rebid TWO HEARTS and play in the Magic Fit.

4) HOW HIGH: Part-Game. With 7 points you need to find a suitable discouraging rebid.

WHERE: Your choices are Pass or an old suit at the two-level...Two Diamonds or Two Hearts. You cannot bid Two Clubs as that would be a **new** suit at the two-level. Since you don't have a Magic Fit in Diamonds or in Hearts, you should PASS and make the final contract One No Trump.

Responder's Rebid with 11 or 12 Points

When opener has shown a minimum hand (13 - 16 points) and responder has 11 or 12 points, responder knows that the partnership is close to Game. He needs to make a bid that is invitational. Opener can then Pass if he has 13 or 14 points (lower part of his range) or continue to Game if he has 15 or 16 points (upper part of his range). There are two rebids by responder that convey this message:

- Two No Trump ▼
- An old suit at the three-level ▼ *

Since it may also not be clear WHERE the final contract should be played, responder chooses whichever of the above bids is most descriptive.

* Sometimes to get to the three-level, responder has to jump a level of bidding.

For example:

OPENER	RESPONDER	
One Diamond	One Spade	♠ K 9 6 3
Two Spades	?	♥ J 8 3
		♦ A 6
		♣ K 9 7 2

HOW HIGH: Maybe Game. With only 11 points he cannot be certain that there is enough combined strength for Game.

WHERE: Spades. Opener has raised responder's Major, showing 4-card support. Since responder knows that there is a Magic Major Suit Fit, he has the answer to WHERE.

Responder therefore makes an invitational bid of an old suit at the three-level ... Three Spades. If opener has 13 or 14 points, he will reject the invitation by Passing. If opener has 15 or 16 points, he will accept the invitation and bid Four Spades.

Another example:

OPENER	RESPONDER	
One Club	One Heart	♠ 9 6 3
One No Trump	?	♥ A J 8 3
		♦ A 10 6
		♣ K 7 2

HOW HIGH: Maybe Game. With 12 points responder wants to make an invitational rebid.

WHERE: No Trump. Since opener didn't raise responder's Major there cannot be a Magic Major Suit Fit. Responder would choose Two No Trump as his invitational rebid. After the Two No Trump rebid by responder, opener can Pass with 13 or 14 points or carry on to Three No Trump with 15 or 16 points.

Another example:

OPENER	RESPONDER	
One Heart	One Spade	♠ A 9 6 3
Two Hearts	?	♥ Q J 8
		♦ 10 6
		♣ K J 7 2

HOW HIGH: Maybe Game. With 11 points responder wants to make an invitational rebid.

WHERE: Hearts. Since opener has shown more than four Hearts, responder knows that there is a Magic Major Suit Fit in Hearts. Responder would choose Three Hearts as his invitational rebid. After the Three Heart rebid by responder, opener can Pass with 13 or 14 points or carry on to Four Hearts with 15 or 16 points.

Here are more examples. You are responder.

OPENER	RESPONDER
One Heart	One Spade
One No Trump	?

After asking yourself HOW HIGH and WHERE, what do you rebid with the following hands?

1) ♠ A Q J 3   2) ♠ J 9 8 7 3 2
   ♥ 7 2   ♥ A 3
   ♦ Q 9 8   ♦ Q 7 4
   ♣ K 10 8 7   ♣ K 4

1) HOW HIGH: Maybe Game. Opener is showing a minimum hand (13 - 16 points). With 12 points you want to invite opener to Game.

   WHERE: No Trump. Since opener denied 4-card support for Spades through his failure to raise, there cannot be a Magic Major Suit Fit. Your rebid should be TWO NO TRUMP. Opener will either Pass or carry on to Three No Trump depending on the strength of his "minimum" hand.

2) HOW HIGH: Maybe Game. Again you have 12 points, so you want to invite Game.

   WHERE: Spades. Since opener is showing a balanced hand with his rebid, he must have at least two Spades. Knowing you have a Magic Major Suit Fit, you can make an invitational rebid by bidding an old suit at the three-level...THREE SPADES.

Responder's Rebid with 13 or more Points

Since responder knows HOW HIGH...Game...he only need determine WHERE to place the final contract. The key to WHERE is whether or not there is a Magic Major Suit Fit. If there is, bid Game in the Major suit. Otherwise, bid Three No Trump. If responder does not know whether or not there is a Magic Major Suit Fit, he will need more information from opener. There are two rebids responder can make with 13 or more points:

- Game 🛑

- A new suit ✴GO✴

A *new suit* is a suit that has not previously been bid by the partnership during the auction.

Because opener's rebid has given responder a good picture of his shape, responder will often be in a position to determine whether or not there is a Magic Major Suit Fit. For example:

OPENER	RESPONDER	
One Diamond	One Spade	♠ K 9 6 3
Two Spades	?	♥ J 8 3
		♦ A 6
		♣ A Q 7 2

HOW HIGH: Game. Responder has 14 points and opener has at least 13.
WHERE: Spades. Opener has raised responder's Major, showing 4-card support. Responder knows that there is a Magic Major Suit Fit. Responder's rebid would be Four Spades.

Another example:

OPENER	RESPONDER	
One Diamond	One Spade	♠ K 9 6 3
One No Trump	?	♥ J 8 3
		♦ A 6
		♣ A J 7 2

HOW HIGH: Game. With 13 points, responder knows there are 26 or more combined points.
WHERE: No Trump. Opener has shown a balanced hand. There cannot be a Magic Major Suit Fit. Responder would rebid Three No Trump.

In both examples, responder's rebid is a sign-off bid. Opener has described his hand and responder has selected the appropriate Game contract. Opener should not bid again.

What if responder is still not certain whether there is a Magic Major Suit Fit? Responder needs to get more information from opener. Since responder knows that the partnership should be in a Game contract but does not know which Game contract, he wants to make a rebid below the Game level that will get more information and that **opener will not Pass**. To do this, responder uses the following principle:

A BID OF A NEW SUIT BY RESPONDER, ON THE SECOND ROUND OF BIDDING, IS A MARATHON BID

This is a great tool for responder. Whenever responder bids a new suit opener must make another bid. This is very useful when responder needs additional information from opener. Sometimes responder can even bid a suit of three cards or less with the knowledge that he will not be left to play there.

Here is an example of bidding a new suit:

OPENER	RESPONDER	
One Diamond	One Spade	♠ K 9 6 3 2
One No Trump	?	♥ J 8
		♦ A 6
		♣ A Q 7 2

HOW HIGH: Game. With 15 points, responder knows that he wants to be in Game.

WHERE: Does the partnership have a Magic Major Suit Fit? Opener doesn't have 4-card support for Spades because he would have raised responder's Major if he did. However, opener could have 3-card support which, in this case, would be sufficient.

To get more information, responder should bid a new suit... Two Clubs. Since this bid is marathon, opener must bid again. If opener does have 3-card support for Spades, he will be able to show it by bidding Two Spades at his next turn. Since he didn't raise immediately, this shows only 3-card support. Responder will now have sufficient information to place the final contract... Four Spades.

If opener only has two Spades, he will make some other descriptive bid at his next turn such as Two Diamonds (to show a 5-card suit) or Two Hearts (to show a second 4-card suit) or Two No Trump (to say he has nothing further to add). Responder will now know that there is no Magic Major Suit Fit and be able to place the final contract... Three No Trump.

Let's see another example:

OPENER	RESPONDER	
One Club	One Heart	♠ K 9 3
Two Clubs	?	♥ A J 9 8 6
		♦ K 7 6
		♣ J 2

HOW HIGH: Game. With 13 points responder wants to be in Game.

WHERE: Is there a Magic Major Suit Fit? Responder knows from opener's failure to raise immediately that he doesn't have 4-card support for Hearts. In this case three Hearts would be sufficient but opener could have fewer.

Responder needs more information and will have to bid a new suit. Since responder doesn't have a new 4-card suit to bid he will have to bid Two

Diamonds. If opener's next bid is Two Hearts, responder will know that opener has support and will be able to place the final contract...Four-card Hearts.

If opener does not bid Two Hearts, responder can give up on the search for a Magic Major Suit Fit and place the final contract as Three No Trump.

Here are more examples:

Opener bids One Heart and you respond One Spade. Opener then rebids One No Trump. Ask HOW HIGH and WHERE to determine what to rebid with the following hands:

1) ♠ A Q J 3	2) ♠ J 9 8 7 3 2	3) ♠ A 9 7 6 5	4) ♠ K J 7 5 4
♥ 7 2	♥ A 3	♥ 3	♥ Q 9 5
♦ Q J 8	♦ A 7 4	♦ A K 9 8 2	♦ A 5
♣ K 10 8 7	♣ K 4	♣ J 5	♣ Q 7 2

1) HOW HIGH: Game. Opener's rebid shows 13 - 15 points. With 13 points you want to get the partnership to Game.

   WHERE: No Trump. Since opener denied 4-card support for Spades through his failure to raise immediately, there cannot be a Magic Major Suit Fit. Your rebid should be THREE NO TRUMP. Opener will accept your decision and Pass.

2) HOW HIGH: Game. Here you have 14 points so you want to be in Game.

   WHERE: Spades. Since opener is showing a balanced hand with his rebid, he must have at least two Spades. Knowing you have a Magic Major Suit Fit, you can place the final contract...FOUR SPADES.

3) HOW HIGH: Game. Your 14 points combined with opener's minimum of 13 points indicate that the partnership should be in Game.

   WHERE: Is there a Magic Major Suit Fit? Maybe. Partner cannot have 4-card support for Spades but may have three of them. You would rebid a new suit, TWO DIAMONDS, to get opener to describe his hand further. If he rebids Two Spades, you can go on to Four Spades. If he rebids anything else, you can bid Three No Trump at your next bid.

4) HOW HIGH: Game. With 13 points, you want the partnership in a Game contract.

   WHERE: What's the best Game contract? You don't yet have sufficient information. Opener could have 3-card support for your Spade suit or could possibly have a 5-card Heart suit and a balanced hand.

Even though you don't have a new 4-card suit to bid you can bid...TWO CLUBS. If opener now bids Two Spades to show 3-card support, you can bid Four Spades. If opener rebids Two Hearts to show a 5-card Heart suit, you can raise to Four Hearts. If opener bids anything else, you can bid Three No Trump confident that there is no Magic Major Suit Fit.

After Opener Shows a Minimum or Medium Hand

Sometimes opener makes a bid which shows a hand that could be either minimum (13 - 16 points) or medium (17 - 18 points). For example:

	OPENER	RESPONDER
• A new suit at the one-level	One Club **One Spade**	One Heart
• A new suit at the two-level if it lower-ranking than opener's first suit	One Heart **Two Clubs**	One Spade

How does responder deal with these two cases? Responder's general approach is to treat them as though opener is showing a minimum hand. If opener has a medium hand, opener can clarify the ambiguity with his next bid. Thus:

- Responder assumes that the hand should be played in Part-Game when he has a minimum hand of 6 - 10 points and makes a discouraging rebid.
- Responder makes an invitational bid with a medium hand of 11 - 12 points.
- Responder makes sure the partnership gets to Game when he has a maximum hand of 13 or more points.

Let's look at how responder rebids in both cases:

- After a new suit at the one-level
- After a new suit at the two-level

Responder's Rebid After Opener Bids a New Suit at the One-Level

Assuming that opener has a minimum hand, responder wants to make a discouraging rebid when he has 6 - 10 points. There are three rebids by responder that convey this message:

- Pass
- One No Trump ▼
- An old suit at the two-level ▼

Responder chooses whichever of the above bids is most descriptive. Note that the rebid of One No Trump is available to show 6-10 points. Let's look at some examples:

OPENER	RESPONDER	
		♠ J 6 3
One Diamond	One Heart	♥ A J 8 3
One Spade	?	♦ 8 6
		♣ K 10 7 4

HOW HIGH: Part-Game. With 9 points, responder knows that there are not enough combined points for Game if opener has a minimum hand.

WHERE: No Trump. Since opener didn't raise responder's Major, there cannot be a Magic Major Suit Fit. Responder would choose One No Trump as his discouraging rebid. If opener has a minimum hand, he will Pass unless he is not satisfied with responder's choice of Part-Game contract. For example, opener might return to Two Diamonds if he had an unbalanced hand with a 6-card Diamond suit.

If opener has a medium hand, he can show his additional strength by making an invitational bid. In the above example, he might now raise to Two No Trump to show that he has 17 or 18 points. With 9 points, responder accepts the invitation by carrying on to Three No Trump. With only 6, 7 or 8 points, responder would Pass and the partnership would stop safely in Part-Game.

Another example:

OPENER	RESPONDER	
		♠ 6 3
One Club	One Diamond	♥ 9 2
One Heart	?	♦ K 10 9 7 3
		♣ A 10 8 3

HOW HIGH: Part-Game. Responder has 8 points. This will not be enough for Game if opener has a minimum hand.

WHERE: Clubs. At the Part-Game level any Magic Fit is acceptable. Responder should choose Two Clubs as his discouraging rebid.

If responder has 11 or 12 points, he makes an invitational rebid:

- Two No Trump ▼
- An old suit at the three-level

Responder chooses whichever bid is the most descriptive. For example:

OPENER	RESPONDER		
One Club	One Diamond	♠	A 6
One Spade	?	♥	Q 7 3 2
		♦	Q J 4 2
		♣	Q 10 3

HOW HIGH: Maybe Game. With 11 points, responder has to choose an invitational rebid.

WHERE: No Trump. There is no Magic Major Suit Fit. Responder's choice would be Two No Trump.

Another example:

OPENER	RESPONDER		
One Diamond	One Heart	♠	7 3
One Spade	?	♥	A 10 9 8 6 3
		♦	K 10
		♣	K 9 2

HOW HIGH: Maybe Game. With 12 points, responder wants to make the most descriptive invitational rebid.

WHERE: Hearts. With an unbalanced hand, he should bid an old suit at the three-level, Three Hearts. Opener can Pass with 13 or 14 points or bid Game with 15 or 16 points.

When responder has 13 or more points, he wants to ensure that the partnership reaches Game. He has two rebids available:

- Game ▼
- A new suit 〈GO〉

If responder knows WHERE, he bids Game. If responder doesn't know WHERE, he bids a new suit. For example:

OPENER	RESPONDER		
One Club	One Heart	♠	K J 10 4
One Spade	?	♥	A 10 9 8
		♦	K 9
		♣	Q 6 2

HOW HIGH: Game. With 14 dummy points, responder knows there is enough combined strength for Game.

WHERE: Spades. Having found a Magic Major Suit Fit, responder knows where to play the hand. Responder has enough information to place the contract...Four Spades.

Another example:

OPENER	RESPONDER	♠	3
One Club	One Heart	♥	K Q 10 7 4
One Spade	?	♦	Q J 7 4
		♣	A 8 2

HOW HIGH: Game. With 13 points, responder knows there are enough combined points for Game.

WHERE: Responder is not sure WHERE. He needs more information. Responder can get the additional information he needs by bidding a new suit, Two Diamonds. This is a forcing bid and opener's next bid should give responder all the information he needs to make the final selection (Three No Trump or Four Hearts).

Here are more examples of what to bid after opener's rebid in a new suit at the one-level:

OPENER	RESPONDER
One Diamond	One Heart
One Spade	?

After considering HOW HIGH and WHERE, what do you rebid with the following hands?

1) ♠ A Q J 3   2) ♠ 10 9 5   3) ♠ J 3
   ♥ K 9 8 7 2   ♥ A J 8 7 5 4   ♥ A Q 10 3
   ♦ 6 4   ♦ 6   ♦ 10 9 2
   ♣ 9 7   ♣ Q 6 5   ♣ A Q 5 2

1) HOW HIGH: Maybe Game. After finding your Spade fit, your hand revalues to 12 dummy points. Since opener may have a minimum hand, you want to make an invitational rebid.

   WHERE: Spades. You can make an invitational bid by bidding THREE SPADES, an old suit at the three-level.

2) HOW HIGH: Part-Game. With 9 points you need to find a suitable discouraging rebid.

   WHERE: Hearts. Since you don't care much for either of opener's suits and you have an unbalanced hand, the most appropriate rebid is TWO HEARTS, an old suit at the two-level. If partner has one or two Hearts, this should prove to be a satisfactory Part-Game contract. Of course, partner could have three Hearts (excellent!) or none at all (unlucky!).

3) HOW HIGH: Game. With 13 points, you want to be in Game.

WHERE: No Trump. You already know that there is no Magic Major Suit Fit so you would rebid THREE NO TRUMP, the most likely Game contract.

Responder's Rebid After Opener Bids a New Suit at the Two-Level

Assuming, for the sake of safety, that opener has a minimum hand, responder wants to make a discouraging rebid when he has 6 - 10 points. After opener bids a new suit at the two-level, there are two rebids by responder that convey this message:

- Pass (STOP)

- An old suit at the two-level

Responder chooses whichever bid is more descriptive. Let's look at some examples:

OPENER	RESPONDER	
		♠ 8 6 3
One Diamond	One Heart	♥ Q J 7 4
Two Clubs	?	♦ 7 4
		♣ A 8 7 2

HOW HIGH: Part-Game. With 7 points, responder knows that the partnership does not have enough combined strength for Game.

WHERE: Clubs. Since he knows there is a Magic Fit in Clubs and that any Magic Fit is suitable for Part-Game, responder would Pass.

Here's another example that introduces an important concept:

OPENER	RESPONDER	
		♠ K 8 7 4
One Heart	One Spade	♥ 10 7 4
Two Diamonds	?	♦ A 7 4
		♣ J 8 2

HOW HIGH: Part-Game. With 8 points responder knows that Game is unlikely since opener has shown a minimum or medium hand.

WHERE: Responder has to choose an appropriately discouraging rebid. The choice is between saying Pass or bidding an old suit at the two-level.

Since opener bid Hearts first and then Diamonds, responder can infer that opener has at least a 5-card Heart suit. If he had a 4-card Heart suit and a 4-card Diamond suit, he would have opened the lower-ranking suit first... Diamonds. Thus responder should return opener to his first suit by rebidding Two Hearts.

Generally, when you have a choice of playing the contract in one of opener's suits, you should prefer playing in opener's first bid suit since it will be as long as, or longer than, any of his other suits. This is called *giving preference* to opener's first suit.

If responder has 11 or 12 points, he makes an invitational rebid:

- Two No Trump ▼
- An old suit at the three-level ▼

Responder chooses whichever bid is the most descriptive. For example:

OPENER	RESPONDER	
One Diamond	One Heart	♠ K 10 7 3
Two Clubs	?	♥ K J 7 4
		♦ Q 4
		♣ Q 10 2

HOW HIGH: Maybe Game. With 11 points, responder wants to make an invitational rebid.

WHERE: No Trump. Opener's failure to raise Hearts or bid Spades indicates that there is no Magic Major Suit Fit so responder invites to Game by bidding Two No Trump. If opener has 13 or 14 points, he will Pass. If opener has 15 or more points, he will carry on to Game.

Another example:

OPENER	RESPONDER	
One Diamond	One Heart	♠ 8 3
Two Clubs	?	♥ Q J 10 3
		♦ A J 7 6 4
		♣ Q 2

HOW HIGH: Maybe Game. With 11 points, responder must choose an invitational rebid.

WHERE: Diamonds. Here the most descriptive rebid is a jump to Three Diamonds...an old suit at the three-level. Note that responder does not bid Two Diamonds, an old suit at the two-level because that would be a discouraging rebid showing 6 - 10 points.

When responder has 13 or more points, he wants to ensure that the partnership reaches Game. He has two rebids available:

- Game ▼
- A new suit

If responder knows WHERE, he bids Game. If responder doesn't know WHERE, he bids a new suit. For example:

OPENER	RESPONDER	
One Diamond	One Heart	♠ A J 10 4
Two Clubs	?	♥ K 8 7 4
		♦ Q 9
		♣ K 8 4

HOW HIGH: Game. With 13 points, responder knows there is enough combined strength for Game.

WHERE: No Trump. Responder knows there is no Magic Major Suit Fit. Responder has enough information to place the contract...Three No Trump

Another example:

OPENER	RESPONDER	
One Heart	One Spade	♠ Q 10 9 6 4 3
Two Diamonds	?	♥ K 8
		♦ A K
		♣ Q 6 3

HOW HIGH: Game. Responder's 16 points should be more than enough for Game.

WHERE: Responder is not sure WHERE. Needing more information, responder bids a new suit, Three Clubs. Opener's next bid should give responder the information he needs to settle on the final contract.

Here are more examples after a new suit by opener at the two-level:

OPENER	RESPONDER
One Heart	One Spade
Two Clubs	?

What do you rebid with the following hands?

1) ♠ Q J 8 7 2	2) ♠ A Q J 3	3) ♠ A 10 9 5	4) ♠ K J 9 8 6 4
♥ K 10	♥ K 9 8	♥ K J 8	♥ A Q
♦ 6 2	♦ 6 4 3 2	♦ A 8 6	♦ 10 9 2
♣ A J 5 4	♣ J 7	♣ Q 6 5	♣ 5 2

1) HOW HIGH: Maybe Game. With 12 points, you need to make an invitational rebid.

   WHERE: Clubs. Your choices are Two No Trump or an old suit at the three-level. The most descriptive bid on this hand is THREE CLUBS, telling opener about the Magic Fit in Clubs while showing a hand of invitational strength. If opener has only 13 or 14 points, he can Pass and play Part-Game in Three Clubs.

2) HOW HIGH: Maybe Game. You have 11 points, enough to make an invitational rebid.

   WHERE: Hearts. Opener's sequence implies that he has at least five Hearts since he bid that suit first and then showed an unbalanced hand (this will be explained more clearly in the next chapter). You can therefore assume that you have a Magic Major Suit Fit. You would rebid THREE HEARTS...an old suit at the three-level.

3) HOW HIGH: Game. This time you have 14 points.

   WHERE: Hearts. This example is similar to the previous one. Bid FOUR HEARTS, Game in the Magic Major Suit Fit.

4) HOW HIGH: Maybe Game. With 12 points, you need to make an invitational rebid.

   WHERE: Spades. You want to tell opener about your extra length in Spades. A bid of THREE SPADES, an old suit at the three-level, will get the appropriate message across to opener.

Summary

When your partner is the opening bidder and makes a rebid that shows he could have a minimum hand (13 - 16 Points), you, as responder, can determine your rebid as follows:

**RESPONDER'S REBID WHEN OPENER
COULD HAVE A MINIMUM HAND**

Ask yourself HOW HIGH and WHERE:

With 6 - 10 points, Game is unlikely so make a discouraging rebid:
- Pass
- An *old* suit at the two-level
- One No Trump

With 11 - 12 points, Game is likely so make an encouraging rebid:
- An old suit at the three-level
- Two No Trump

With 13 or more points, Game is certain so make sure you get there:
- Bid Game if you know WHERE
- Bid a *new* suit if you don't know WHERE

Exercises

1) Partner opens the bidding One Diamond. You respond One Heart. Partner raises you to Two Hearts. What is your rebid with each of the following hands?

a)♠ J 9 4 3	b)♠ A 6 3	c)♠ 7 2	d)♠ 8 3
♥ K J 3 2	♥ K 9 8 2	♥ K Q J 9	♥ 9 8 7 3
♦ J 9 4	♦ 7 3	♦ A Q 3	♦ A Q 7 5 3
♣ 9 2	♣ K J 7 3	♣ K 9 7 3	♣ 9 3

2) Partner opens the bidding One Club, you respond One Diamond and your partner rebids One Spade. What do you do next with the following hands?

a)♠ Q 9 8 5	b)♠ K Q 10 2	c)♠ A K 9 3
♥ A 5	♥ Q 3 2	♥ A 7
♦ K 7 6 3	♦ A 7 5 4	♦ Q J 9 8 4
♣ 8 7 3	♣ 6 3	♣ 7 3

3) Partner opens the bidding One Heart and you respond One Spade. Your partner now bids One No Trump. What do you rebid with the following hands?

a)♠ A 7 4 2	b)♠ J 7 6 5 3 2	c)♠ A Q J 2	d)♠ K 7 6 5 2
♥ 7 3	♥ 5 3	♥ 5 3 2	♥ Q 9 3
♦ K 9 8	♦ 8 3	♦ K 8 3	♦ K Q
♣ Q 7 6 2	♣ A 5 3	♣ Q 9 3	♣ A 8 3

4) Partner opens One Spade and you respond One No Trump. Partner now bids Two Clubs. What do you do with the following hands?

a)♠ A 7 4	b)♠ 3	c)♠ Q 3	d)♠ 2
♥ Q 9 6 3	♥ J 8 5	♥ K 9 4 3 2	♥ K 9 3 2
♦ J 7 4	♦ Q J 8 4	♦ J 7 3 2	♦ J 8 5 3 2
♣ J 9 7	♣ Q J 7 6 3	♣ Q 6	♣ J 6 2

5) Partner opens One Diamond, you respond One Heart and partner rebids Two Diamonds. What do you rebid with the following hands?

a)♠ A 3 2	b)♠ A 10	c)♠ A 6 3 2	d)♠ 9
♥ A 10 9 8	♥ A J 10 7 6 4	♥ 9 7 5 4 3	♥ A J 9 7 5
♦ Q 8	♦ 8 3	♦ 3	♦ K 3
♣ K Q 3 2	♣ J 4 2	♣ Q 9 3	♣ K Q 9 7 2

12

Responder's Rebid After Opener's Medium or Maximum Rebid

While opener will most frequently show a minimum (13 - 16 point) hand with his rebid, there will be times when his rebid promises a medium (17 - 18 point) or maximum (19 - 21 point) hand.

Responder's Rebid After Opener Shows a Medium Hand

Since responder needs at least 6 points to make his initial response, whenever opener's rebid shows a medium hand (17 - 18 points) there will usually be enough combined strength to play in a Game contract. Only if responder has 6, 7 or 8 points will he allow the auction to stop in a Part-Game contract. With 9 or more points, responder should always make sure the partnership gets to Game.

How does responder recognize when opener is showing a medium hand? The following rebids by opener describe a medium hand after responder has bid at the one-level:

	OPENER	RESPONDER
• A jump raise of responder's Major to the three-level	One Diamond **Three Spades**	One Spade
• A jump rebid of opener's suit at the three-level	One Heart **Three Hearts**	One Spade
• A new suit at the two-level if it is higher-ranking than opener's first suit	One Diamond **Two Hearts**	One Spade

132

Let's look at these situations one at a time.

Rebid After a Jump Raise of Responder's Major

OPENER	RESPONDER
One Diamond	One Spade
Three Spades	?

WHERE has been decided...there is a Magic Major Suit Fit in Spades. Responder need only decide HOW HIGH. Since opener is showing 17 or 18 points, responder can rebid as follows:

RESPONDER'S REBID AFTER A JUMP RAISE

- With 6 - 8 points: Pass (STOP). Game is unlikely...settle for Part-Game.
- With 9 or more points: Bid 4 of the Major (STOP). There will be at least enough combined strength for Game.

A couple of notes:

- If responder has exactly 8 points, it is possible that opener has exactly 18 and there is enough combined strength for Game. There is no way to be 100% accurate. You can use your judgement and, if you wish, you can carry on to Game with 8 points.
- If responder has 15 or more points he should consider bidding a Slam. More on this in a later chapter.

For example, partner opens the bidding One Diamond and you respond One Heart. Partner now rebids Three Hearts. Ask yourself HOW HIGH and WHERE to decide what would you do with each of the following hands:

1) ♠ 9 7 4	2) ♠ 7 5	3) ♠ A J 9 8
♥ K 7 5 4	♥ Q 9 8 6 5	♥ A 9 7 3
♦ 8 6	♦ K J 8	♦ 10 9
♣ Q J 9 3	♣ J 3 2	♣ J 6 2

1) HOW HIGH: Part-Game. With only 6 points, there is not enough combined strength for Game even if opener has 18 points.

   WHERE: Hearts. Opener's raise has told you that there is a Magic Major Suit Fit. PASS and play in a Part-Game contract of Three Hearts.

2) HOW HIGH: Part-Game. Here you have 7 high card points plus 1 for the fifth Heart. Since partner is showing 17 - 18 points you have a combined total of 25 or 26 points.

   WHERE: Hearts. You have a Magic Fit. You should probably say PASS. However, there would be nothing wrong if you took an aggressive view and carried on to FOUR HEARTS. If partner has only 17 points, it will give you a challenge to play the hand!

3) HOW HIGH: Game. With 10 points there should be more than enough combined strength for Game.

   WHERE: Hearts. Accept partner's invitation and bid on to FOUR HEARTS.

Rebid After a Jump Rebid of Opener's Suit

OPENER	RESPONDER
One Heart	One Spade
Three Hearts	?

It is important to realize that opener's jump rebid in his own suit shows:

- A medium hand (17 - 18 points)
- A 6-card or longer suit

Responder decides HOW HIGH and rebids as follows:

RESPONDER'S REBID AFTER OPENER'S JUMP REBID

- With 6 - 8 points: Pass ⬢ . Game is unlikely…settle for Part-Game.
- With 9 or more points: Bid Game ⬢ . Raise opener's Major suit to Game with 2-card support (6 + 2 = 8). Choose Three No Trump if there is no Magic Major Suit Fit.

For example, partner opens the bidding One Heart and you respond One Spade. Partner now rebids Three Hearts. What would you do with each of the following hands?

1) ♠ K 9 7 4 3   2) ♠ Q J 7 5   3) ♠ A J 9 4
   ♥ 5   ♥ Q 5   ♥ 3
   ♦ J 8 6   ♦ A 9 4 3   ♦ Q 10 6 4
   ♣ Q 9 7 3   ♣ 5 3 2   ♣ K 7 6 2

1) HOW HIGH: Part-Game. With only 7 points, there is not enough combined strength for Game even if opener has 18 points.

WHERE: Hearts. You should PASS and play in the acceptable Part-Game contract of Three Hearts.

2) HOW HIGH: Game. Here you have 9 points, enough for Game.

WHERE: Hearts. Since partner has an unbalanced hand with no second suit to bid, he has at least a 6-card suit. You have a Magic Major Suit Fit and should raise partner to FOUR HEARTS.

3) HOW HIGH: Game. With 10 points there should be more than enough combined strength for Game.

WHERE: No Trump. Since partner did not support your Spade suit, there cannot be a Magic Major Suit Fit there. There is also unlikely to be a Magic Major Suit Fit in Hearts unless partner has seven or more. Rebid THREE NO TRUMP, the most likely Game contract.

The '5-4' Inference

When opener bids two suits, he must have at least four cards in each suit. Sometimes, however, responder should assume opener has **five** cards in his first suit even though opener has not rebid his first suit.

When opener rebids a new suit **at the two-level** he has an unbalanced hand because he must have answered "No" to the third question, "Is my hand balanced?". Responder can **infer** that opener has '5-4' shape: five or more cards in the first suit and four or more cards in the second suit. For example, suppose the auction goes:

OPENER	RESPONDER
One Heart	One Spade
Two Diamonds	?

Opener might have one of the following hands:

♠ 6 4	♠ 9	♠ 5
♥ A Q 6 4 2	♥ K Q 7 5 4	♥ Q J 9 7 5 4
♦ K J 8 3	♦ A Q 8 4 2	♦ A K J 3 2
♣ K 3	♣ J 6	♣ 3

On rare occasions, opener will have an unbalanced hand with only 4-card suits (i.e. 4-4-4-1 shape) but, in general, responder can assume:

'5-4' INFERENCE

If opener bids a new suit at the two-level, he has at least
five cards in his first suit and at least four cards in his second suit.

The value of the '5-4' inference is that it makes responder's bidding easier in many situations. For example:

OPENER	RESPONDER		
One Heart	One Spade	♠	J 7 6 4
Two Diamonds	?	♥	K 4 3
		♦	A K 2
		♣	Q 6 3

With 13 points, responder knows HOW HIGH...Game. In deciding WHERE, responder can take advantage of the '5-4' inference to determine that opener has at least five Hearts. Knowing that there is a Magic Major Suit Fit, responder can bid Four Hearts.

Another example:

OPENER	RESPONDER		
One Heart	One Spade	♠	J 8 6 3
Two Diamonds	?	♥	J 2
		♦	Q 4
		♣	Q 8 4 3 2

Holding only 7 points, responder wants to play in the best Part-Game. When deciding WHERE, responder can infer that opener has at least a 5-card Heart suit. Responder should bid Two Hearts (an old suit at the two-level) rather than passing and leaving opener in his second suit. The concept of choosing between opener's two suits is called preference.

The '5-4' inference does not apply when opener bids a new suit at the one-level. For example:

OPENER	RESPONDER
One Club	One Heart
One Spade	?

Here opener could have a balanced hand because the second question, "Can I bid a new suit at the one-level?", comes before the third question, "Is my hand balanced?".

Rebid After Opener Bids a Higher-Ranking Suit at the Two-Level

OPENER	RESPONDER
One Diamond	One Spade
Two Hearts	?

In this case, opener is making an invitational rebid with an unbalanced hand. Using the '5-4' inference, opener should have at least five Diamonds and at least four Hearts. Keeping in mind that opener's first suit is longer than his second suit, responder can rebid as follows:

RESPONDER'S REBID AFTER OPENER BIDS
A HIGHER-RANKING SUIT AT THE TWO-LEVEL

- With 6 - 8 points: Choose the best Part-Game:
  - Put opener back into his first suit if you like it better
  - Pass if you like the second suit better
  - Rebid a 5-card or longer suit
  - Bid Two No Trump

- With 9 or more points: The choices are familiar:
  - Bid Game if you know WHERE
  - Bid a new suit if you need more information

For example, partner opens the bidding One Diamond and you respond One Spade. Partner now rebids Two Hearts. What would you do with each of the following hands?

1) ♠ K 9 7 4   2) ♠ K 9 7 4 3 2   3) ♠ A J 6 2
   ♥ 5 4   ♥ 6 3   ♥ 7 6 3
   ♦ K 8 6   ♦ 6 4   ♦ 7 3
   ♣ 9 8 7 3   ♣ K 7 6   ♣ K Q 7 4

1) HOW HIGH: Part-Game. With only 6 points, Game is unlikely even if opener has 18 points.

   WHERE: Diamonds. Even though you have only 6 points, you should not Pass since you are not in the best Part-Game. Partner should have at least five Diamonds ('5-4' inference), so the best rebid is THREE DIAMONDS, putting the partnership in the Magic Fit.

3) HOW HIGH: Part-Game (Maybe Game?). With 8 points, Game is unlikely if opener has 17 points but is possible if opener has 18 points. The more conservative view is to assume the contract should be played in Part-Game.

   WHERE: Spades. With a 6-card suit, you should rebid TWO SPADES. This will tell opener that you have 6 - 8 points, at least five Spades and no support for his suits.

4) HOW HIGH: Game. Holding 10 points you have enough for Game (10 + 17 = 27).

   WHERE: No Trump. Since opener did not raise your Spade suit and you do not have good support for either of opener's suits, you should bid the most likely Game...THREE NO TRUMP.

Note: If responder's initial response is a new suit at the two-level, he must have at least 11 points. If opener describes a medium strength hand of 17 or 18 points, there must be enough combined strength for a Game contract. Since opener is also aware of this, neither partner will stop the auction below Game. Thus, any rebid by responder below the Game level is forcing.

Responder's Rebid After Opener Shows a Maximum Hand

| 13 | 14 | 15 | 16 | 17 | 18 | 19 | 20 | 21 |

If opener's rebid shows a maximum hand (19 - 21 points), he is making a marathon bid **GO**. There should always be enough combined strength for a Game contract, even if responder has as few as 6 points. Responder must always make sure that the bidding reaches a Game contract.

How does responder recognize when opener is showing a maximum hand? The following rebids by opener describe a maximum hand after responder has bid at the one-level:

	OPENER	RESPONDER
• A jump rebid in a new suit (Jump Shift)	One Heart **Three Clubs**	One Spade
• A jump rebid in No Trump	One Heart **Two No Trump**	One Spade
• A jump to Game in a Major or in No Trump	One Heart **Four Hearts**	One Spade

Since the partnership has enough combined strength for Game, the answer to HOW HIGH has been settled...Game. Responder only needs to determine whether or not there is a Magic Major Suit Fit to determine WHERE. Since both opener and responder know that they are headed for Game, any bid below the Game level is marathon (even old suit bids at the three-level). This makes responder's task relatively easy and he rebids as follows:

RESPONDER'S REBID
AFTER OPENER SHOWS A MAXIMUM HAND

- Bid Game if you know WHERE
- Bid an old suit (opener's rebid is marathon) or a new suit if you don't know WHERE.

Note that, if opener jumps to the three-level in a new suit, he should have at least five cards in his first suit ('5-4' inference).

Here are some examples. Partner opens the bidding One Heart and you respond One Spade. Partner now rebids Three Clubs. What would you do with each of the following hands?

1) ♠ K 9 7 4   2) ♠ Q J 5 2   3) ♠ K 7 6 4 3
   ♥ 5 4   ♥ K 7 3   ♥ 6 3
   ♦ K 8 6 3   ♦ 7 4 3   ♦ 6 4 3
   ♣ 9 8 3   ♣ 8 6 3   ♣ K 7 2

1) HOW HIGH: Game. Even though you only have 6 points, you cannot Pass since partner's rebid is marathon.

   WHERE: No Trump. Since partner did not raise your suit, you don't have a Magic Major Suit Fit in Spades. Unless partner has a 6-card or longer Heart suit, you don't have a Magic Major Suit Fit in Hearts either. You would rebid THREE NO TRUMP.

2) HOW HIGH: Game. Again you have 6 points, but opener's bid is forcing to the Game level.

   WHERE: Hearts. Since partner should have at least five Hearts ('5-4' inference), rebid FOUR HEARTS.

3) HOW HIGH: Game. Here you have 8 points. You must get to Game.

   WHERE: Opener has denied 4-card support for Spades through his failure to raise, but he could have three. Rebid THREE SPADES and give opener an opportunity to support your suit.

The Rest of the Auction

If the bidding continues past responder's rebid, the partnership is probably heading for at least Game and perhaps Slam. Use the principles that have guided both opener and responder so far to complete any auction. There are numerous possibilities, which is part of what makes the game intriguing. We will look at one example before we move on to new topics.

	OPENER	RESPONDER
	♠ A 10 3	♠ K J 7 6 5
	♥ K Q 8	♥ A J 5
	♦ J 8 7 4	♦ 2
	♣ K J 3	♣ A 9 5 4
The bidding:	One Diamond	One Spade
	One No Trump	Two Clubs
	Two Spades	Four Spades

Opener, holding 14 points, starts by bidding his longest suit. Responder can bid a new suit at the one-level and does so. Opener now shows his minimum strength and balanced distribution with a rebid of One No

Trump. Responder knows there is enough combined strength for Game but is uncertain whether or not there is a Magic Major Suit Fit. He therefore bids a new suit, marathon, to get more information.

Opener, having already described his balanced hand and denied 4-card Spade support, has a second chance to show 3-card support for responder's suit. This tells responder what he needs to know to place the final contract.

Look at what happens if we change opener's hand slightly:

OPENER	RESPONDER
♠ A 3	♠ K J 7 6 5
♥ K Q 8	♥ A J 5
♦ J 10 8 7 4	♦ 2
♣ K J 3	♣ A 9 5 4

The bidding:		
	One Diamond	One Spade
	One No Trump	Two Clubs
	Two Diamonds	Three No Trump

Our bidding is becoming quite sophisticated! Of course, the opponents have been very quiet to date. In the next section, we will look at what happens when both sides are competing to win the contract.

Summary

When opener's rebid shows a medium hand (17 - 18 points), responder rebids as follows:

RESPONDER'S REBID
WHEN OPENER SHOWS A MEDIUM HAND

- With 6 - 8 points:　　　　Choose the best Part-Game.
- With 9 or more points:　　Bid Game or make a marathon bid (new suit).

When opener's rebid shows a maximum hand (19 - 21 Points), responder rebids as follows:

RESPONDER'S REBID
WHEN OPENER SHOWS A MAXIMUM HAND

- With 6 or more Points:　　Bid Game or make a descriptive bid. The bidding must continue until Game is reached.

If responder is uncertain whether or not a specific rebid by him will be forcing, he can always make sure by **bidding a new suit**.

Exercises

1) Partner opens the bidding One Diamond. You respond One Heart. Partner raises you to Three Hearts. What is your rebid with each of the following hands?

a) ♠ J 9 4 3	b) ♠ A 6 3	c) ♠ 7 2	d) ♠ 8 3
♥ K J 3 2	♥ K 9 8 2	♥ K J 9 3	♥ J 8 7 3
♦ J 9 4	♦ 7 3	♦ A Q 3	♦ A Q 7 5 3
♣ 9 2	♣ K J 7 3	♣ K 9 7 3	♣ 9 3

2) Partner opens the bidding One Heart, you respond One Spade and your partner rebids Three Hearts. What do you do next with the following hands?

a) ♠ J 9 5 3	b) ♠ Q 9 8 5	c) ♠ K 10 9 5 2	d) ♠ A Q 9 3
♥ Q 4 2	♥ A 5	♥ 2	♥ 7
♦ Q 10 9 8	♦ K 7 6 3	♦ A 7 5 4	♦ Q J 9 8 4
♣ J 10	♣ 8 7 3	♣ Q 6 3	♣ K 7 3

3) Partner opens the bidding One Heart and you respond One Spade. Your partner now bids Three Diamonds. What do you rebid with the following hands?

a) ♠ A 7 4 2	b) ♠ J 7 6 5 3 2	c) ♠ A J 6 2	d) ♠ K Q 6 5 2
♥ 7 3	♥ 5 3	♥ 5 3 2	♥ 9 3
♦ K 9 8	♦ 8 3	♦ K 8 3	♦ Q 5 2
♣ Q 7 6 2	♣ A 5 3	♣ Q 9 3	♣ 9 8 5

4) Partner opens One Spade and you respond One No Trump. Partner now bids Three Spades. What do you do with the following hands?

a) ♠ Q 4	b) ♠ 3	c) ♠ Q 3	d) ♠ J 2
♥ Q 10 9 6 3	♥ K 8 5	♥ K Q 3 2	♥ K 9 3 2
♦ J 7 4	♦ Q J 8 4	♦ 9 7 3 2	♦ K 8 5 3 2
♣ J 9 7	♣ Q J 7 6 3	♣ Q 6 3	♣ 9 2

5) Partner opens One Diamond, you respond One Heart and partner rebids Two No Trump. What do you rebid with the following hands?

a) ♠ J 3 2	b) ♠ J 10	c) ♠ 6 3 2	d) ♠ K J 9 2
♥ A 10 9 8	♥ A J 10 7 6 4	♥ A Q 5 4 3	♥ A 9 7 5
♦ Q 8	♦ 8 3	♦ 4 2	♦ Q 3
♣ J 8 3 2	♣ J 4 2	♣ 9 6 3	♣ 9 7 2

B. COMPETITIVE BIDDING

13

The Double

We are about to enter the world of competitive bidding...both sides bidding at the same time. Before we start, it will be useful to add a few details about scoring that will be important when considering competitive auctions.

Penalty for Undertricks

In Chapter 3 we discussed what happens when, for example, you bid to a contract of Four Spades and do not take ten tricks. Your contract has gone down and the opponents get a bonus, called a penalty, for every trick (undertrick) by which your contract was defeated. The penalty depends on the vulnerability of the defeated side as follows:

- Vulnerable: 100 points per undertrick
- Not vulnerable: 50 points per undertrick

The Double

There is a way to increase the penalty for defeating an opponent's contract. If an opponent reaches a contract which you feel cannot be made, instead of saying Pass, you can say "*double*" when it is your turn to bid.

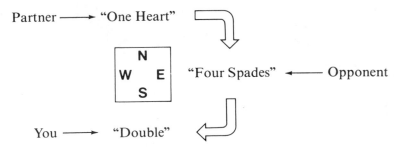

Here are some important points about the Double:

- A Double does not necessarily end the auction. Like any other bid, it must be followed by three Passes before the final contract is settled.
- You can only double when it is your turn to bid.
- You can only double an opponent's bid, not your partner's bid.

The effect of doubling a contract is a change in the value of undertricks. If the final contract is doubled, the penalty for defeating it is as follows:

- Vulnerable: 200 points for the first undertrick
                  300 points for each subsequent undertrick
- Not vulnerable: 100 points for the first undertrick
                  200 points for each subsequent undertrick

For example, if you are not vulnerable and bid Three Hearts and are defeated by three tricks, the opponents would get 150 points (50 + 50 + 50). If one of the opponents doubled the final contract, they would get 500 points (100 + 200 + 200). The opponents would score an additional 350 points by doubling your contract! Using the Double in this way is called making a *penalty double*. Another use of the Double will be discussed in Chapter 17.

Making a Doubled Contract

What happens if you make your contract after it has been doubled? Then:

- The trick score for making the contract is doubled.
- A bonus of 50 points is awarded (for the insult of having been doubled!).
- Any overtricks are scored with the following value:
  — Vulnerable: 200 points per overtrick
  — Not vulnerable: 100 points per overtrick

For example, if you made your contract of Three Hearts after the opponents had doubled, you would receive the following score:

Trick Score (2 x 90)	180
+ Bonus for a not vulnerable Game	300
+ Bonus for the insult of being doubled	50
= Total score	530

Note that the Double has turned your Part-Game of Three Hearts into a Game contract since your doubled trick score is more than 100 points if you make it. A Double is a two-way proposition: it increases the amount that can be won and also increases the amount that can be lost.

The Redouble

The redouble is used infrequently. If you are doubled and feel that you can make your contract, instead of saying Pass you can say *'redouble'* when it is your turn to bid.

Here are some important points about the Redouble:
- A Redouble does not necessarily end the auction. Like any other bid, it must be followed by three Passes before the final contract is settled.
- You can only redouble when it is your turn to bid.
- You can only redouble a double.

The effect of redoubling:
- If you don't make it, the doubled penalty is multiplied by two.
- If you do make it the doubled trick score is multiplied by two.

Summary

Points can be scored for defeating the opponents' contracts. The value of the points won or lost can be increased by *doubling* the final contract for penalties.

Exercises

1) You are not vulnerable and bid to a contract of Three No Trump. You take seven tricks. How would this be scored?

2) You are vulnerable and bid to a contract of Four Hearts. The opponents defeat your contract by three tricks. How many points do they receive?

3) Not vulnerable, your opponents bid to a contract of Four Spades. You double and they only take eight tricks. How many points do you receive for defeating their contract?

4) Your side is vulnerable and bids to a contract of Four Hearts. The opponents double and defeat you by two tricks. How many points do they receive?

5) You are not vulnerable and bid to a contract of Two Hearts. One of the opponents doubles and you end up taking nine tricks. How would this be scored?

14

The Overcall

In Section A we discussed bidding without *competition*. You or your partner opened the bidding and you exchanged information back and forth until you reached a final contract. The opponents were quiet throughout. Now let's look at the auction when both sides are competing for the contract.

Suppose you were planning to open the bidding but one of your opponents beat you to it. What can you do? One of your choices is to go ahead and bid your own suit. Since you are making a *call* (bid) over the opponent's bid, this is called an *overcall*.

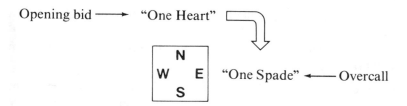

Opening bid ⟶ "One Heart"

"One Spade" ◀—— Overcall

You could also overcall One No Trump. In this case, you would be making a No Trump Overcall.

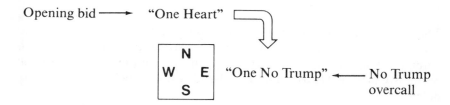

Opening bid ⟶ "One Heart"

"One No Trump" ◀—— No Trump overcall

An overcall can be made by either partner at any time during the auction.

For example:

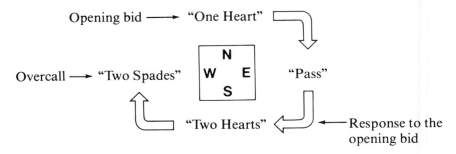

Before looking at the requirements for making an overcall, let's take a look at the advantages and risks of coming into the auction when the opponents have opened the bidding.

The Advantages

There are several good reasons to enter the auction even though the opponents have opened the bidding:

- You might be able to make a Part-Game or Game contract
- You might make it more difficult for the opponents to exchange information
- You may push the opponents to a higher contract than they can make
- You may provide your partner with enough information to help him defeat the opponents' contract

Let's look at each situation in turn. For example, suppose the opponent on your right (*right-hand opponent*) opens One Club and you hold the following hand:

♠ A K Q J 7 6
♥ 7 3
♦ A 6 3
♣ 9 2

There is an excellent chance that you can make at least seven tricks with Spades as trump, more if your partner has some strength. If you do not enter the auction, the opponents will end up naming the trump suit, perhaps Clubs or Hearts, and your hand will be much less effective on defense.

If you bid One Spade, look at the effect this might have on the opponent on your left (*left-hand opponent*). Suppose he holds:

♠ 3
♥ K 9 8 7 3 2
♦ K J 6
♣ 4 3 2

After his partner opened the bidding One Club, he was planning to bid One Heart ... a new suit at the one-level. By bidding One Spade you have taken away this option. Since he has less than 11 points, he cannot bid a new suit at the two-level. What can he do? Bid One No Trump? That looks unappetizing since your side will take Spade tricks right away. You can see how your overcall of One Spade can make it difficult for the opponents.

Further, suppose your partner has some support for you and the auction proceeds:

NORTH	EAST	SOUTH	WEST
(Dealer)	(You)		
One Club	One Spade	Two Clubs	Two Spades
?			

If your opponents want to play with Clubs as trump, they will have to bid Three Clubs. This will prove too high if all they can take is eight tricks. So instead of letting the opponents score points for bidding and making Two Clubs, you will score 50 points (100 if they are vulnerable) for defeating them in Three Clubs. Their other option is to let you play in Two Spades and make a Part-Game.

Finally, suppose the opponents do buy the contract and your partner has to make the opening lead. It will be useful for him to know something about your hand.

The Risks

While there is much to be said for competing when the opponents open the bidding, there is also some danger. The opening bidder has promised a better than average hand with at least 13 points. He has started to describe his hand to his partner while you have not yet exchanged any information. Opener's partner will be in a good position to double if you come into the auction. You will have to take action without knowing anything about your partner's hand. The major risks are:

- You might be doubled (or left to go down undoubled)
- You might give the opponents useful information

For example, suppose your right-hand opponent opens One Heart and you hold:

♠ K J 7 3 2
♥ Q 9
♦ 7 6 4
♣ K J 2

If you overcall One Spade, it might warn the opponents that you have some strength and help them get to the correct contract or play the hand with the knowledge of where the missing high cards are located.

Alternatively, partner may have very little strength and you will be left to play in One Spade. You will probably be defeated by several tricks whereas, if you don't overcall, the opponents might get to a contract you can defeat and you will collect some points.

Your left-hand opponent may hold a hand like this:

♠ A Q 10 9 8
♥ 7 3
♦ A K 3
♣ Q 5 4

Knowing his partner has at least 13 points, he may decide to double your contract.

NORTH ·	EAST	SOUTH	WEST
(Dealer)	(You)		
One Heart	One Spade	Double	Pass
Pass	Pass		

If partner has a poor hand (very likely!) you may take only three tricks and be defeated four tricks. If you were not vulnerable, the penalty would be 700 points (100 + 200 + 200 + 200). If you were vulnerable, the penalty would be 1,100 points (200 + 300 + 300 + 300)!

The Overcall

How do you balance the advantages of making an overcall versus the risks? You can minimize the risks by ensuring that you have the following:

- A five-card suit or longer
- Sufficient strength

The longer your suit, the less danger that an opponent will be able to double you. If you have at least a 5-card suit, you reduce this possibilty. This will also make it easier for your partner to compete since he will be able to raise with only 3-card support if he knows you have at least five.

The stronger your hand, the more tricks you are likely to take and the safer it will be to overcall. This will also make it easy for your partner to decide what to do as we shall see in the next chapter.

> **REQUIREMENTS FOR MAKING**
> **AN OVERCALL**
>
> A 5-card suit or longer **and**
> An opening bid (13 - 21 points)

Let's look at some examples. Your right-hand opponent opens the bidding One Diamond. What would you bid with the following hands?

1) ♠ A Q J 7 3   2) ♠ A 6 3   3) ♠ K 9 8 7 2   4) ♠ A 9 6 5 3
   ♥ A 2   ♥ K 2   ♥ Q 8   ♥ Q 5
   ♦ 7 4 3   ♦ 7 3   ♦ K J 6 3   ♦ 3
   ♣ Q 9 2   ♣ A J 7 5 4 3 ♣ 7 3   ♣ A K 7 5 3

1) ONE SPADE. Your hand is worth 14 points and you have a 5-card suit. Overcall One Spade to compete for the right to name the final contract. Partner will know that you have an opening bid and at least five Spades.

2) TWO CLUBS. With 14 points you would have opened the bidding One Club. However, when the opponents open the bidding, you will have to overcall Two Clubs to show your good suit. Note that you have to start the bidding for your side at the two-level.

3) PASS. Even though you have a 5-card suit, you do not have an opening bid. You should Pass. Coming into the auction with this hand would run the risk that an opponent might double you and also that partner would expect you to have a better hand.

4) ONE SPADE. With an opening bid and two 5-card suits, do the same thing as if you were opening the bidding. Bid the higher-ranking suit, One Spade.

The One No Trump Overcall

Suppose you have the following hand:

♠ K J 7 2
♥ A 9 4
♦ K Q 4
♣ K J 2

Your right-hand opponent opens the bidding One Club. With a balanced hand of 17 points, you were planning to open the bidding One No Trump.

There is nothing to stop you from conveying this information to partner by overcalling One No Trump. Partner can treat this as if you had opened One No Trump.

> ### REQUIREMENTS FOR A
> ### ONE NO TRUMP OVERCALL
>
> 16 - 18 points
> Balanced hand

Let's look at some examples. Your right-hand opponent opens the bidding One Heart. What do you bid with each of the following hands?

1) ♠ A K 3	2) ♠ K 3	3) ♠ 8 7 2	4) ♠ A Q 6 5 3
♥ A Q 2	♥ A J 10	♥ A Q 8	♥ A J 6 5
♦ A 7 4 3	♦ 9 7 3	♦ K Q J 3 2	♦ 2
♣ J 9 2	♣ A K 5 4 3	♣ J 3	♣ A J 3

1) ONE NO TRUMP. You have a balanced hand with 18 points.

2) ONE NO TRUMP. Your hand is worth 16 points...15 in high cards and 1 for the fifth Club. Although you could overcall Two Clubs with your 5-card suit, an overcall of One No Trump is far more descriptive. Partner will know you have a balanced hand with 16 to 18 points.

3) TWO DIAMONDS. While you have a balanced hand, you only have 14 points. Settle for a simple overcall of Two Diamonds.

4) ONE SPADE. Your hand is worth 17 points. However, your hand is not balanced. Overcall One Spade.

The 13+ Point Pass

Suppose you hold the following hand:

♠ K J 9 7 2
♥ Q 9
♦ K 6 4
♣ K J 2

You are planning to open the bidding One Spade when your right-hand opponent opens the bidding One Spade. What should you do? Since your opponent must have at least a 4-card Spade suit and is contracting to take 7 tricks with Spades as trump, it does not make sense for you to bid Two

Spades and contract to take 8 tricks with Spades as trump. Pass and be content to defend. **You do not have to overcall just because you have an opening bid and a 5-card suit.** You should not overcall in the same suit that your opponent bid.

Summary

When the opponents open the bidding, you can compete by making an *overcall*.

REQUIREMENTS FOR MAKING AN OVERCALL

A 5-card suit or longer **and**
An opening bid (13 - 21 points)

You can also make a No Trump overcall with the same type of hand with which you would open One No Trump.

REQUIREMENTS FOR A ONE NO TRUMP OVERCALL

16 - 18 points
Balanced hand

Exercises

1) Your right-hand opponent opens the bidding One Diamond. What should you bid with each of the following hands?

a) ♠ A J 9 4 3
♥ K J 3 2
♦ 9 4
♣ A 2

b) ♠ Q J 6 3
♥ 8 2
♦ A K 7 3
♣ Q J 3

c) ♠ A 7 2
♥ K 9
♦ 9 6 3
♣ K Q J 7 3

d) ♠ Q 4
♥ A Q 9
♦ K Q 3
♣ Q J 9 7 6

e) ♠ 3
♥ K Q 9 4 2
♦ Q 8
♣ A Q 10 7 5

f) ♠ Q 9 5
♥ A 5
♦ K Q 10 7 3
♣ J 8 3

g) ♠ Q 10 3 2
♥ J 7 6 4 2
♦ A 4
♣ K 3

h) ♠ A 9 3
♥ A 10 8 7
♦ A J 6 3
♣ 9 8

2) The bidding proceeds:

NORTH	EAST	SOUTH	WEST
(You)	(Opener)		
—	One Spade	Pass	Two Diamonds
?			

You are North. What do you do with the following hands?

a) ♠ A 4 2
   ♥ K Q J 9 7 3
   ♦ 9 8
   ♣ Q 2

b) ♠ K J 7 6 4
   ♥ A Q
   ♦ 8 3
   ♣ A 9 5 3

c) ♠ J 2
   ♥ A 3 2
   ♦ K 8
   ♣ A K J 7 5 3

15

Responding to a One-Level Overcall

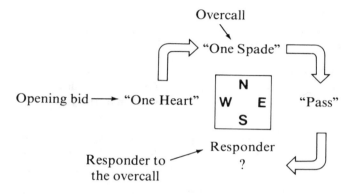

When your partner makes an overcall at the one-level, you know that he has:

- A 5-card suit or longer
- An opening bid (13 - 21 points)

Thus, when you are responding to partner's overcall, treat it in the same fashion as responding to an opening bid. Ask yourself Responder's Four Questions:

> ### RESPONDER'S FOUR QUESTIONS
> 1. CAN I RAISE PARTNER'S MAJOR?
> 2. DO I HAVE A WEAK HAND (0 - 5 POINTS)?
> 3. CAN I BID A NEW SUIT AT THE ONE-LEVEL?
> 4. DO I HAVE A MINIMUM HAND (6 - 10 POINTS)?

Some minor modifications occur because partner has promised a 5-card suit and your left-hand opponent opened the bidding. Let's see how it all works.

Question One

> ### 1. CAN I RAISE PARTNER'S MAJOR?

Because partner has promised at least a 5-card suit, **you only need 3-card support to raise**...5 + 3 = 8. If you have 3-card support or more, revalue your hand using dummy points and raise to the appropriate level.

You can determine HOW HIGH to raise in the same fashion as if partner had opened the bidding:

<table>
<tr><td colspan="3" align="center">RAISING
OVERCALLER'S MAJOR</td></tr>
<tr><td>DUMMY POINTS</td><td>BID</td><td></td></tr>
<tr><td>0 - 5</td><td>Pass</td><td>🛑</td><td>Game is very unlikely, so stop at the lowest Part-Game</td></tr>
<tr><td>6 - 10</td><td>Raise to the two-level ▼</td><td></td><td>Game is possible if partner has a medium (17 - 18) or maximum (19 - 21) hand</td></tr>
<tr><td>11 - 12</td><td>Raise to the three-level ▼</td><td></td><td>Game is very likely unless partner has only 13 or 14 points</td></tr>
<tr><td>13 - 16</td><td>Raise to the four-level ▼</td><td></td><td>Game should be bid as there are at least 26 combined points</td></tr>
</table>

For example, the auction starts off:

NORTH	EAST	SOUTH	WEST
(Dealer)			(You)
One Diamond	One Heart	Pass	?

You are West. What would you respond with the following hands?

1) ♠ 9 4 3	2) ♠ K 6 3	3) ♠ A 7 2	4) ♠ —
♥ J 6 3 2	♥ K 8 2	♥ Q 9 4 2	♥ A J 9
♦ Q 9 4	♦ 9 8 7 4 3	♦ 3	♦ K 9 7 6 3
♣ J 7 2	♣ J 3	♣ Q J 8 7 3	♣ Q J 9 7 6

1) PASS. Even though you have 4-card support for partner's Major, with only 4 dummy points Game is unlikely.

2) TWO HEARTS. Here you have 3-card support, which is sufficient since partner must have at least five. Your hand is worth 8 dummy points...7 HCPs and 1 for the doubleton Club. Raise to Two Hearts. This will allow partner to carry on to Game with a maximum hand (19 - 21) or make an invitational try with a medium hand (17 - 18) by bidding Three Hearts.

3) THREE HEARTS. You have 4-card support and 12 dummy points...9 HCPs and 3 for the singleton Diamond. Game is likely, so make a highly invitational raise of Three Hearts. Partner will only decline if he has a 13 or 14 points.

4) FOUR HEARTS. With 3-card support and a hand worth 16 dummy points...11 HCPs and 5 Points for the Spade void...you should have enough combined strength for Game.

Question Two

2. DO I HAVE A WEAK HAND (0 - 5 POINTS)?

If the answer is yes, Pass; Game is very unlikely. For example, the auction starts off:

NORTH	EAST	SOUTH	WEST
(Dealer)			(You)
One Club	One Heart	Pass	?

You are West. Combining the first two questions, what would you respond with the following hands?

1) ♠ K 7 4 3
   ♥ 3 2
   ♦ Q 7 5 4
   ♣ 9 8 2

2) ♠ Q 8 4 3
   ♥ K 9 8 2
   ♦ 3
   ♣ 9 7 6 3

3) ♠ K J 8 7 2
   ♥ 4 2
   ♦ 5 3
   ♣ K 9 8 7

1) PASS. You can't raise partner's Major and you only have 5 points. Pass to prevent the partnership from getting too high.

2) TWO HEARTS. You have 4-card support for partner's Major. Revaluing with dummy points you have 8 points...5 in high cards and 3 for the singleton. That is enough to raise partner to Two Hearts.

3) You can't support partner's Major and you don't have a weak hand ...you have 8 points. You'll have to go on to the third question.

Question Three

> ### 3. CAN I BID A NEW SUIT AT THE ONE-LEVEL?

If you can, bid the appropriate 4-card or longer suit. For example, the auction goes:

NORTH	EAST	SOUTH	WEST
(Dealer)			(You)
One Club	One Heart	Pass	?

As West, use the first three questions to determine what you would respond with the following hands:

1) ♠ A Q 8 4 3	2) ♠ K 9 8 4 3	3) ♠ K 9 7 3 2	4) ♠ J 9 4
♥ 3 2	♥ 8 2	♥ K 4 2	♥ 7 4
♦ 9 4	♦ 8 7 4 3	♦ Q 5 3	♦ K 9 7 6
♣ K J 8 2	♣ 7 3	♣ J 8	♣ K J 9 3

1) ONE SPADE. You can't raise partner's Major and you don't have a weak hand (0 - 5 points). You can bid a new suit at the one-level... One Spade.
2) PASS. With only 4 points you don't have enough to say anything except Pass.
3) TWO HEARTS. With 3-card support for partner's suit and 10 dummy points, raise to the appropriate level...Two Hearts. Don't worry about looking for a second Magic Major Suit Fit, one is enough.
4) You can't raise partner's Major, don't have a weak hand and can't bid a new suit at the one-level. Time to look at the fourth question.

Question Four

> ### 4. DO I HAVE A MINIMUM HAND (6 - 10 POINTS)?

If the answer is Yes, you have 6 - 10 points. Since you can't raise partner's Major and can't bid a new suit at the one-level, you are left with only two choices:

- Supporting partner's Minor suit ▼
- Responding One No Trump ▼

You can support partner's Minor with 3-card support by raising to the two-level. Otherwise, you are left with the "catch-all" response of One No Trump.

For example, the auction goes:

NORTH	EAST	SOUTH	WEST
(Dealer)			
One Club	One Diamond	Pass	?

As West, what would you respond with the following hands?

	1)		2)		3)
♠	K 4 3	♠	K 4 3	♠	K Q 3
♥	Q 3 2	♥	8 2	♥	K 7 4
♦	Q 4	♦	K 7 4 3	♦	9 7 6
♣	J 9 7 4 2	♣	J 8 7 3	♣	A Q J 9

1) ONE NO TRUMP. Can you raise partner's Major? No, he hasn't bid one. Do you have a weak hand (0 - 5 points)? No, you have 9...8 in high cards and 1 for the fifth Club. Can you bid a new suit at the one-level? No, you don't have one you can bid. Do you have a minimum hand (6 - 10 points)? Yes, you have 9. With only two cards in partner's Minor suit, respond One No Trump.

2) TWO DIAMONDS. You can't support partner's Major, don't have 0 - 5 points and can't bid a new suit at the one-level. You do have a minimum hand... you have 7 points. Your choice is to raise partner's Minor suit or bid One No Trump. You only need 3-card support to raise, so you have more than enough. Raise partner to Two Diamonds.

3) You can't raise partner's Major, you don't have less than 6 points and you can't bid a new suit at the one-level. You also don't have a minimum hand...you have 15 points. It's time to look at what happens if you answer no to all four questions.

The Final Choice

If you answered No to all four questions, you must have at least 11 points. Since partner has at least 13 points, you must be close to Game. If partner overcalled at the one-level, you can respond as if partner opened the bidding at the one-level:

- Raising overcaller's Minor suit to the three-level or to Game level (Three No Trump)
- Bidding a new suit at the two-level

Raising partner's Minor to the three-level is an invitational bid and shows:

- 3-card or longer support for partner's Minor suit
- 11 - 12 points ▼

A jump to Three No Trump over partner's Minor suit overcall is an invitational bid and shows:

- 3-card or longer support for partner's Minor suit
- 13 - 16 points ▼

A new suit at the two-level is a forcing bid and shows:

- A 4-card or longer suit
- 11 or more points (GO)

Here are some examples. The bidding proceeds:

NORTH	EAST	SOUTH	WEST
(Dealer)			(You)
One Diamond	One Spade	Pass	?

As West, what would you respond with the following hands?

1) ♠ A 7
   ♥ 8 6 2
   ♦ 7 6 3
   ♣ A K J 4 3

2) ♠ K Q
   ♥ Q 10 9 7 2
   ♦ 9
   ♣ K 7 6 3 2

1) TWO CLUBS. You can't raise partner's Major, don't have a weak hand, can't bid a new suit at the one-level and do not have a minimum hand...you have 13 points. You should respond Two Clubs, a new suit at the two-level.

2) TWO HEARTS. Can you raise partner's Major? No, you have only 2-card support. Do you have a weak hand? No, you have 12 points ...10 HCPs plus 2 points for the two 5-card suits. Can you bid a new suit at the one-level? No, you don't have any room. Do you have a minimum hand? No, you have 12 points. With a choice of suits to bid at the two-level, bid the higher-ranking and respond Two Hearts.

Some more examples:

NORTH	EAST	SOUTH	WEST
(Dealer)			(You)
One Club	One Diamond	Pass	?

As West, what would you respond with the following hands?

3) ♠ A 7 6
   ♥ 4 2
   ♦ K J 4 3
   ♣ K 8 7 3

4) ♠ A Q 8
   ♥ 7 3 2
   ♦ A J 7 2
   ♣ K 9 8

3) THREE DIAMONDS. You can't support partner's Major, don't have less than 6 points, can't bid a new suit at the one-level and do not have a minimum hand…you have 11 points. You should respond Three Diamonds, telling partner that you have 11 or 12 points and three or more Diamonds.

4) THREE NO TRUMP. You can't raise partner's Major, don't have a weak hand, can't bid a new suit at the one-level and don't have a minimum hand. You have 14 points, too many points to raise partner to the three-level. So respond Three No Trump to show a hand of 13 - 16 points and at least 3-card support for partner's Minor.

After a No Trump Overcall

When partner overcalls One No Trump, he is showing a balanced hand with 16 - 18 points. Thus you can respond almost exactly as if partner had opened One No Trump (see Chapter 5). The only difference is that you do not choose the opponent's suit as trump.

RESPONSES TO AN OVERCALL OF ONE NO TRUMP

- With 0 - 7 points: Bid Two Diamonds or Two Hearts or Two Spades with a 5-card or longer suit. Otherwise, Pass.

- With 8 - 9 points: Bid Two No Trump (or bid Two Clubs*.)

- With 10 - 14 points: Bid Four Hearts or Four Spades with a 6-card or longer Major suit. Bid Three Hearts or Three Spades with a 5-card Major suit. (Bid Two Clubs with a 4-card Major suit*.) Otherwise bid Three No Trump.

---

* The Two Club response will be discussed in Chapter 20.

For example, the auction goes:

NORTH	EAST	SOUTH	WEST
(Dealer)			(You)
One Diamond	One No Trump	Pass	?

As West, what would you respond with the following hands?

1) ♠ K 4 3   2) ♠ K J 6 4 3   3) ♠ A Q 8 6 3   4) ♠ 3
   ♥ J 4 2   ♥ 4 2   ♥ 3 2   ♥ 10 9 8 6 4 3
   ♦ 8 5 3   ♦ 4 3   ♦ 5 3   ♦ A 7 4
   ♣ J 7 6 2   ♣ Q 8 7 3   ♣ A 8 7 2   ♣ A 4 2

1) PASS. With only 5 points, there is not enough combined strength for Game. With no 5-card suit, Pass. The final contract will be One No Trump.

2) TWO SPADES. With 7 points you do not have quite enough to hope for Game. With a 5-card suit, bid Two Spades. If partner has three or more Spades you will have found a Magic Major Suit Fit. Even if partner only has two, the 7-card fit should prove adequate.

3) THREE SPADES. With 11 points, there should be enough combined strength for Game. By bidding Three Spades, which is marathon, you will find out whether or not partner has 3-card support. If partner has three or more Spades, he will bid Four Spades. Otherwise he will bid Three No Trump.

4) FOUR HEARTS. With 10 points...8 in high cards and 2 for the 6-card Heart Suit...there are enough combined points for Game. Since partner must have at least two Hearts, you can bid Four Hearts and be assured of playing in a Magic Major Suit Fit.

Summary

If partner overcalls at the one-level in a suit, you can determine the appropriate response by asking yourself Responder's Four Questions:

Question One: CAN I RAISE PARTNER'S MAJOR? (You only need 3-card support)

If the answer is YES: Revalue your hand using dummy points and raise to the appropriate level.

DUMMY POINTS

Ace	4 points	Void	5 points
King	3 points	Singleton	3 points
Queen	2 points	Doubleton	1 point
Jack	1 point		

APPROPRIATE LEVEL

0 - 5 points	Pass
6 - 10 points	Raise to the two-level
11 - 12 points	Raise to the three-level
13 - 16 points	Raise to the four-level

16

Responding to a Two-Level Overcall

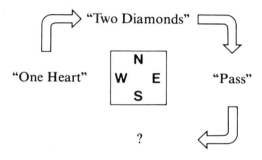

"Two Diamonds"

"One Heart"

N
W E
S

"Pass"

?

When your partner makes an overcall at the two-level, you know that he has:

- A 5-card suit or longer **and**
- An opening bid (13 - 21 points)

You can respond as if to an opening bid **except that the first bid for your side is at the two-level.** This has taken away some of your bidding room on the Bidding Ladder. You can still use Responder's Four Questions to guide you to the appropriate response:

```
RESPONDER'S FOUR QUESTIONS

1. CAN I RAISE PARTNER'S MAJOR?
2. DO I HAVE A WEAK HAND (0 - 5 POINTS)?
3. CAN I BID A NEW SUIT AT THE ONE-LEVEL?
4. DO I HAVE A MINIMUM HAND (6 - 10 POINTS)?
```

Question One

---

1. CAN I RAISE PARTNER'S MAJOR?

As when responding to an overcall at the one-level, you only need 3-card support to raise...5 + 3 = 8. If you have 3-card support or more, revalue your hand using dummy points.

When determining **HOW HIGH** to raise, take into account that you no longer have sufficient room to show all the possible point-count ranges. You are already at the two-level, so a two-level raise, showing 6 - 10 points, becomes a Pass. Use the following chart as a guide:

RAISING
OVERCALLER'S MAJOR

DUMMY POINTS	BID		
0 - 10	Pass	STOP	Game is unlikely
11 - 12	Raise to the three-level	▼	Game is likely unless partner has only 13 or 14 points.
13 - 16	Raise to the four-level	▼	Game should be bid as there are at least 26 combined points.

For example, the auction starts off:

NORTH	EAST	SOUTH	WEST
(Dealer)			(You)
One Spade	Two Hearts	Pass	?

You are West. What would you respond with the following hands?

1) ♠ K 4 3	2) ♠ K Q 4 3	3) ♠ A 7 2	4) ♠ A Q 9
♥ J 6 3 2	♥ K J 2	♥ A 4 2	♥ 6 5
♦ Q 9 4	♦ 9 8 7 4 3	♦ 5 3	♦ K 9 6 3
♣ J 7 2	♣ 3	♣ K J 8 7 3	♣ Q J 7 6

1) PASS. Even though you have 4-card support for partner's Major and 7 dummy points you should say Pass. You will only miss a Game if partner has a maximum hand (19 - 21)...unlikely. If you raise to the three-level, you are more likely to get the partnership too high when partner has a minimum hand (13 - 16).

2) THREE HEARTS. With 3-card support and 12 dummy points...9 HCPs and 3 for the singleton Club...you should make a try for Game by bidding Three Hearts. Partner will carry on to Game unless he has 13 - 14 points.

3) FOUR HEARTS. With 13 dummy points and 3-card support, there should be enough combined strength for Game. Respond Four Hearts to partner's overcall.

4) Here you can't raise partner's Major. Time to move on to the next question.

Question Two

> ### 2. DO I HAVE A WEAK HAND (0 - 5 POINTS)?

If the answer is yes, Pass. Game is very unlikely.

Question Three

> ### 3. CAN I BID A NEW SUIT AT THE ONE-LEVEL?

Since you are already at the two-level, you can ignore this question and go on to the fourth question.

Question Four

> ### 4. DO I HAVE A MINIMUM HAND (6 - 10 POINTS)?

If the answer is yes, **Pass.**

When responding to an opening bid or a one-level overcall, you only Pass if you have less than 6 points, in case partner has a maximum hand (19 - 21 points). If partner overcalls at the two-level, you have to give up on the possibility of partner holding a medium (17 - 18) or maximum (19 - 21) hand and Pass with up to 10 points. In the more frequent cases where partner has a minimum hand (13 - 16), you may get the partnership too high if you bid.

For example, if the bidding goes:

NORTH	EAST	SOUTH	WEST
(Dealer)			(You)
One Heart	Two Diamonds	Pass	?

Pass with any of these hands:

1) ♠ Q 7 4 3   2) ♠ K 9 4 3   3) ♠ K J 8 7 2
   ♥ K 6 3 2   ♥ 8 2   ♥ 4 2
   ♦ 4   ♦ Q 7 4 3   ♦ 5 3
   ♣ Q 8 7 2   ♣ 9 6 3   ♣ K J 8 7

The Final Choice

If you answered no to all four questions, you must have at least 11 points.
Partner has at least 13 points, so you must be close to Game. Since partner
overcalled at the two-level, you are left with these choices:

- Bidding a new suit at the two-level or higher
- Raising overcaller's Minor suit — to the three-level
  — to Game
  (Three No Trump)

A new suit at the two-level or higher is a forcing bid and shows:

- A 4-card or longer suit
- 11 or more points

Raising partner's Minor to the three-level is an invitational bid and shows:

- 3-card or longer support for partner's Minor suit
- 11 - 12 points

A jump to Three No Trump over partner's Minor suit overcall is an
invitational bid and shows:

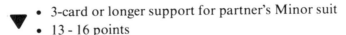

- 3-card or longer support for partner's Minor suit
- 13 - 16 points

Here are some examples after partner overcalls at the two-level.

The auction goes:

NORTH	EAST	SOUTH	WEST
(Dealer)			(You)
One Heart	Two Diamonds	Pass	?

As West, use Responder's Four Questions to determine what you would
respond with the following hands:

1) ♠ K 4 3   2) ♠ A J 3   3) ♠ A J 7 3 2   4) ♠ K Q 3
   ♥ Q 3 2   ♥ 8 3 2   ♥ J 2   ♥ K 7 4
   ♦ Q 4 3   ♦ K 8 4 3   ♦ J 3   ♦ 9 7 6 3
   ♣ J 9 7 2   ♣ Q J 7   ♣ K Q 8 3   ♣ A Q J

1) PASS. You can't raise partner's Major, he hasn't bid one. You don't have a weak hand. You ask yourself the third question: "Do I have a minimum hand (6 - 10 points)?". Here the answer is Yes...you only have 8 points... so you should Pass. You may miss a Game if partner has a maximum hand but you are more likely to get too high if you bid and partner has a minimum hand.

2) THREE DIAMONDS. You can't raise partner's Major, don't have a weak hand and don't have a minimum hand...you have 11 points. With 4-card support for partner's Minor you raise to Three Diamonds.

3) TWO SPADES. You can't raise partner's Major and don't have a weak or minimum hand. You have 13 points. Bid a new suit at the two-level, Two Spades.

4) THREE NO TRUMP. You can't support partner's Major and you don't have less than 11 points...you have 15. With no 4-card suit or longer other than Diamonds, raise partner to Game by bidding Three No Trump.

Summary

If partner overcalls at the two-level in a suit, you can determine the appropriate response by asking yourself Responder's Four Questions:

Question One: CAN I RAISE PARTNER'S MAJOR? (You only need 3-card support)

If the answer is YES: Revalue your hand using dummy points and raise to the appropriate level.

DUMMY POINTS

Ace	4 points	Void	5 points
King	3 points	Singleton	3 points
Queen	2 points	Doubleton	1 point
Jack	1 point		

APPROPRIATE LEVEL

0 - 10 points	Pass
11 - 12 points	Raise to the three-level
13 - 16 points	Raise to the four-level

If the answer is NO: Go on to the next question.

Question Two: DO I HAVE A WEAK HAND (0 - 5 POINTS)?

If the answer is YES: Pass.

If the answer is NO: Go on to the next question.

Question Three: CAN I BID A NEW SUIT AT THE ONE-LEVEL?

The answer is always NO: Go on to the next question.

Question Four: DO I HAVE A MINIMUM HAND (6 - 10 POINTS)?

If the answer is YES: Pass.

If the answer is NO:
- Bid a new suit at the two-level or higher
- Raise partner's Minor suit:
  — to the three-level with 11 - 12 points and 3-card or longer support
  — to the Game level (Three No Trump) with 13 - 16 points and 3-card or longer support for partner's Minor

Exercises

1) The auction goes:

NORTH (Dealer)	EAST	SOUTH	WEST (You)
One Spade	Two Hearts	Pass	?

As West, what would you respond with the following hands?

a) ♠ K 9 8 3
♥ 9 8
♦ J 9 4
♣ Q 8 7 2

b) ♠ K 9
♥ Q 8 2
♦ A 10 8 3
♣ J 7 3 2

c) ♠ K J 2
♥ K 9 4 2
♦ A Q 7
♣ 9 5 3

d) ♠ 7 6 4 3 2
♥ K Q 9 4 3
♦ A 7 6
♣ —

2) The auction goes:

NORTH (Dealer)	EAST	SOUTH	WEST (You)
One Spade	Two Clubs	Pass	?

As West, what would you respond with the following hands?

a) ♠ Q 9 8 3
♥ J 8
♦ Q 9 4
♣ J 8 7 2

b) ♠ K 9 8
♥ Q J 2
♦ A 10 8 3 2
♣ J 7

c) ♠ 7 3 2
♥ K Q 7 4 3 2
♦ A 7
♣ K Q

d) ♠ 3
♥ A J 9 4 3
♦ A K 9 7 6
♣ 8 3

e) ♠ 9 8 3
♥ K Q 8
♦ Q 9 7
♣ A 5 4 2

f) ♠ K 5 3
♥ A 8
♦ K 8 3
♣ Q J 6 4 3

17

The Take-Out Double

Suppose your right-hand opponent opens the bidding with One Heart and you have the following hand:

- ♠ A 5 4 2
- ♥ 6
- ♦ A Q 9 4
- ♣ A 6 5 3

With 14 points, you were planning to open the bidding. However, your right-hand opponent beat you to the punch. Can you overcall? No, because you don't have a 5-card suit. What can you do? You would like to make a bid which shows your strength and **asks partner to pick the trump suit in which to compete**. What bid is available that could carry this message? The **Double**. When you double the opponent's opening bid you are saying:

- "I have an opening hand (13 - 21 points)"
- "Bid your best suit, partner"

Used in this manner, the Double is called a *take-out double* because you are asking partner to 'take-out' your Double and bid his best suit. It is the perfect bid to get across the message because it doesn't take up any bidding room. But can we use it to have this meaning? After all, in Chapter 13 we discussed how the Double is used to increase the penalty for defeating the opponents' contract.

Penalty or Take-out?

There are several reasons why the Double of a Part-Game contract is not usually used for penalties. Suppose an opponent opens One Heart and you have the following hand:

♠ 4 3 2
♥ A Q J 10 3
♦ A K 3
♣ 3 2

It would not be wise to double for penalties because:

- You may not be able to defeat their contract...you know nothing about your partner's hand
- Even if you defeat the contract, the penalty might not be very large
- You might warn the opponents that they are in a poor contract ...they might escape to a better contract

How is partner to tell whether a Double is for penalty or take-out?

A Double is for take-out if:

- Neither you nor your partner has bid (other than Pass) **and**
- You are doubling a Part-Game contract

A Double is for penalty if:

- Either you or your partner has bid (Pass doesn't count) **or**
- You are doubling a Game contract or higher

The following Doubles are for **take-out**:

NORTH (Opener)	EAST (Partner)	SOUTH	WEST (You)
One Heart	**Double**		

NORTH (Opener)	EAST (You)	SOUTH	WEST (Partner)
One Heart	Pass	Two Hearts	**Double**

NORTH (Opener)	EAST (You)	SOUTH	WEST (Partner)
Pass	Pass	One Diamond	**Double**

NORTH (Opener)	EAST (You)	SOUTH	WEST (Partner)
One Heart	Pass	One No Trump	**Double**

These Doubles are for **penalty**:

NORTH (Opener)	EAST (You)	SOUTH	WEST (Partner)
One Heart	Pass	Four Hearts	**Double**

NORTH	EAST	SOUTH	WEST
(Opener)	(You)		(Partner)
Pass	One Heart	Two Clubs	**Double**

NORTH	EAST	SOUTH	WEST
(Opener)	(You)		(Partner)
One Heart	One Spade	Two Hearts	**Double**

Now that you can see how the Double can be used as a penalty Double in some situations and as a take-out Double in other situations, let's take a closer look at the types of hand on which you would use a take-out Double.

To make a take-out Double you need to consider two features of your hand:

- Distribution
- Strength

Distribution Required for a Take-out Double

Since you are making a bid that will ask partner to pick a trump suit, other than that bid by the opponents, you should have at least **3-card support for any unbid suit**. Since partner, as we will see in the next chapter, will strain to bid a Major suit, this requirement is especially important with respect to the unbid Major suit(s). You can sometimes relax the requirement for the unbid Minor suit(s).

The ideal distribution is to have 4-card support for all the unbid suits. For example, if your right-hand opponent opens the bidding One Heart, the following hand has the ideal distribution for a take-out Double:

♠ A 5 4 2
♥ 6
♦ A Q 9 4
♣ A 6 5 3

Whichever suit your partner picks as the trump suit, you will have 4-card support. Thus you are bound to land in a Magic Fit.

The above hand would not be suitable for a take-out Double if your right-hand opponent opened the bidding with anything other than One Heart. For example, if the opening bid were One Spade, you could not use a take-out Double. If partner were to choose Hearts as the trump suit, you would not have support.

Because the take-out Double is a very flexible tool, you do not need to wait for the perfect distribution before using it. For example, on any of the following hands you would make a take-out Double after your opponent opened the bidding One Heart:

♠ A J 8 3	♠ A 5 3 2	♠ A 9 4 3
♥ 3 2	♥ —	♥ 8 7 4
♦ Q 9 4 2	♦ A 9 7 3	♦ A K 9 6
♣ A K 3	♣ K J 8 6 4	♣ A 3

The first hand has 4-card support for Spades or Diamonds and 3-card support for Clubs. You will be happy whichever suit partner chooses.

On the second hand, you could overcall your 5-card suit, Two Clubs. However, the Double is more flexible. By leaving the decision of where to play the hand up to partner, you have tripled the probability that you will end up in your best trump fit.

On the last hand, you only have 2-card support if partner chooses Clubs. However, if you want to compete, this is the chance you must take. Maybe partner will bid Spades or Diamonds. If he does bid Clubs, you'll have to hope that he has at least five of them!

Strength Required for a Take-out Double

When it comes to strength, you will need to have at least the strength of an opening bid to compete since you know that your opponent who opened the bidding has a hand of that strength or greater. However, since partner is going to pick the trump suit, your hand will be going down as the dummy. Thus, you can **value your hand using dummy points for your shortness in the opponent's suit**.

For example, if your right-hand opponent opens the bidding One Heart and you have the following hand:

| ♠ A 5 4 2 |
| ♥ 6 |
| ♦ K 10 9 4 |
| ♣ A 6 5 3 |

You can make a take-out Double even though you only have 11 high card points. When you revalue your hand using dummy points, you have 14 points...11 in high cards and 3 for the singleton Heart. Thus we have:

> REQUIREMENTS FOR A TAKE-OUT DOUBLE
> * Support for the unbid suits
> * 13 - 21 dummy points

Let's look at some examples:

Your right-hand opponent opens the bidding One Spade. Should you double, overcall or Pass with each of the following hands?

1) ♠ 3
   ♥ A J 3 2
   ♦ A 9 7 4
   ♣ Q 6 3 2

2) ♠ 3
   ♥ K 8 7 2
   ♦ K 9 8 3
   ♣ Q 10 7 3

3) ♠ 3 2
   ♥ K Q J 4 2
   ♦ 7 3
   ♣ A K J 8

4) ♠ —
   ♥ A 10 4 3
   ♦ J 9 7 6
   ♣ K 10 9 8 3

5) ♠ A Q J 9 8
   ♥ 3 2
   ♦ A K 9 4
   ♣ 5 2

6) ♠ A K 9 3
   ♥ 8 2
   ♦ K 8 3
   ♣ K J 7 3

1) DOUBLE. With 14 dummy points...11 in high cards and 3 for the singleton Spade...and support for all the unbid suits, you have just the right type of hand to use a take-out Double.

2) PASS. Even though you have support for all the unbid suits, you cannot afford to say Double. Partner will assume that you have at least the strength for an opening bid and, even valuing with dummy points, you have only 11 points.

3) TWO HEARTS. Here you have 15 points...14 in high cards and 1 for the fifth Heart. With a 5-card Heart suit your hand is more suited for an overcall of Two Hearts than a take-out Double. Note that you value your hand using length points when overcalling. You only use dummy points if you have the distribution required for a take-out Double.

4) DOUBLE. Even though you have only 8 HCPs, you can add 5 dummy points for your void. With support for whichever suit partner picks, you have enough to compete with a take-out Double.

5) PASS. Here you might like to make a penalty Double of the opening bid. As mentioned earlier, this is not usually successful. Worse, partner will interpret your Double as a take-out Double and bid his best suit. To avoid this you must say Pass. You will not be disappointed if you end up defending a contract of One Spade.

6) Here you have a hand that is not suited to a take-out Double. You do not have support for all the unbid suits. In addition, you cannot overcall because you do not have a 5-card suit. Let's take a look at how you handle this type of hand.

Hands That Don't Qualify

If your opponent opens the bidding One Spade and you hold a hand of opening bid strength like the following:

♠ A K 9 3
♥ 8 2
♦ K 8 3
♣ K J 7 3

- You do not have a balanced hand with 16 - 18 points
- You do not have a 5-card suit to overcall
- You do not have support for all the unbid suits

In this case, **Pass**.

If the opponents open the bidding, you do not have to bid just because you have a hand of opening bid strength. You have two competitive tools available:

- The overcall
- The take-out Double

If these do not apply, you should not compete. The auction is not over yet. Maybe partner will bid something. If he doesn't, you will continue to Pass... it is even more dangerous to compete later.

Summary

If the opponents open the bidding, you have a tool other than the overcall with which to compete in the auction... the *take-out Double*.

Partner will be able to distinguish your take-out Double from a penalty Double provided it satisfies the following criteria:

PENALTY OR TAKE-OUT?

A Double is for Take-out if:
- Neither you nor your partner has bid **and**
- You are doubling a Part-Game contract

A Double is for Penalty if:
- Either you or your partner has bid **or**
- You are doubling a Game contract or higher

You can use a take-out Double if you have:

REQUIREMENTS FOR A TAKE-OUT DOUBLE
- Support for the unbid suits
- 13 - 21 dummy points

Exercises

1) You are West. How would you interpret your partner's double in each of the following auctions:

a)
NORTH	EAST	SOUTH	WEST
(Dealer)	(Partner)		(You)
One Diamond	**Double**	Pass	?

b)
NORTH	EAST	SOUTH	WEST
	(Partner)	(Dealer)	(You)
—	—	One Heart	Pass
Two Clubs	**Double**	Pass	?

c)
NORTH	EAST	SOUTH	WEST
	(Partner)	(Dealer)	(You)
—	—	One Spade	Two Hearts
Two Spades	**Double**	Pass	?

d)
NORTH	EAST	SOUTH	WEST
	(Partner)	(Dealer)	(You)
—	—	One Heart	Pass
Four Hearts	**Double**	Pass	?

2) You are East. What would you do with the following hands after the auction has gone:

NORTH	EAST	SOUTH	WEST
(Dealer)	(You)		(Partner)
One Diamond	?		

a) ♠ K J 9 8 3
♥ J 8 3 2
♦ 4
♣ Q 9 3

b) ♠ K J 8 4
♥ K Q 8 2
♦ 8
♣ A 8 7 3

c) ♠ K Q 9 8 4
♥ K 2
♦ A 7 3
♣ Q 9 8

d) ♠ K J
♥ A J 4
♦ A Q 9
♣ Q 8 7 4 3

e) ♠ K 9 8 4
♥ 2
♦ A K 8 3
♣ Q J 7 3

f) ♠ K 7 3 2
♥ K 9 7 2
♦ —
♣ K J 8 6 2

g) ♠ K 4 3
♥ 7 4
♦ A K Q 7 6
♣ J 8 2

18

Responding to a Take-Out Double

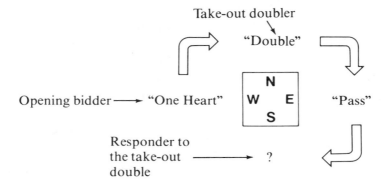

Take-out doubler

"Double"

Opening bidder ⟶ "One Heart"

N
W   E
S

"Pass"

Responder to
the take-out ⟶ ?
double

When your partner makes a take-out Double, he is saying "Bid your best suit, partner". What should you do as responder?

What's Changed?

You must think about responses to a take-out Double in a different way from responses to an opening bid of one in a suit...the usual rules about responses don't apply:

- Opening bids at the one-level are invitational but take-out Doubles are forcing
- A new suit response to an opening bid of one in a suit is forcing but a new suit response to a take-out Double is invitational

Why is partner's take-out Double a forcing bid? Look at what happens if you Pass:

NORTH	EAST	SOUTH	WEST
	(Partner)		(You)
One Heart	Double	Pass	**Pass**
Pass!			

Now the contract is One Heart doubled. Defeating this contract will be difficult for your side. Your partner said he wanted to compete in any suit **except Hearts**. For example, partner's hand might be:

♠ A 9 7 4
♥ 2
♦ A 7 6 3
♣ A 7 5 3

Partner will only be able to take three tricks on defense against Hearts so you shouldn't Pass.

Why is responder's bid of a new suit invitational when responding to a take-out Double? It is easy to understand if you think of it this way:

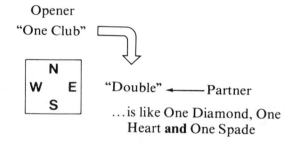

Opener
"One Club"

"Double" ◄──── Partner

...is like One Diamond, One
Heart **and** One Spade

Three opening bids at once! Partner is asking you to raise one of his suits:

- 0 - 10 points: raise without jumping: One Spade, One Heart
or One Diamond in the
above example.

- 11 - 12 points: raise with a jump: Two Spades, Two Hearts
or Two Diamonds in the
above example.

- 13 or more points: raise to Game: Four Spades, Four
Hearts or Three No
Trump in the above
example.

Because a take-out Double is forcing, a raise without jumping includes hands with 0 - 5 points as well as hands with 6 - 10 points. Also, "raises" in response to a take-out Double can be made at a lower level than the corresponding raise of an opening bid. For example, compare the following auctions:

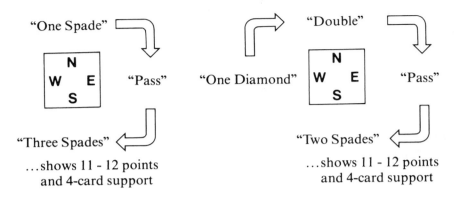

"One Spade" → "Pass"

"One Diamond" → "Double"

"Three Spades" ← ...shows 11 - 12 points and 4-card support

"Two Spades" ← ...shows 11 - 12 points and 4-card support

In each case, the "raise" skips one level. In summary, new suit responses to a take-out Double are invitational because they are "raises" of one of the take-out doubler's promised suits.

Responding with 0 - 10 Points

Since the take-out Double is a forcing bid, you must bid something. Partner has asked you to pick a trump suit other than the one(s) bid by the opponents. Which suit should you pick?

You and your partner are interested in playing in a Magic Major Suit Fit so **your first priority is to bid a 4-card or longer Major suit**, if you have one. Partner has promised at least 3-card support for any unbid Major suit and likely has 4-card support. Since you want to tell partner you don't have a very strong hand, bid the Major suit at **the cheapest available level**.

If you do not have a 4-card or longer Major suit to bid, you should bid a 4-card or longer Minor suit. Again, bid at the cheapest available level.

The cheapest available level may be the two-level. It may seem strange to bid a new suit at the two-level without 11 or more points but, because partner has made a take-out Double, the situation is comparable to raising partner's suit.

In summary:

RESPONDING TO A TAKE-OUT DOUBLE WITH 0 - 10 POINTS

- Bid a suit at the cheapest level:
  — Bid a 4-card or longer unbid Major suit or (lacking one)
  — Bid a 4-card or longer unbid Minor suit or (lacking one)
- Bid One No Trump (rare response)

Let's look at some examples.

NORTH	EAST	SOUTH	WEST
	(Partner)		(You)
One Diamond	Double	Pass	?

What would you respond with each of the following hands:

1) ♠ A J 9 8 3	2) ♠ A 9 8 4	3) ♠ 9 8 4 3	4) ♠ J 7
♥ J 3 2	♥ 8 7 5 4 2	♥ 6 2	♥ 8 5 4
♦ 9 4	♦ 8 6	♦ A 7	♦ J 8 3
♣ 9 7 3	♣ 7 3	♣ Q 9 8 7 4	♣ Q 10 7 4 3

5) ♠ Q 7 5	6) ♠ 9 8 4
♥ 8 3 2	♥ 9 7 4 2
♦ K Q 10 4	♦ 8 6 3
♣ J 9 3	♣ 8 7 3

1) ONE SPADE. With 7 points...6 in high cards and 1 for the fifth Spade...you would bid your Major suit at the cheapest available level. Your response of One Spade will tell partner that you have a hand in the 0 - 10 point range. Notice that, as responder, you don't count dummy points...the take-out doubler does.

2) ONE HEART. With a choice of suits, bid the longest Major suit at the cheapest available level, One Heart.

3) ONE SPADE. Even though your Clubs are longer than your Spades, you should bid a 4-card or longer Major suit if you have one. By responding One Spade you are giving the partnership the best chance of finding a Magic Major Suit Fit. Four Spades is a possible Game if partner has a maximum hand.

4) TWO CLUBS. With no 4-card or longer Major suit to bid, you should bid your minor suit at the cheapest available level, Two Clubs. **This is one time you don't need 11 or more points to bid a new suit at the two-level.**

5) ONE NO TRUMP. Here you have reasonable strength...8 HCPs. Your only 4-card suit is the one bid by the opponents.

6) ONE HEART. Unappetizing though this hand may be, you cannot Pass. Partner's take-out Double is forcing. You'll have to bid your 4-card Major suit, One Heart. Because you bid at the cheapest available level, partner will be aware that you are in the range of 0 - 10 points.

Responding with 11 - 12 Points

Since partner has promised at least 13 points with his take-out Double, you are close to having enough combined strength for Game when you hold 11 - 12 points. You want to make a strongly invitational bid that tells your partner you would like to be in Game unless he has only 13 - 14 points. You do this by **jumping one level** when you bid your suit. This is similar to the way you respond to a One Heart opening bid when you have 11 -12 points and 4-card support...you jump to Three Hearts.

The emphasis is on finding a Magic Major Suit Fit, so:

RESPONDING TO A TAKE-OUT DOUBLE WITH 11 - 12 POINTS

- Bid a suit **jumping a level** with:
  — 4-card or longer unbid Major suit or (lacking one)
  — A 4-card or longer unbid Minor suit or (lacking one)
- Jump to Two No Trump (rare response)

Let's look at some examples.

NORTH	EAST	SOUTH	WEST
	(Partner)		(You)
One Diamond	Double	Pass	?

What would you respond with each of the following hands:

1) ♠ A J 9 8 3	2) ♠ A 9 8 4	3) ♠ K Q 4	4) ♠ K 9 7
♥ J 3 2	♥ 4 2	♥ 6 2	♥ J 5 4
♦ 9 4	♦ J 6	♦ 7 3	♦ A Q 10 3
♣ A 7 3	♣ K Q 9 7 3	♣ A J 9 8 7 4	♣ Q 10 7

1) TWO SPADES. With 11 points... 10 HCPs and 1 for the fifth Spade ...you should jump to Two Spades to strongly invite your partner to carry on to Game unless he has only 13 - 14 points.

2) TWO SPADES. With 11 points... 10 in high cards and one for the fifth Club ...you want to jump to show partner a hand of invitational strength. You jump to Two Spades rather than Three Clubs because you are trying to play in a Magic Major Suit Fit whenever possible.

3) THREE CLUBS. With 12 points and no 4-card or longer Major suit, you can jump in your Minor suit to Three Clubs.

4) TWO NO TRUMP. Here you have 12 points and you have no 4-card unbid suit. Tell partner that you have 11 - 12 points by jumping to Two No Trump.

Responding with 13 or More Points

When partner makes a take-out Double and you have 13 or more points, you know the answer to HOW HIGH...Game. The choices are familiar ...Four Spades, Four Hearts and Three No Trump. For example, if the auction goes:

NORTH	EAST (Partner)	SOUTH	WEST (You)
One Heart	Double	Pass	?

and you hold:

♠ K Q 8 6
♥ 6 5
♦ A 9 5
♣ K J 7 4

Bid Four Spades. You have 13 points and partner has at least 13 points. You probably have a Magic Major Suit Fit in Spades. Even if partner has only three Spades, you still have seven trumps, an acceptable fit.

RESPONDING TO A TAKE-OUT DOUBLE WITH 13 OR MORE POINTS

- Jump to Game in a 4-card or longer unbid Major suit or (lacking one)
- Jump to Three No Trump

Let's look at some examples:

NORTH	EAST (Partner)	SOUTH	WEST (You)
One Diamond	Double	Pass	?

What would you respond with each of the following hands:

1) ♠ 8 3	2) ♠ 9 8 4	3) ♠ 9 8 6 4 3 2	4) ♠ A 8 5
♥ A K 9 3 2	♥ Q 4	♥ A 6	♥ K J 5 4
♦ A 9 4	♦ K Q 10 6	♦ K 3	♦ 8
♣ J 9 3	♣ A Q 7 3	♣ A J 7	♣ A J 9 7 3

1) FOUR HEARTS. You have 13 points...12 HCPs and 1 for the fifth Heart. With a 5-card Heart suit, you know that there is a Magic Major Suit Fit. Since you know HOW HIGH...Game...and WHERE...Hearts...bid Four Hearts.

2) THREE NO TRUMP. Again you have 13 points but this time there is unlikely to be a Magic Major Suit Fit. Bid Three No Trump, the most likely Game.

3) FOUR SPADES. With 14 points...12 HCPs plus 2 for the 6-card Spade suit... you have enough for Game. You know there is a Magic Major Suit Fit, so bid Four Spades.

4) FOUR HEARTS. With 14 points you know that there is enough combined strength for Game. You have four cards in Hearts, an unbid Major suit, so jump to Four Hearts.

Rebids by the Take-out Doubler

As with an opening bid, the take-out doubler's hand will fall into one of three ranges:

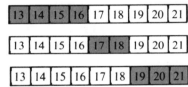

- MINIMUM HAND (13 - 16 points)
- MEDIUM HAND (17 - 18 points)
- MAXIMUM HAND (19 - 21 points)

If you make a take-out Double and partner bids at the cheapest available level (0 - 10 points), keep this in mind: **You forced partner to bid, so he could have very few points.** Take this into account by **bidding one level lower than if you were rebidding as the opening bidder.**

REBIDS BY THE TAKE-OUT DOUBLER
WHEN PARTNER SHOWS 0 - 10 POINTS

Minimum hand (13 - 16)	Pass (STOP). Since partner has at most 10 points, Game is unlikely.
Medium hand (17 - 18)	Raise partner's suit ▼. This is a "mild" invitational bid. Partner can bid Game with 9 or 10 points, otherwise stop in Part-Game.
Maximum hand (19 -21)	Jump in partner's Major suit ▼ or bid No Trump* ▼. These are "strong" invitational rebids. Partner can bid Game with 6 - 10 points, otherwise stop in Part-Game.

---

* This shows a balanced hand of 19 - 21 points, too strong to overcall One No Trump.

If partner shows a hand in the 11 - 12 point range by jumping in a suit or to Two No Trump, you should plan to get to Game unless you have only 13 or 14 points. You should rebid as follows:

REBIDS BY THE TAKE-OUT DOUBLER WHEN PARTNER SHOWS 11 - 12 POINTS

13 - 14 points

| 13 | 14 | 15 | 16 | 17 | 18 | 19 | 20 | 21 |

Pass (STOP). You are unlikely to have enough combined strength for Game.

15 - 21 points

| 13 | 14 | 15 | 16 | 17 | 18 | 19 | 20 | 21 |

Raise partner's Major suit to Game (STOP) or bid Three No Trump (STOP).

If partner shows 13 or more points by jumping to Game, you should rebid as follows:

REBIDS BY THE TAKE-OUT DOUBLER WHEN PARTNER SHOWS 13 OR MORE POINTS

Minimum hand (13 - 16) or medium hand (17 - 18)

| 13 | 14 | 15 | 16 | 17 | 18 | 19 | 20 | 21 |

Pass (STOP).

Maximum hand (19 - 21)

| 13 | 14 | 15 | 16 | 17 | 18 | 19 | 20 | 21 |

Search for Slam. More on this in Chapter 22.

Let's look at some examples. The auction goes:

NORTH	EAST (You)	SOUTH	WEST (Partner)
One Diamond	Double	Pass	One Spade
Pass	?		

What would you bid with each of the following hands?

1) ♠ A 9 8	2) ♠ A K 8 3	3) ♠ A K 8 3
♥ K J 3 2	♥ K J 3 2	♥ A K 3 2
♦ 9 4	♦ 4	♦ 4
♣ A 9 3 2	♣ A 9 3 2	♣ A 9 3 2

1) PASS. You have a minimum hand…12 HCPs plus 1 for the doubleton Diamond. Since partner has at most 10 points, you should
settle for Part-Game and Pass.

2) TWO SPADES. With 18 points…15 in high cards and 3 for the
singleton Diamond…you have enough to make an invitational
raise of Two Spades. If partner has 9 - 10 points, he can carry on to
Game. Remember…raise one level lower than you would as opening
bidder.

3) THREE SPADES. Even though you have 21 points…18 in high cards
and 3 for the singleton Diamond…partner may have zero. Jump to
Three Spades to make a strongly invitational raise. Partner will only
Pass if he has 0 -5 points.

Summary

Take-out Doubles are forcing bids.

```
                 RESPONDING TO A TAKE-OUT DOUBLE

 0 - 10 points:        • Bid a 4-card or longer unbid Major suit at
                         the cheapest available level
                       • Bid a 4-card or longer unbid Minor suit at
                         the cheapest available level
                       • Bid One No Trump (rare response)

 11 - 12 points:       • Jump in a 4-card or longer unbid Major
                         suit
                       • Jump in a 4-card or longer unbid Minor
                         suit
                       • Jump to Two No Trump (rare response)

 13 or more points:    • Jump to Game in a 4-card or longer unbid
                         Major suit
                       • Jump to Three No Trump
```

If you make a take-out Double, your rebid depends on the strength shown
by partner's response as follows:

YOUR STRENGTH	PARTNER'S STRENGTH	HOW HIGH	YOUR REBID
13 - 16	0 - 10	Part-Game	Pass (STOP). Partner has chosen the best Part-Game.
	11 - 12	Maybe Game	Pass (STOP) with 13 - 14 or bid Game (STOP) with 15 - 16.
	13 or more	Game	Pass (STOP). Partner has chosen the best Game.
17 - 18	0 - 10	Maybe Game	Raise partner's Suit ▼.
	11 - 12	Game	Raise to Game (STOP), or bid Three No Trump (STOP).
	13 or more	Game	Pass (STOP).
19 - 21	0 - 10	Maybe Game	Jump Raise partner's Suit or bid No Trump ▼.
	11 - 12	Game	Raise to Game (STOP), or bid Three No Trump (STOP).
	13 or more	Maybe Slam	Search for Slam (See Chapter 22).

Exercises

1)

NORTH	EAST	SOUTH	WEST
(Dealer)	(Partner)		(You)
One Club	Double	Pass	?

What would you respond with each of the following hands:

a) ♠ 9 8 7 3
   ♥ J 2
   ♦ 9 6 5 4
   ♣ J 9 3

b) ♠ J 8 4
   ♥ K Q 4 2
   ♦ K Q 10 6
   ♣ 7 3

c) ♠ 9 8 6 5 4
   ♥ A Q 2
   ♦ A Q 6
   ♣ 7 4

d) ♠ 8 5 3
   ♥ J 5 4
   ♦ J 7 5 3 2
   ♣ 9 7

e) ♠ 8 3 2
   ♥ 9 3 2
   ♦ Q 4
   ♣ A J 9 5 3

f) ♠ 9 8 6
   ♥ J 4 2
   ♦ K Q 10
   ♣ A Q 7 3

g) ♠ A 8 4　　h) ♠ J 9 8 7 4　　i) ♠ A 8 4
　♥ K 6 2　　　　♥ Q 8 4 3 2　　　♥ J 2
　♦ K 9 3　　　　♦ 6　　　　　　　♦ K Q 8 6 3
　♣ A J 9 8　　　♣ 7 3　　　　　　♣ 8 7 4

2)

NORTH	EAST	SOUTH	WEST
(Dealer)	(You)		(Partner)
One Club	Double	Pass	One Heart
Pass	?		

What would you rebid with each of the following hands:

a) ♠ A Q 7 3　　b) ♠ K 9 8 4　　c) ♠ A Q 6
　♥ A J 2　　　　♥ K Q 4 2　　　　♥ A J 9 2
　♦ A 6 5 4　　　♦ A Q 6 3　　　　♦ A Q 6 3 2
　♣ 9 3　　　　　♣ 3　　　　　　　♣ 4

d) ♠ A 9 8 6　　e) ♠ A 8 4
　♥ Q 8 4 2　　　♥ K J 6 2
　♦ K J 10 3 2　　♦ K Q J 9 3
　♣ —　　　　　　♣ A

For the Curious

When your only Suit has been bid by the Opponents

Occasionally, you will have 0 - 5 points and no unbid 4-card suit when your partner makes a take-out double. For example, suppose the auction goes:

NORTH	EAST	SOUTH	WEST
	(Partner)		(You)
One Club	Double	Pass	?

and you hold:

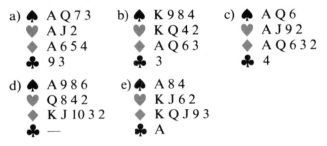

♠ 7 5 4
♥ K 6 4
♦ 7 3 2
♣ J 5 3 2

Or the auction goes:

NORTH	EAST	SOUTH	WEST
	(You)		(Partner)
One Diamond	Pass	One Spade	Double
Pass	?		

and you hold:

♠ 8 5 3 2
♥ 8 5
♦ J 9 5 3
♣ Q 8 7

Your partner's take-out Double is forcing, so you must bid. In each example, you must bid a 3-card suit! This is unfortunate, but there is no better alternative. Partner will usually have 4-card support, giving you an adequate 7-card fit. In any case, it is better than defending a doubled one-level contract. If responder has 6 - 10 points and no 4-card or longer unbid suit, he can respond One No Trump.

On rare occasions, responder will have a long and strong enough holding in the opponent's trump suit to Pass partner's take-out Double. Suppose the auction goes:

NORTH	EAST	SOUTH	WEST
	(Partner)		(You)
One Club	Double	Pass	?

and you hold:

♠ A 5
♥ 7 5
♦ 9 6 4
♣ Q J 10 9 8 7

With only 9 points...7 in high cards and 2 for the 6-card Club suit...it looks like you are headed for Part-Game. What is the best Part-Game? Even though partner probably doesn't have too many, it looks like Clubs! You should be able to take four trump tricks and the Ace of Spades. Partner should come up with two or three tricks since he has promised the strength of an opening bid. What should you do? In this case, you should **Pass. This has the effect of converting partner's take-out Double into a penalty Double**:

NORTH	EAST	SOUTH	WEST
	(Partner)		(You)
One Club	Double	Pass	**Pass**
Pass			

The final contract (assuming North elects to Pass) will be One Club doubled. If you can take at least seven tricks on defense, you will defeat this contract.

Passing partner's take-out Double to convert it to a penalty Double is very rare. You should have at least five good trumps before considering this.

Bidding the Opponent's Suit: the Cue Bid Response

When partner makes a take-out Double and you have 13 or more points, we recommended that you jump to Game in any 4-card or longer unbid Major suit. Lacking one, you bid Three No Trump. This approach is easy to remember and works well on most hands.

For greater accuracy, you can adopt a slight modification when you are not certain WHERE to play the contract after partner makes a take-out Double. For example, suppose the auction goes:

NORTH	EAST	SOUTH	WEST
	(Partner)		(You)
One Club	Double	Pass	?

and you hold:

♠ A Q 7 6
♥ K J 6 5
♦ 7 6 5
♣ K 6

With 13 points, you want to be in Game but, since partner may only have 3-card support for the unbid suits, you are uncertain what the best Game contract is. Partner might hold any of these hands:

1) ♠ K 5 4   2) ♠ K J 5 4   3) ♠ K 8 3
   ♥ A Q 3 2   ♥ A 4 3   ♥ A 9 2
   ♦ A K 8 4   ♦ A K 4 2   ♦ A 8 3 2
   ♣ 7 5   ♣ 5 3   ♣ Q J 8

If partner has the first hand, you have a Magic Major Suit Fit in Hearts but not in Spades. If partner has the second hand, you should be playing in your Magic Major Suit Fit in Spades. If partner has the third hand, you have no Magic Major Suit Fit and should play Game in Three No Trump.

In order to get additional information from partner to help you decide WHERE, you need a forcing bid. Since partner has asked you to pick any suit **other than the suit bid by the opponents**, you do have a bid which could be used for this purpose. You could **bid the opponent's suit!** Such a bid is called a *cue bid* of the opponent's suit. Since neither you nor partner have any intention of playing with the opponent's suit as trump, partner will not Pass.

A CUE BID RESPONSE TO A TAKE-OUT DOUBLE
IS A MARATHON BID SAYING "I KNOW WE BELONG
IN GAME BUT I AM NOT SURE WHERE"

What will partner do when you cue bid the opponent's suit? He will provide you with the additional information you need. For example, suppose partner holds one of the above hands and the auction goes:

NORTH	EAST (Partner)	SOUTH	WEST (You)
One Club	Double	Pass	**Two Clubs**
Pass	?		

With the first two hands, partner will bid his 4-card Major and you will raise to Game. With the third hand, he has no 4-card Major so he will bid Two No Trump and you will raise to Three No Trump.

Used in this manner, the cue bid response to partner's take-out double is often very useful. However, it does add some complexity to the auction.

19

The Competitive Auction

We've come a long way! First we looked at bidding by opener and responder without competition. Then we looked at what to do if your opponents open the bidding. Now we'll tie it all together by looking at the most common competitive situations:

OPENER'S TEAM	{	• Partner opens the bidding and right hand opponent — overcalls — makes a take-out double
OVERCALLER OR DOUBLER'S TEAM	{	• Left-hand opponent opens the bidding — partner overcalls and right-hand opponent bids — partner doubles and right-hand opponent bids

Let's look at each of these situations in turn.

Partner Opens the Bidding and Right-hand Opponent Overcalls

What effect does the overcall have on responder's choice of bid? You should still use Responder's Four Questions. However, you must sometimes make an adjustment because of the overcall.

> **RESPONDER'S FOUR QUESTIONS**
>
> 1. CAN I RAISE PARTNER'S MAJOR?
> 2. DO I HAVE A WEAK HAND (0 - 5 POINTS)?
> 3. CAN I BID A NEW SUIT AT THE ONE-LEVEL?
> 4. DO I HAVE A MINIMUM HAND (6 - 10 POINTS)?

Let's look at some examples.

The first question is:

1. CAN I RAISE PARTNER'S MAJOR?

If you can support partner's major, the overcall will rarely affect your response. Here is an example:

NORTH (Partner)	EAST	SOUTH (You)	WEST
One Heart	One Spade	?	

You hold:

♠ 7 6 5
♥ K J 5 3
♦ A 9 6
♣ K 4 3

Respond Three Hearts to show 4-card support for partner's Major and 11 - 12 points, just as you would have done if East had passed.

The second question is:

2. DO I HAVE A WEAK HAND (0 - 5 POINTS)?

Again, there is no effect. For example:

NORTH (Partner)	EAST	SOUTH (You)	WEST
One Diamond	One Heart	?	

You hold:

♠ 10 8 7 6 5
♥ J 3
♦ Q J 8
♣ 10 7 4

Pass. The overcall has not changed your response.

The third question is:

3. CAN I BID A NEW SUIT AT THE ONE-LEVEL?

You may be able to answer yes if the overcall still allows you enough room to bid a new suit at the one-level. For example, sometimes the overcall does not affect your response:

NORTH	EAST	SOUTH	WEST
(Partner)		(You)	
One Club	One Heart	?	

What do you do with the following hand?

♠ K J 5 4 2
♥ A 10 6
♦ 8 6 4
♣ 9 6

Bid One Spade. The overcall has not interfered with your normal response. At other times, the overcall does interfere but you may be able to find a suitable alternative bid. For example:

NORTH	EAST	SOUTH	WEST
(Partner)		(You)	
One Club	One Heart	?	

This time, you have the following hand:

♠ A 10 6 3
♥ 9 2
♦ Q 10 8 6 4
♣ 7 3

You were originally planning to respond One Diamond but, since that option has been taken away, you can still bid a new suit at the one-level …One Spade. The fourth question is:

---

4. DO I HAVE A MINIMUM HAND (6 - 10 POINTS)?

Again, you may have to find a suitable substitute bid (i.e. one that is "close" to being correct) when the overcall interferes. For example:

NORTH	EAST	SOUTH	WEST
(Partner)		(You)	
One Diamond	One Spade	?	

You have the following hand:

♠ K J 3
♥ Q 7 4 2
♦ 10 3
♣ Q 9 7 4

You were going to respond One Heart, a new suit at the one-level but you had to answer no to the third question because the overcall prevented this. With only 8 points, you are not strong enough to bid a new suit at the two-level. But you do have available the response of One No Trump to show 6 - 10 points.

Sometimes you may have to stretch a little further in a competitive situation to find a suitable substitute bid. For example, the auction goes:

NORTH	EAST	SOUTH	WEST
(Partner)		(You)	
One Heart	Two Clubs	?	

and you hold:

♠ Q 9 7 4 2
♥ A Q 3
♦ 9 8 5
♣ 3 2

You have 9 points. If your right-hand opponent had passed, you would have been able to respond One Spade. After the overcall, you do not have enough strength to bid your suit at the two-level. While you could Pass, it is better to tell partner you have 6 - 10 points if you can find a suitable substitute bid. With the above hand, you should raise to Two Hearts. Partner will often have a 5-card or longer suit in which case you will have found a Magic Fit. If partner has a 4-card suit, you will still have an adequate 7-card fit.

The "3-card raise" is so important in competitive situations that it deserves special emphasis:

IN A COMPETITIVE AUCTION YOU CAN RAISE PARTNER'S SUIT WITH ONLY 3-CARD SUPPORT

If you are in the 6 - 10 point range and have no suitable substitute for your planned response, you can Pass. For example:

NORTH	EAST	SOUTH	WEST
(Partner)		(You)	
One Diamond	Two Clubs	?	

You hold:

♠ 6 5 3
♥ K 10 7 3
♦ 9 6
♣ K 4 3 2

You were planning to respond One Heart but the opponent's overcall has eliminated that possibility. With a minimum hand (6 - 10 points), you can't bid a new suit at the two-level. Here you are best to Pass.

If you do not have a minimum hand, you must bid something. If you Pass, a Game may be missed. With 11 or more points, you have enough strength to bid a new suit at the two-level or higher so there will usually be no problem. However, suppose the bidding goes:

NORTH	EAST	SOUTH	WEST
(Partner)		(You)	
One Diamond	Two Clubs	?	

and you hold:

♠ A 6 5
♥ 6 5 3
♦ 9 6
♣ A Q J 7 5

The opponent has taken away your intended response. In this case, you can make use of the penalty Double:

NORTH	EAST	SOUTH	WEST
(Partner)		(You)	
One Diamond	Two Clubs	**Double**	

You expect to take three or four Club tricks and the Ace of Spades. Since partner has opened the bidding, he should be able to take at least two or three tricks. You should have no trouble defeating the opponents' contract.

After a two-level overcall, you sometimes have 11 or 12 points but no convenient bid. For example, the bidding goes:

NORTH	EAST	SOUTH	WEST
(Partner)		(You)	
One Heart	Two Diamonds	?	

and you hold:

♠ A J 5
♥ Q 9
♦ K 10 9 5
♣ J 9 6 4

With 11 points, you must say something. Bidding Three Clubs does not seem appropriate. If partner has no fit, you may get the partnership too high with no suitable place to play the contract. A penalty Double is also not attractive. To cater to these hands:

IN COMPETITION, A RESPONSE OF TWO NO TRUMP
IS AN INVITATIONAL BID SHOWING
11 - 12 POINTS

In summary:

RESPONSES AFTER RIGHT-HAND OPPONENT OVERCALLS

Use RESPONDER'S FOUR QUESTIONS:

1. Can I raise partner's Major?
   - The overcall won't interfere

2. Do I have a weak hand (0 - 5 points)?
   - The overcall won't interfere

3. Can I bid a new suit at the one-level?
   - If the overcall interferes, find another suit to bid at the one-level, where possible

4. Do I have a minimum hand (6 - 10 points)?
   - With 6 - 10 points, find a substitute bid if possible:
     — Raise partner's suit with 3-card support (or longer)
     — Bid One No Trump
   - With 11 or more points, find a suitable substitute bid if necessary:
     — Two No Trump with 11 - 12 points
     — Penalty double with lots of the opponents' trumps if you don't feel they can make their contract

---

Here are some examples after a one-level overcall:

NORTH	EAST	SOUTH	WEST
(Partner)		(You)	
One Club	One Heart	?	

and you hold:

1) ♠ K 9 8 7 3	2) ♠ Q 7 6 4	3) ♠ Q 8 3
♥ A 6 2	♥ J 8 6 4	♥ K J 2
♦ J 5 4	♦ A 9 7 5	♦ Q 9 8 3
♣ Q 9	♣ 3	♣ 7 6 4

1) ONE SPADE. Can you raise partner's Major? No, he hasn't bid one. Do you you have a weak hand? No, you have 11 points. Can you bid a new suit at the one-level? Yes. Respond One Spade. The opponent's overcall has not affected your response.

2) ONE SPADE. You can't support partner's Major and don't have a weak hand. Can you bid a new suit at the one-level? Yes. Respond One Spade. Without the overcall, you would have responded One Heart.

3) ONE NO TRUMP. You can't support partner's Major, don't have a weak hand and can't bid a new suit at the one-level. Do you have a minimum hand (6-10 points)? Yes, you have 8 points. In this case, bid One No Trump.

Here are some examples after a two-level overcall:

NORTH	EAST	SOUTH	WEST
(Partner)		(You)	
One Spade	Two Diamonds	?	

and you hold:

1) ♠ K J 7 3	2) ♠ Q 4 3	3) ♠ A Q 9	4) ♠ 3
♥ A 9 6 2	♥ K J 4	♥ 9 7 6 2	♥ A 5 4
♦ 5 4	♦ K J 5 3	♦ 8 3	♦ K J 10 9 7
♣ K 8 6	♣ J 8 7	♣ Q 7 6 4	♣ A 8 6 3

1) THREE SPADES. Can you raise partner's Major? Yes, you have 4-card support. With 12 dummy points...11 in high cards and 1 for the doubleton Diamond...make an invitational raise to Three Spades.

2) TWO NO TRUMP. You don't have 4-card support for partner's Major, don't have a weak hand and can't bid a new suit at the one-level. You do not have a minimum hand...you have 11 points. Since you can't bid a new suit at the two-level, bid Two No Trump to show 11-12 points. This is more appealing than raising partner to the three-level with only 3-card support.

3) TWO SPADES. Can you support partner's Major? In competition, you only need 3-card support to raise. Since nothing else is appealing, bid Two Spades.

4) DOUBLE. You can't raise partner's Major, don't have a weak hand, can't bid a new suit at the one-level and don't have a minimum hand ...you have 13 points. When you look at bidding a new suit at the two-level, you notice it has already been bid, by your opponent. You have an effective countermeasure, the penalty Double.

Partner Opens the Bidding and Right-hand Opponent Makes a Take-out Double

If the bidding goes:

NORTH (Partner)	EAST	SOUTH (You)	WEST
One Heart	Double	?	

what effect does the opponent's take-out Double have on your auction? It has taken away none of your bidding room. On the other hand, it has announced that your right-hand opponent has at least the strength of an opening bid and intends to compete for the contract.

Since none of your bidding room has been taken away, you can respond in the same manner as if your right-hand opponent had passed, using Responder's Four Questions. For example:

NORTH (Partner)	EAST	SOUTH (You)	WEST
One Heart	Double	?	

and you hold:

♠ A 8
♥ J 10 8 3
♦ Q 6 3
♣ 8 6 5 3

Raise to Two Hearts to show your 4-card support for partner's Major and 8 dummy points.

Another example:

NORTH (Partner)	EAST	SOUTH (You)	WEST
One Heart	Double	?	

What would you do with the following hand?

♠ K Q 8 7 4
♥ J 4
♦ A 5 3
♣ 8 7 3

You can't raise partner's Major and you don't have a weak hand. You can bid a new suit at the one-level. Respond One Spade.

Now we turn to situations you may encounter when the opponents open the bidding and your partner bids.

Left-hand Opponent Opens the Bidding, Partner Overcalls and Right-hand Opponent Bids

If the auction goes:

NORTH	EAST	SOUTH	WEST
	(Partner)		(You)
One Heart	One Spade	Two Hearts	?

What is the effect of your right-hand opponent's bid? It has taken away some of your bidding room. You can no longer bid One No Trump, Two Clubs or Two Diamonds. For compensation, you don't have to bid with less than 11 points since partner will get another opportunity to bid. Otherwise, you can still use Responder's Four Questions:

RESPONSES AFTER PARTNER OVERCALLS AND RIGHT-HAND OPPONENT BIDS

Use Responder's Four Questions:

1. Can I raise partner's Major?
    - Right-hand opponent's bid shouldn't interfere. You can raise with only 3-card support since partner must have a 5-card suit

2. Do I have a weak hand (0 - 5 points)?
    - Pass

3. Can I bid a new suit at the one-level?
    - If right-hand opponent's bid interferes, find another suit to bid at the one-level, where possible

4. Do I have a minimum hand (6 - 10 points)?
    - With 6 - 10 points, find a substitute bid if possible:
      — Raise partner's suit with 3-card support (or longer)
      — Bid One No Trump
    - With 11 or more points, find a suitable substitute bid if necessary:
      — New suit at the two-level or higher
      — Two No Trump with 11 - 12 points

Here are some examples:

NORTH	EAST	SOUTH	WEST
	(Partner)		(You)
One Heart	One Spade	Two Hearts	?

What would you do with the following hands?

1)	♠ K 7 3	2)	♠ K J 7 4	3)	♠ J 4	4)	♠ A 9
	♥ 10 2		♥ 9 8		♥ 10 5 4		♥ 6 2
	♦ A 9 8 5 4		♦ A 10 5 3		♦ K 9 8 3		♦ A K J 8 5 4
	♣ J 8 6		♣ K 9 6		♣ Q 8 6 3		♣ 9 8 6

1) TWO SPADES. Since partner has at least five Spades, you have enough to support his suit. With 9 dummy points, you should raise to Two Spades.

2) THREE SPADES. Again you have adequate trump support. This time you should jump to Three Spades to show a hand in the 11 - 12 point range.

3) PASS. With only 6 points and no convenient bid available, the best tactic is to Pass. You will hear again from partner if he has a strong hand.

4) THREE DIAMONDS. You can't support partner's Major and you can't bid a new suit at the one-level. With 14 points, you are strong enough to bid a new suit at the two-level or higher. Bid Three Diamonds.

Left-hand Opponent Opens the Bidding, Partner Doubles and Right-hand Opponent Bids

If the auction goes:

NORTH	EAST (Partner)	SOUTH	WEST (You)
One Heart	Double	Two Hearts	?

What effect does your right-hand opponent's bid have on the auction?

Partner's take-out Double is a forcing bid so you would have to respond if your right-hand opponent said Pass. **Since your right-hand opponent has bid, you do not have to bid.** Partner will get an opportunity to bid again in case he has a medium or maximum hand. For example:

NORTH	EAST (Partner)	SOUTH	WEST (You)
One Heart	Double	Two Hearts	?

and you hold:

♠ 8 6 5 4
♥ 8 6 4
♦ 7 5
♣ 10 7 4 2

You would have bid One Spade if your right-hand opponent had passed, but now you can safely say Pass.

Does that mean that you should always Pass? No. Partner's take-out Double is an invitation for your side to compete for the contract. Suppose the auction starts:

NORTH	EAST	SOUTH	WEST
	(Partner)		(You)
One Heart	Double	Two Hearts	?

You hold:

♠ A J 8 6 5
♥ 6 4
♦ 10 8 6
♣ Q 5 2

Bid Two Spades. This is not really a new suit at the two-level since partner's Double invites you to support one of his suits. Your 8 points combined with partner's opening bid should give your side enough strength to compete for the contract. Not only is there a good chance that you will make your contract, but, if the opponents want to compete for the contract, they will have to bid Three Hearts which you may be able to defeat. In general, bid a 4-card or longer unbid suit with 6 - 10 points. Pass with 0 - 5.

With 11 - 12 points, jump in your suit, as you would do if your right-hand opponent had passed.

For example:

NORTH	EAST	SOUTH	WEST
	(Partner)		(You)
One Heart	Double	Two Hearts	?

You hold:

♠ A J 8 6 5
♥ 7 5
♦ K 6 5
♣ Q 8 6

Bid Three Spades. This is an invitational bid showing 11 - 12 points. Partner can Pass with 13 or 14 points. Otherwise he will carry on to Game.

With 13 or more points, bid Game. The choices are familiar...Four Spades or Four Hearts with a 4-card or longer Major; otherwise Three No Trump. For example:

NORTH	EAST	SOUTH	WEST
	(Partner)		(You)
One Heart	Double	Two Hearts	?

You hold:

♠ A J 8 6 5
♥ 7 5
♦ K 6 5
♣ A 8 6

Bid Four Spades. There is enough combined strength for Game and you know there is a Magic Major Suit Fit since partner has promised at least 3-card support for Spades.

In summary:

RESPONSE TO A TAKE-OUT DOUBLE
IF RIGHT-HAND OPPONENT BIDS

- 0 - 5 points: Pass
- 6 - 10 points: Bid an unbid suit or, rarely, bid One No Trump
- 11 - 12 points: Jump in an unbid suit or, rarely, bid Two No Trump
- 13 or more points: Bid Game

Competition for Part-Game

When both sides are competing for the contract, you will be faced with two choices:

- Pass, planning to defend against their contract
- Bid higher, hoping to get the contract. It may be that your opponents will compete further and you can hope they "overbid"

Choices such as these make Bridge challenging and fascinating. You will have to judge which action is likely to get the best result for your side. If you are wrong, don't worry...even experts go wrong sometimes.

For example, if the auction goes:

NORTH	EAST	SOUTH	WEST
(Partner)		(You)	
One Heart	One Spade	Two Hearts	Two Spades
Pass	Pass	?	

If the opponents had not competed, you and your partner would be in a contract of Two Hearts. Now you are faced with the choice of saying Pass and defending Two Spades, or bidding Three Hearts if you want to play with your suit as trumps.

In the above auction you might hold:

♠ 7
♥ A 9 6 5
♦ Q J 8 5 4
♣ 7 5 4

You have 10 dummy points…7 high card points plus 3 for your singleton Spade. With the maximum for your promised range, a good fit with partner's suit and little defense against the opponents' contract, you should compete to Three Hearts. This has three advantages: you may make Three Hearts; you may push the opponents to Three Spades which you might be able to defeat; you may go down a trick but the opponents would have made their contract and scored a Part-Game.

On the other hand, if you hold:

♠ K 8 5
♥ Q 6 4
♦ 7 5
♣ Q 6 4 3 2

You should Pass. You have already "stretched" to raise partner with only 3-card support, you only have 8 points and you have some defense against Two Spades.

As a general guide when both sides are competing for Part-Game:

- Use your best judgement
- If in doubt, compete at the two-level and Pass at the three-level

Summary

If your partner opens the bidding and your right-hand opponent overcalls, use Responder's Four Questions:

RESPONDER'S FOUR QUESTIONS

1. CAN I RAISE PARTNER'S MAJOR?
2. DO I HAVE A WEAK HAND (0 - 5 POINTS)?
3. CAN I BID A NEW SUIT AT THE ONE-LEVEL?
4. DO I HAVE A MINIMUM HAND (6 - 10 POINTS)?

If the opponent's bid has interfered with your normal response, try to find a suitable substitute. With 6 - 10 points, you may Pass if you have no suitable bid. With 11 or more points, you must bid something.

If your partner overcalls and your right-hand opponent bids, you can also use Responder's Four Questions.

When an opponent bids after your partner has made a take-out Double:

• 0 - 5 points:	Pass
• 6 - 10 points:	Bid an unbid suit or, rarely, bid One No Trump
• 11 - 12 points:	Jump in an unbid suit or, rarely, bid Two No Trump
• 13 or more points:	Bid Game

When an opponent makes a take-out Double of your partner's opening bid, respond exactly as you would have if the opponent had said Pass.

When both sides are competing for Part-Game:

- Use your best judgement
- If in doubt, compete at the two-level and Pass at the three-level

Exercises

1)
NORTH	EAST	SOUTH	WEST
(Partner)		(You)	
One Diamond	One Heart	?	

What would you bid with the following hands?

a) ♠ K 8 7 3
   ♥ 9 6 2
   ♦ J 5 4
   ♣ Q 10 9

b) ♠ Q 7 4
   ♥ K J 4
   ♦ 5 3
   ♣ K 9 7 5 3

c) ♠ Q 8 3
   ♥ J 2
   ♦ Q J 8 3 2
   ♣ 7 6 4

d) ♠ A K
   ♥ 9 5 4
   ♦ 5 3 2
   ♣ A Q 9 7 3

2)
NORTH	EAST	SOUTH	WEST
(Partner)		(You)	
One Heart	Two Diamonds	?	

What would you respond with the following hands?

a) ♠ K 8 7 3
   ♥ A 9 6 2
   ♦ A 5 4
   ♣ Q 9

b) ♠ Q J 6 4 2
   ♥ J 6 4
   ♦ A 9 7
   ♣ K 3

c) ♠ A 8 3
   ♥ K 9 2
   ♦ Q J 8 3
   ♣ Q 10 4

d) ♠ Q 6 3
   ♥ 4
   ♦ A Q 10 9 7
   ♣ A 9 7 3

3) NORTH   EAST   SOUTH   WEST
(Partner)   (You)
One Club   Double   ?

What would you do with the following hands?

a) ♠ 7 5 3   b) ♠ Q 7 6 4   c) ♠ 8 3   d) ♠ A Q 3
    ♥ J 9 7 6 2   ♥ J 8 6 4   ♥ K J 2   ♥ K Q 4
    ♦ J 7 5 4   ♦ A 7 5   ♦ 9 8 3   ♦ Q 5 3
    ♣ 9   ♣ 3 2   ♣ K 9 7 6 4   ♣ J 7 3 2

4) NORTH   EAST   SOUTH   WEST
            (Partner)   (You)
One Club   One Spade   Two Clubs   ?

How would you respond with the following hands?

a) ♠ A 2   b) ♠ Q 7 6 4   c) ♠ K J 3 2   d) ♠ 7 4 3
    ♥ J 7 3   ♥ A K 8 6 4   ♥ 8 3   ♥ K J 5
    ♦ K 5 4 3 2   ♦ 7 5   ♦ A 9 8 3   ♦ A Q J 2
    ♣ 10 9 3   ♣ 9 3   ♣ K Q J   ♣ J 7 5

5) NORTH   EAST   SOUTH   WEST
            (Partner)   (You)
One Club   Double   One No Trump   ?

How would you respond with the following hands?

a) ♠ 7 3   b) ♠ Q 7 6 4   c) ♠ Q J 8 3   d) ♠ 7 3
    ♥ 9 6 2   ♥ K J 8 6 4   ♥ K J 2   ♥ 9 5
    ♦ J 5 4 3 2   ♦ 7 5   ♦ A 9 8 3   ♦ A Q J 8 3 2
    ♣ Q 10 9   ♣ 9 3   ♣ 7 4   ♣ K 9 7

For the Curious

The Redouble

When an opponent makes a take-out Double, he makes a new bid available to you...the Redouble. The Redouble is not needed and we advise you not to use it. However, some players use the Redouble to say:

- "Partner I have 10 or more high card points"
- "I hope to describe my hand in more detail at my next opportunity"

We mention this so you will know what players who have learned elsewhere are doing if they use the Redouble.

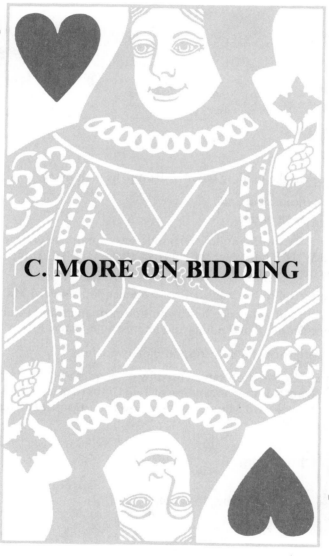

C. MORE ON BIDDING

20

The Stayman Convention

If partner opens the bidding One No Trump, he is showing:

- A balanced hand and
- 16, 17 or 18 points

In Chapter 5, we looked at how responder, as captain, determined HOW HIGH and WHERE to place the contract after a One No Trump opening. Two problems were left unsolved:

- Finding out if the One No Trump opener had a **4-card** Major suit
- Finding out if opener has a minimum or maximum hand when responder has 8 or 9 points and interest in a Magic Major Suit Fit

We also carefully reserved the response of Two Clubs.

The Stayman Convention can be used by responder after an opening bid of One No Trump. It uses a response of Two Clubs to discover whether or not opener has a 4-card Major. Let's see how this response can be applied to the above problems.

The Two Club Response

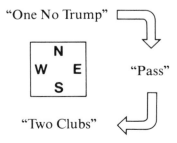

If your partner opens the bidding One No Trump, by agreement with your partner you use a response of Two Clubs to ask the question:

DO YOU HAVE A 4-CARD MAJOR SUIT?

Used in this manner, the Two Club response is an **artificial** or *conventional* bid. It is called the *Stayman Convention*. It is only used if responder has at least 8 points and is interested in Game in a Major suit.

For example, responder might hold the following hand when opener bids One No Trump:

♠ A 8 6 4
♥ K 9 7 6
♦ 6 3
♣ A 10 5

The above hand is suited to a Stayman Two Club response.

Rebids by Opener

How does opener rebid after his partner uses the Two Club (Stayman) response? If opener has a 4-card or longer Major suit, he bids that suit. If not, opener bids Two Diamonds. Like the response of Two Clubs, the rebid of Two Diamonds is an artificial or conventional bid. Opener has three possible rebids:

OPENER'S REBID AFTER A TWO CLUB (STAYMAN) RESPONSE	
• Two Hearts:	4-card or longer Heart suit
• Two Spades:	4-card or longer Spade suit
• Two Diamonds:	No 4-card Major

What if opener has both a 4-card Heart suit and a 4-card Spade suit? Opener uses the general rule of bidding the lower-ranking of two 4-card suits and rebids Two Hearts.

Let's look at some examples. You are North and the auction starts off:

NORTH	EAST	SOUTH	WEST
(You)		(Partner)	
One No Trump	Pass	**Two Clubs**	Pass
?			

What would you rebid with the following hands?

1) ♠ K 8 7 3   2) ♠ A J   3) ♠ A Q 3   4) ♠ A Q 7 3
   ♥ A 6 2   ♥ J 9 8 3   ♥ A J 2   ♥ Q 9 5 4
   ♦ A 5 4   ♦ A K 5 3   ♦ J 2   ♦ K J 2
   ♣ K Q 9   ♣ K J 3   ♣ K Q 7 6 4   ♣ A 10

1) TWO SPADES. The Two Club response asks you to bid a 4-card Major suit if you have one. With a 4-card Spade suit, rebid Two Spades.

2) TWO HEARTS. With a 4-card Heart suit, you would rebid Two Hearts when partner uses the Stayman Convention.

3) TWO DIAMONDS. Responder has asked if you have a 4-card Major suit and you don't have one. Bid Two Diamonds. This is an artificial response and has nothing to do with the number of Diamonds in your hand. It merely says: "I don't have a 4-card Major suit".

4) TWO HEARTS. With a choice of 4-card Major suits, bid the lower-ranking...Two Hearts.

Using Stayman With 10 or More Points

When partner opens One No Trump and you have 10 or more points, you know the answer to HOW HIGH...Game. To determine WHERE, you need to know whether or not there is a Magic Major Suit Fit. If there is, Game should be played in the Major suit. If there isn't, Game should be played in Three No Trump.

The only time responder uses the Stayman Convention when he has 10 or more points is when he has a 4-card Major suit and needs to know if opener has 4-card support. For example, opener bids One No Trump and responder holds:

♠ A 8 6 4
♥ K 9 7 6
♦ 6 3
♣ A 10 5

With 11 points, responder knows there is enough combined strength for Game. To determine WHERE, responder can use the Stayman Convention and bid Two Clubs. If opener bids Two Hearts, responder now knows that there is a Magic Major Suit Fit and can bid Four Hearts. Similarly, if opener bids Two Spades, responder bids Four Spades. If opener doesn't have a 4-card Major suit and rebids Two Diamonds, responder knows there is no Magic Major Suit Fit and bids Three No Trump.

Another example. Opener bids One No Trump and responder has:

♠ J 6 4 3
♥ 6 3
♦ K Q 8 5 3
♣ K 4

With 10 points, responder knows there is enough for Game. Since there may be a Magic Major Suit Fit in Spades, responder bids Two Clubs. If opener bids Two Spades, responder can raise to Four Spades. If opener bids Two Diamonds, responder can bid Three No Trump, knowing that there is no Magic Major Suit Fit. What if opener rebids Two Hearts? Again responder should bid Three No Trump.

Here are some more examples:

NORTH	EAST	SOUTH	WEST
(Partner)		(You)	
One No Trump	Pass	?	

What would you respond with the following hands?

1) ♠ J 8 7 3	2) ♠ K Q 8 6 4	3) ♠ A 9 3
♥ J 9 6 2	♥ 8 3	♥ K 7 4 2
♦ A 5 4	♦ J 5 3	♦ A 6 4
♣ A 9	♣ A 8 3	♣ 7 6 4

1) TWO CLUBS. With 10 points there should be enough combined strength for Game. WHERE? If partner has a 4-card Major suit, there will be a Magic Major Suit Fit. Respond Two Clubs to find out. If opener bids Two Hearts you raise to Four Hearts. If opener bids Two Spades, you raise to Four Spades. If opener bids Two Diamonds, you raise to Three No Trump, secure in the knowledge that there is no Magic Major Suit Fit.

2) THREE SPADES. With 11 points, you want to be in Game. Here there is no need to use the Stayman Convention. With a 5-card Major suit, you only need 3-card support from opener. The bid that finds out whether or not opener has 3-card or longer support is Three Spades. Opener will bid Four Spades if he has three or more Spades, otherwise, he will bid Three No Trump.

3) TWO CLUBS. Again, with 11 points you want to get to Game. Since there may be a Magic Major Suit Fit in Hearts, bid Two Clubs. If opener bids Two Hearts, you raise to Four Hearts. If opener bids Two Diamonds or Two Spades, you bid Three No Trump.

Using Stayman With 8 or 9 Points

Suppose opener bids One No Trump and responder has:

♠ A 7 5 3
♥ K 6 5 2
♦ J 4 2
♣ 6 3

With 8 points, when responder asks himself HOW HIGH the answer is "Maybe Game". Responder wants to make an invitational bid. While the raise to Two No Trump is one way to invite to Game, this does not give responder an opportunity to uncover a Magic Major Suit Fit. Instead, responder should start by bidding Two Clubs.

If opener rebids Two Hearts, responder can raise to Three Hearts as an invitational bid. Opener will Pass with 16 or 17 points and carry on to Four Hearts with 18 points. Similarly, if opener bids Two Spades, responder can invite to Game by raising to Three Spades. What if opener rebids Two Diamonds? Now responder knows that there is no Magic Major Suit Fit and can bid Two No Trump to show an invitational hand of 8 or 9 points.

Here are some more examples. Partner opens One No Trump. What would you do with the following hands?

1) ♠ A J 2   2) ♠ A 7 2
   ♥ J 9 8   ♥ 10 9 7 2
   ♦ 7 6 5 3   ♦ J 2
   ♣ K 8 3   ♣ K 6 5 4

  1) TWO NO TRUMP. Since it is very unlikely that there is a Magic Major Suit Fit, raise to Two No Trump to invite opener to bid Game.

  2) TWO CLUBS. With 8 points and interest in finding a Magic Major Suit Fit, bid Two Clubs. If opener rebids Two Hearts, invite to Game by raising to Three Hearts. If opener rebids Two Diamonds or Two Spades, invite to Game by bidding Two No Trump.

There is another way you can make use of the Stayman Convention when you have a hand in the 8 - 9 point range. Suppose partner opens One No Trump and you have:

♠ K 9 5 4 2
♥ 7 5
♦ Q 7 5
♣ Q 6 3

Here you have 8 points. You want to make an invitational bid but, at the same time, you don't want to miss a Magic Major Suit Fit if you have one.

You can't bid Two Spades because that shows 0 - 7 points and is a signoff bid. Partner will Pass even with 18 points. You can't bid Three Spades because that shows 10 - 14 points and is a forcing bid. Partner will carry on to Four Spades or Three No Trump even if he has only 16 points. What can you do?

The way around this dilemma is to start off by bidding Two Clubs. If partner rebids Two Spades, you can make an invitational raise to Three Spades. You know that you have a Magic Major Suit Fit. What if partner bids Two Diamonds or Two Hearts? Now you can bid Two Spades:

NORTH	EAST	SOUTH	WEST
(Partner)		(You)	
One No Trump	Pass	Two Clubs	Pass
Two Diamonds	Pass	**Two Spades**	

This will tell partner you have a hand of invitational (8 - 9 points) strength with at least five Spades. Why? If you had a weak hand (0 - 7 points), you would bid Two Spades directly as a sign-off bid. If you had a strong hand (10 - 14 points), you would bid Three Spades with a 5-card suit or Four Spades with a 6-card or longer suit. Thus, you must have a hand in the 8 - 9 point range. If you only had a 4-card Spade suit you would rebid Two No Trump. So, partner can Pass with a minimum hand (16 - 17 points) or bid Three No Trump or Four Spades with a maximum hand (18 points).

Another example. Partner opens the bidding One No Trump and you have:

♠ K 7
♥ Q 9 7 5 4 2
♦ J 5 3
♣ 6 3

With 8 points and interest in a Major suit, bid Two Clubs. If partner rebids Two Hearts, raise to Three Hearts to invite him to carry on to Game. If partner bids Two Diamonds, bid Two Hearts to show an invitational hand with five or more Hearts. Similarly, if partner bids Two Spades, bid Three Hearts to show an invitational hand with five or more Hearts.

Here are some more examples. Partner opens One Trump. What do you respond with the following hands?

1) ♠ 10 8 7 3 2
    ♥ Q 5 2
    ♦ 5 4
    ♣ K Q 3

2) ♠ J 2
    ♥ J 9 8 6 4
    ♦ 7 6 5 3
    ♣ 8 3

3) ♠ Q 7 2
    ♥ Q 7 2
    ♦ J 2
    ♣ K 6 5 4 3

1) TWO CLUBS. With 8 points...7 HCPs and 1 for the fifth Spade...and interest in finding a Magic Major Suit Fit, bid Two Clubs. If partner bids Two Spades, invite to Game by bidding Three Spades. If partner bids Two Diamonds or Two Hearts, bid Two Spades to show an invitational hand with at least five Spades.

2) TWO HEARTS. With only 3 points, you don't have enough to bid Two Clubs and then bid Hearts. That would show an invitational hand. Just make a sign-off bid of Two Hearts. Partner will Pass.

3) TWO NO TRUMP. With 9 points and no interest in a Major suit, make an invitational raise to Two No Trump.

Why You Don't Use Stayman With 0 - 7 Points

Suppose partner opens One No Trump and you have:

♠ J 7 5 4
♥ Q 9 7 5
♦ 6 3
♣ 8 6 3

With only 3 points you want to play in Part-Game. Should you bid Two Clubs to look for a Magic Major Suit Fit? On the surface, this looks reasonable. If partner bids Two Hearts, you can Pass and play in the Magic Fit. Similarly, if partner bids Two Spades, you can Pass. But what if partner bids Two Diamonds? Since Two Diamonds is an artificial response, partner might have as few as two of them. You don't want to leave partner there. What about bidding Two No Trump? As you saw earlier, partner would interpret that as an invitational bid and would carry on to Three No Trump with 18 points.

Thus, you cannot use the Stayman Convention with a hand in the 0 - 7 point range. You must Pass with one or two 4-card Majors. You can still sign-off in Two Diamonds, Two Hearts or Two Spades with a 5-card or longer suit.

Summary

After partner opens the bidding One No Trump, you can bid Two Clubs (the *Stayman Convention*) if you have 8 or more points and are interested in knowing whether or not opener has a 4-card Major suit. Opener rebids as follows:

OPENER'S REBID AFTER A TWO CLUB (STAYMAN) RESPONSE

- Two Hearts: 4-card (or longer) Heart suit
- Two Spades: 4-card (or longer) Spade suit
- Two Diamonds: No 4-card Major

You can also use the Stayman Convention to show an invitational hand (8 - 9 points) with a 5-card or longer Major suit.

Exercises

1) You open the bidding One No Trump and your partner responds Two Clubs (Stayman). What do you rebid with the following hands?

a) ♠ K 7 3 2
♥ A Q
♦ A 9 5 4
♣ A 7 3

b) ♠ A K Q
♥ J 8 6 4
♦ K 5 3
♣ K 8 3

c) ♠ A K J 3
♥ J 8 7 2
♦ Q 9
♣ A K 3

d) ♠ Q J 3
♥ A J 2
♦ J 9 6
♣ A K 7 4

2) Your partner opens the bidding One No Trump. What would you respond with the following hands?

a) ♠ K 7 3 2
♥ 5 2
♦ Q 9 5 4
♣ 9 7 3

b) ♠ K 8 6 5 3
♥ 6 4
♦ J 5 3
♣ J 8 3

c) ♠ A 10 7
♥ 7 2
♦ Q 9 6 2
♣ Q 6 5 3

d) ♠ Q 9 8 3
♥ 4 2
♦ A 9 6
♣ A 10 7 4

e) ♠ K 7 3 2
♥ 5 2
♦ A 9 5 4
♣ J 7 3

f) ♠ K 8
♥ K 9 8 6 4
♦ Q 5 3
♣ 9 8 3

g) ♠ 7 2
♥ 2
♦ A Q J 9 6 2
♣ J 6 5 3

h) ♠ K J 9 8 3
♥ 2
♦ A J 9 6
♣ 10 7 4

i) ♠ K 7 3
♥ A J 9 7 5 2
♦ 4
♣ J 7 3

j) ♠ K 8 6 5
♥ Q 8 6 4
♦ K 5 3
♣ 8 3

k) ♠ J 10 7 6 3
♥ 7 2
♦ Q 9 6 2
♣ A 3

For the Curious

Can Opener Show Both Major Suits?

Suppose you open the bidding One No Trump with the following hand:

♠ A J 9 8
♥ K J 8 6
♦ A 7
♣ A 8 6

Your partner bids Two Clubs and you rebid Two Hearts, the lower-ranking of your two 4-card Major suits. Partner now bids Three No Trump. What do you do?

Bid Four Spades! Why? Responder must have a 4-card Major to use Stayman. It isn't Hearts because responder didn't raise your Two Heart bid. So responder must have a 4-card Spade suit. Since you know there is a Magic Major Suit Fit, you 'correct' the final contract to Four Spades.

Can You Use Stayman If Partner Overcalls One No Trump?

Suppose the auction goes:

NORTH	EAST	SOUTH	WEST
(Opener)	(Partner)		(You)
One Diamond	One No Trump	Pass	?

Here partner has overcalled One No Trump. You can respond as if partner opened the bidding One No Trump:

- Two Clubs is the Stayman convention
- Two Hearts and Two Spades are sign-off bids (stop) with a 5-card or longer suit and 0 - 7 points
- Two No Trump is an invitational bid ♥ with 8 - 9 points
- Three Hearts and Three Spades are marathon bids (go) with a 5-card suit and 10 - 14 points
- Four Hearts and Four Spades are sign-off bids (stop) with a 6-card or longer suit and 10 - 14 points
- Three No Trump is a sign-off bid (stop) with 10 - 14 points

A Two Diamond response, the opponent's suit, is not generally used. You don't want to choose their suit as trump.

21

Powerhouse Hands

As opener, you sometimes pick up a hand that looks like this:

- ♠ A K Q 9 8
- ♥ A K Q 6 5
- ♦ A
- ♣ 9 8

If you open the bidding One Spade, you run the risk that the auction will end there because responder will Pass with less than 6 points. With a hand worth 24 points...22 in high cards and 1 for each 5-card suit...you have enough strength to make Game even if partner has only 2 points.

If you open the bidding Four Spades, you will get to a Game contract but will not leave the partnership much room to explore for the best Game or for the possibility of a Slam. As you will see in the next chapter, bidding to a Slam contract requires room to exchange information before commiting the partnership to the Slam level.

What is the solution? Strong hands of 22 or more points are opened at the two-level. An opening bid at the two-level in a suit is called a *strong two-bid*. This is a signal to responder that opener has a very strong hand and, at the same time, leaves sufficient room to explore for the best Game and the possibility of a Slam. Let's see how it works.

Choosing the Best Powerhouse Opening Bid

With balanced hands (no voids, no singletons, no more than one doubleton) of 22 or more points, you open the bidding in No Trump at the appropriate level:

> ### RULE FOR A TWO NO TRUMP OPENING BID
>
> To open the bidding Two No Trump you need:
>
> - A balanced hand and
> - 22, 23 or 24 points

> ### RULE FOR A THREE NO TRUMP OPENING BID
>
> To open the bidding Three No Trump you need:
>
> - A balanced hand and
> - 25, 26 or 27 points*

* Balanced hands of 28 points or more are extremely rare.

Let's look at some examples.

You are the opening bidder. What do you do with each of the following hands?

1) ♠ A K 7 3   2) ♠ K 7
   ♥ A J 3   ♥ A K Q
   ♦ K J 3   ♦ K Q J 9 3
   ♣ K Q J   ♣ A Q J

1) TWO NO TRUMP. With a balanced hand of 22 points, open the bidding Two No Trump (22 - 24 points). This is an invitational bid. Partner knows that you have at most 24 points so he can Pass if there is not enough combined strength for Game.

2) THREE NO TRUMP. With 26 points and a balanced hand, open the bidding Three No Trump. Although you are already in Game, this is an invitational bid. Partner may want to play Game in a Major suit or bid a Slam.

Unbalanced hands of 22 or more points are opened at the two-level in a suit:

> ### RULE FOR OPENING THE BIDDING
> ### TWO OF A SUIT (STRONG TWO-BID)
>
> With an unbalanced hand of 22 or more points, open the bidding at the two-level in your longest suit.
>
> With two 5-card or 6-card suits, open the higher-ranking suit.
>
> With three 4-card suits, open the middle-ranking suit.

With only two 4-card suits, you would have a balanced hand and would open Two No Trump or Three No Trump, not two of a suit.

An opening two-bid shows at least 22 points so the partnership will be close to Game even if responder has little or no strength. Because the opening two-bid has no upper limit in strength, it is a marathon bid. Thus, **responder must keep bidding, even with no points, until Game is reached.**

> AN OPENING TWO-BID IN A SUIT
> IS MARATHON (FORCING TO GAME)

Let's look at some examples.

You have an opportunity to open the bidding. What do you bid with each of the following hands?

1) ♠ A 8 7	2) ♠ 3	3) ♠ A K 2	4) ♠ A K J 7 3
♥ A K	♥ A Q 9 6 4	♥ A 2	♥ —
♦ 4	♦ A K Q J 10	♦ K Q J 9 8 4	♦ A K 9 3
♣ A K Q J 8 7 3	♣ A 4	♣ J 3	♣ A K 10 8

1) TWO CLUBS. With 24 points...21 in high cards and 3 for the 7-card Club suit, you are strong enough to open the bidding Two Clubs. This will commit the partnership to Game even if responder has no points but, with 10 likely tricks in your own hand, you cannot risk playing in Part-Game.

2) TWO HEARTS. Here you have 22 points...20 in high cards and 1 for each of the 5-card suits. With two 5-card suits, bid the higher-ranking Two Hearts.

3) ONE DIAMOND. Your hand is only worth 20 points...18 in high cards and 2 for the 6-card Diamond suit. This is not enough to open a two-bid. Instead, open the bidding at the one-level, One Diamond. If partner does not have enough to respond (i.e. less than 6 points), it is unlikely that your side can make a Game contract. If partner does respond, you will show your strong hand by the rebid you make.

4) TWO SPADES. With 23 points, you are strong enough to open at the two-level. Bid your longest suit, Two Spades.

Responding to Two No Trump and Three No Trump Opening Bids

If your partner opens the bidding Two No Trump, he is showing:

- A balanced hand and
- 22, 23 or 24 points

As responder, look at your points to determine HOW HIGH:

- Pass with 0 - 2 points
- Get to Game with 3 or more points

Responses to Two No Trump are almost the same as the responses to One No Trump:

- Four Hearts and Four Spades are sign-off bids (STOP) showing a 6-card or longer suit
- Three No Trump is a sign-off bid (STOP)
- Three Hearts and Three Spades are marathon bids (GO) showing a 5-card suit
- Three Clubs is the Stayman Convention*

After a Three No Trump opening bid, showing a balanced hand of 25 - 27 points, there is not much room to explore the various possibilities. In general, bid Four of a Major suit if you have a 6-card or longer suit. Otherwise, Pass unless you are interested in Slam.

Here are some examples. What do you respond with the following hands if your partner opens Two No Trump?

1) ♠ 7 3 2   2) ♠ 5 3   3) ♠ J 10 7 6 3 2
   ♥ 7 5 2   ♥ 6 4   ♥ 7 2
   ♦ J 9 5 4   ♦ K 5 3 2   ♦ Q 6 2
   ♣ 8 7 3   ♣ 9 8 7 5 4   ♣ 5 3

4) ♠ 7 3   5) ♠ 3 2
   ♥ A Q 8 7 3   ♥ Q 10 5 2
   ♦ J 9 6   ♦ J 6 5 4
   ♣ 10 7 4   ♣ A 7 5

1) PASS. With only 1 point, even if partner has 24 there will not be enough combined strength for Game. Pass, and wish partner luck!

2) THREE NO TRUMP. You have 4 points and no interest in looking for a Magic Major Suit Fit. Raise partner to Three No Trump. Even if partner has only 22 points, there should be enough combined strength for Game.

3) FOUR SPADES. With 5 points...3 HCPs plus 2 for the 6-card Spade suit...you know there is enough combined strength for Game. Since opener has shown a balanced hand, he must have at least two Spades. You know there is a Magic Major Suit Fit so bid Four Spades.

4) THREE HEARTS. With 8 points you want to be in Game. With a 5-card Major suit, you can find out if there is a Magic Major Suit

---

* You can use the Stayman convention over the Two No Trump opening. Everything is the same except that you start one level higher.

Fit by bidding Three Hearts. This is similar to a response of Three Hearts when partner opens One No Trump. Opener will bid Four Hearts if he has 3-card or longer support. With only two Hearts, opener will bid Three No Trump.

5) THREE CLUBS. You have 7 points, enough for Game. Since there may be a Magic Major Suit Fit in Hearts, use the Stayman Convention to find out if opener has a 4-card Heart suit. After an opening bid of Two No Trump, a response of Three Clubs is Stayman, asking opener for a 4-card Major. If opener bids Three Hearts, raise to Four Hearts. If opener bids Three Diamonds (no 4-card Major) or Three Spades, bid Three No Trump.

Responding to a Two-Bid in a Suit

An opening two-bid in a suit is a marathon bid...responder cannot Pass until Game is reached. Use only the first two of Responder's Four Questions when responding to an opening bid at the two-level:

RESPONDER'S QUESTIONS
AFTER AN OPENING TWO-BID

1. CAN I RAISE PARTNER'S MAJOR?
2. DO I HAVE A WEAK HAND (0 - 5 POINTS)?

Let's look at these one at a time.

Question One

Since you are still trying to find a Magic Major Suit Fit where possible, the first question is:

1. CAN I RAISE PARTNER'S MAJOR?

Opener will almost always have a 5-card Major suit if he opens at the two-level (see 'For the Curious'). If you have 3-card support or longer, value your hand using dummy points.

RAISING PARTNER'S OPENING
TWO-BID IN A MAJOR SUIT

• With 6 or more points raise partner's Major to the three-level

Why only the three-level when you know that there is sufficient combined strength for Game? As you will see in the next chapter, there is a good possibility of bidding to a Slam contract when opener starts with a two-bid and you have 6 or more points. Since opener has already taken up some room on the Bidding Ladder by opening at the two-level, you do not want to waste any more of the room that might be needed to explore the possibility of a Slam contract. Remember that opener's two-bid is **forcing to Game**. Neither of you can Pass until Game (at least) is reached.

What if you have 3-card or longer support for partner's Major but less than 6 points? Then go on to Question Two.

Let's look at some examples of the first question in action.

Your partner opens the bidding Two Hearts. What do you respond with the following hands?

1) ♠ 7 3   2) ♠ 3   3) ♠ 7 6 2
   ♥ Q 10 6 3   ♥ A 7 6   ♥ 8 2
   ♦ 9 7 6   ♦ K 5 4 3   ♦ K 9 7 5 4
   ♣ K 8 7 2   ♣ K J 10 7 6   ♣ 10 9 4

1) THREE HEARTS. Can you raise partner's Major? Yes, you have 4-card support. Valuing with dummy points, you have 6 points...5 in high cards and 1 for the doubleton Spade. Raise to the three-level, Three Hearts, to tell partner that you have found a Magic Major Suit Fit.

2) THREE HEARTS. You can support partner's Major and have 14 dummy points... 11 in high cards and 3 for the singleton Spade. You would raise to Three Hearts, even though you know there is enough combined strength for Game. As you will see in the next chapter, there should be enough combined strength for Slam and the first thing you want to do is agree with partner WHERE the final contract will be played. Then you can go exploring to see if you want to be at the six-level or seven-level.

3) Here you can't raise partner's Major. Time to look at the second question.

Question Two

The next question is designed to warn opener when you have a weak hand:

---
2. DO I HAVE A WEAK HAND (0 - 5 POINTS)?

Even if the answer is Yes, you cannot Pass since opener's bid is forcing to Game. You have to make some other bid that will get the message across and allow the auction to continue. The response that is used for this purpose is **Two No Trump**.

This has no relation to whether or not you wish to play in a No Trump contract. A bid used in this fashion is an artificial or conventional bid. It has a special meaning assigned to it by the partnership...a conventional understanding.

RESPONDING TO AN OPENING TWO-BID WITH A WEAK HAND

- With 0 - 5 points respond **Two No Trump** (GO)

Let's look at some examples combining the first two questions.

Your partner opens the bidding Two Spades. What do you respond with the following hands?

1) ♠ 10 7 3 2	2) ♠ 7 2	3) ♠ 7 6 2	4) ♠ 9
♥ A 6 3	♥ 7 6 4	♥ 8 2	♥ J 9 7
♦ 9 7 3	♦ 8 5 4	♦ K 9 7 5 4	♦ K Q 7 5 3
♣ A 8 5	♣ Q 9 8 7 4	♣ J 3 2	♣ Q 6 4 3

1) THREE SPADES. Can you raise partner's Major? Yes, you have 4-card support. With 8 dummy points, you should raise to Three Spades.

2) TWO NO TRUMP. Can you raise partner's Major? No. Do you have a weak hand? Yes, you have 3 points...2 in high cards and 1 for the fifth Club. Respond Two No Trump. This tells opener that you are in the 0 - 5 point range. Remember, opener could have 26 or more points in his own hand.

3) TWO NO TRUMP. Can you raise partner's Major? Yes. However, after valuing with dummy points, you only have 5. Treat this like any other hand with less than 6 points and respond Two No Trump. Since the partnership is forced to Game, you will get an opportunity to show your support after opener makes his rebid. In the meantime, you won't have unduly encouraged him to go exploring for a Slam.

4) Can you support partner's Major? No. Do you have less than six points? No. Time to see what happens if you answer no to both questions.

The Final Choice

If you answered no to both questions, then you:

- Can't raise opener's Major suit
- Have 6 or more points

Since you are already commited to the Game level, you do not need to concern yourself with the level at which you will have to respond. Your remaining choices are:

- Bidding a new suit at the two-level or higher
- Raising opener's Minor suit with 4-card or longer support

Here are some examples. Your partner opens the bidding Two Clubs. What do you respond with the following hands?

1) ♠ 8 7 3	2) ♠ A J 7 5 2	3) ♠ J 9 7 6 2	4) ♠ J 8 4
♥ 8 6 3	♥ 7 6 4	♥ 2	♥ A 9 7
♦ 9 7 6 3	♦ 8 5	♦ K J 7 5 4	♦ Q 5 3
♣ 9 8 5	♣ Q 9 4	♣ 3 2	♣ Q 6 4 3

1) TWO NO TRUMP. Can you raise partner's Major? No, he didn't bid one. Do you have a weak hand? Yes. Respond Two No Trump to tell opener you have a hand of 0 - 5 points.

2) TWO SPADES. You can't raise partner's Major since he didn't bid one. You don't have a weak hand, you have 8 points...7 in high cards and 1 for the fifth Spade. With a 5-card suit of your own, respond Two Spades.

3) TWO SPADES. You can't support partner's Major and don't have a weak hand ...you have 7 points. With a choice of two 5-card suits, bid the higher-ranking suit, Two Spades.

4) THREE CLUBS. You can't raise partner's Major and don't have a weak hand. With 4-card support for partner's Minor suit, you can raise to the three-level, Three Clubs.

Rebids by Opener and Responder

Since the opening two-bid is marathon, opener can use the remainder of the auction to assist responder in determining WHERE and HOW HIGH (Game or Slam). In order to conserve bidding room, both opener and responder can keep the following principle in mind:

> AFTER AN OPENING TWO-BID, ANY BID
> BELOW THE GAME LEVEL IS MARATHON

Slam bidding will be discussed in the next chapter but here are some examples of the continuation of the auction after an opening two-bid.

OPENER	RESPONDER
♠ A K Q 8 5	♠ 6 4
♥ A K J 5	♥ 9 6 4 3
♦ A K 6	♦ 8 7 5 4
♣ 8	♣ 6 3 2
Two Spades	Two No Trump
Three Hearts	Four Hearts
Pass	

With 25 points and an unbalanced hand, opener starts with a two-bid in his longest suit. Responder, with no points, bids Two No Trump. This is the conventional response to keep the auction going while telling opener that responder has 0 - 5 points. Opener can now show his other suit, Hearts, at the three-level. There is no need to jump to Game. Since the Game level has not been reached, responder must bid again. Responder now knows that there is a Magic Major Suit Fit in Hearts and so tells opener WHERE by raising to Four Hearts. Since opener knows that responder has at most 5 points, he is not interested in exploring a Slam contract and is content to Pass.

OPENER	RESPONDER
♠ A 7 5	♠ K 9 8 6 4
♥ A K 3	♥ 6 4 2
♦ A K Q 7 5 3	♦ 5
♣ 6	♣ 9 8 3 2
Two Diamonds	Two No Trump
Three Diamonds	Three Spades
Four Spades	Pass

With 22 points and an unbalanced hand, openerr starts with a two-bid in his longest suit, Two Diamonds. Responder, with only 4 points, bids Two No Trump. Opener, with no second suit to show, rebids his suit, Three Diamonds. Again, there is no hurry to get to Game. Responder, not yet sure of WHERE to play the contract, now has an opportunity to show his suit by bidding Three Spades. Since opener did not have a 4-card Spade suit to bid at his second opportunity, this implies that responder has at least a 5-card suit since he is still looking for a Magic Fit. Opener now knows that there is a Magic Major Suit Fit in Spades and raises responder's Major to the four-level. Since neither opener nor responder has any extra strength, the auction ends at Four Spades.

OPENER	RESPONDER
♠ 5	♠ K Q 9 6
♥ A K Q 7 5	♥ 4 3
♦ A K J 9 6	♦ 10 4 3
♣ A 4	♣ K 6 3 2

OPENER	RESPONDER
Two Hearts	Two Spades
Three Diamonds	Three No Trump
Pass	

With 23 points...21 in high cards and 1 for each of the 5-card suits... opener starts with a two-bid in the higher ranking of his two 5-card suits. Responder, with 8 points, can't support partner's Major and bids his cheapest 4-card suit, Two Spades. Opener can now show his second suit by bidding Three Diamonds. Since responder can't support opener's Major and opener can't support his Major, responder knows that a Magic Major Suit Fit is unlikely. He settles for the most likely Game contract, Three No Trump. Opener, having had an opportunity to describe his hand, has no reason to over-rule responder's decision and the final contract becomes Three No Trump.

Summary

Opening bids at the two-level show powerhouse hands of 22 or more points:

> ### RULE FOR A TWO NO TRUMP OPENING BID
>
> To open the bidding Two No Trump you need:
>
> - A balanced hand and
> - 22, 23 or 24 points

> ### RULE FOR A THREE NO TRUMP OPENING BID
>
> To open the bidding Three No Trump you need:
>
> - A balanced hand and
> - 25, 26 or 27 points

> ## RULE FOR OPENING THE BIDDING
> ## TWO OF A SUIT
>
> With an unbalanced hand of 22 or more points, open the bidding at the two-level in your longest suit.
>
> With two 5-card or 6-card suits, open the higher-ranking suit.
>
> With three 4-card suits, open the middle-ranking suit.

If partner opens the bidding Two No Trump, you can determine the appropriate response as follows:

> ## RESPONSES TO AN OPENING BID OF TWO NO TRUMP
>
> - With 0 - 2 points: Pass.
> - With 3 - 8 points: Bid Four Hearts or Four Spades with a 6-card or longer Major suit. Bid Three Hearts or Three Spades with a 5-card Major suit. Bid Three Clubs (Stayman) with a 4-card Major suit. Otherwise, bid Three No Trump.

If partner opens with a two-bid in a suit, you can determine the appropriate response by asking the following questions:

Question One: CAN I SUPPORT PARTNER'S MAJOR? (You only need 3-card support)

    If the answer is YES: Value your hand using dummy points.

                With 0 - 5 points go on to the next question.

                With 6 or more points, raise to the three-level.

    If the answer is NO: Go on to the next question.

Question Two: DO I HAVE LESS THAN SIX POINTS?

    If the answer is YES: Respond Two No Trump (conventional).

    If the answer is NO: Bid a new suit at the two-level or higher.

                Raise opener's Minor to the three-level with 4-card or longer support.

Exercises

1) You have an opportunity to open the bidding. What would you bid with the following hands?

a) ♠ A K 3
   ♥ K Q 2
   ♦ A K Q 3
   ♣ Q 9 5

b) ♠ A K J 5 2
   ♥ A K 4
   ♦ —
   ♣ A K Q J 4

c) ♠ A
   ♥ A K Q J
   ♦ A 4
   ♣ K Q 9 7 3 2

d) ♠ Q 4
   ♥ A K J
   ♦ A K Q 5 3
   ♣ K Q J

e) ♠ A Q J 7 3
   ♥ A Q 3
   ♦ A K 6 3
   ♣ 5

f) ♠ A 2
   ♥ K 4
   ♦ A Q J 9 6 4 3
   ♣ A Q

g) ♠ A K Q J
   ♥ 2
   ♦ K Q 5 4
   ♣ A K J 2

h) ♠ K 8 4
   ♥ A K 7
   ♦ Q J 3
   ♣ A Q J 3

2) Your partner opens the bidding Two Hearts. What do you respond with the following hands?

a) ♠ J 7 6 3
   ♥ 6 3
   ♦ 7 6 3
   ♣ J 9 8 5

b) ♠ J 7 5
   ♥ A 10 6 4
   ♦ 8 5
   ♣ Q 9 7 4

c) ♠ 9 7 4
   ♥ K 2
   ♦ 7 5 4
   ♣ K Q 7 3 2

d) ♠ K 10 7 2
   ♥ 10 9 7
   ♦ K Q 3
   ♣ J 4 3

e) ♠ 3
   ♥ 6 3
   ♦ Q 9 7 6 3
   ♣ J 9 8 6 5

f) ♠ 7 5
   ♥ 4
   ♦ K Q 9 8 5
   ♣ Q J 9 7 4

g) ♠ —
   ♥ 9 6 4 2
   ♦ Q 5 4 3
   ♣ J 9 7 3 2

h) ♠ A K
   ♥ 9 7
   ♦ 9 7 4
   ♣ Q J 8 6 4 3

3) Your partner opens the bidding Two No Trump. What would you do with the following hands?

a) ♠ K 7 3 2
   ♥ 9 7 5 2
   ♦ 4
   ♣ J 7 3 2

b) ♠ 9 8
   ♥ Q 8 6 4 3
   ♦ K 5 3
   ♣ 8 3 2

c) ♠ 7 6 3
   ♥ 4 2
   ♦ 9 5 4 2
   ♣ 9 6 4 3

d) ♠ K 8 3
   ♥ Q 7 4
   ♦ J 9 6
   ♣ 6 5 4 3

For the Curious

4-4-4-1 Hands

There is only one case where an opening two-bid in a suit does not promise a 5-card suit. With a 4-4-4-1 hand pattern and 22 or more points, opener is neither balanced nor has a 5-card suit. In this case, opener will have to open in a 4-card suit. However, since this is the exception rather than the rule, responder can assume that opener has a 5-card suit.

For example:

♠ A K 7 3
♥ 3
♦ A K J 3
♣ A K J 8

Even though you have no 5-card suit, you do have 23 points. Since your hand is not balanced, you cannot open the bidding with a No Trump bid. You should open the middle-ranking of your three 4-card suits, Two Diamonds.

Responder can use the assumption that opener normally has a 5-card suit to raise with 3-card support. This will often simplify the problem of determining WHERE to play the hand.

Note, because opener bids the **middle** 4-card suit with three 4-card suits:

- A Two Club or Two Spade opening bid always promises a 5-card or longer suit
- A Two Diamond or Two Heart opening bid could be made with a 4-card suit (Diamonds and Hearts are the "middle" suits).

22

Slam Bidding

The earlier analysis of **HOW HIGH** was limited, for simplicity's sake, to the consideration of whether to play in Part-Game or Game. However, as can be seen by looking at the Bidding Ladder, there is nothing to stop the partnership from bidding up to the six-level or even the seven-level.

Going for the Bonus

In addition to the Game bonus, a considerable bonus is awarded for bidding a Small Slam (six-level contract) or a Grand Slam (seven-level contract).

		Trick Score	Game Bonus	Slam Bonus	Total
Not vulnerable Small Slam	Six No Trump	190	300	**500**	990
	Six Spades	180	300	500	980
	Six Hearts	180	300	500	980
	Six Diamonds	120	300	500	920
	Six Clubs	120	300	500	920
Not vulnerable Grand Slam	Seven No Trump	220	300	**1000**	1520
	Seven Spades	210	300	1000	1510
	Seven Hearts	210	300	1000	1510
	Seven Diamonds	140	300	1000	1440
	Seven Clubs	140	300	1000	1440
Vulnerable Small Slam	Six No Trump	190	500	**750**	1440
	Six Spades	180	500	750	1430
	Six Hearts	180	500	750	1430
	Six Diamonds	120	500	750	1370
	Six Clubs	120	500	750	1370
Vulnerable Grand Slam	Seven No Trump	220	500	**1500**	2220
	Seven Spades	210	500	1500	2210
	Seven Hearts	210	500	1500	2210
	Seven Diamonds	140	500	1500	2140
	Seven Clubs	140	500	1500	2140

There is also a risk associated with moving beyond the Game level in search of the big bonus for a *Slam* contract. If you do not make your contract, you lose not only the bonus for making the Slam but also any score you would have received for bidding and making your Game contract. In addition, the opponents receive points for defeating you.

How can you minimize the risk of bidding to a Slam contract and yet take advantage of the opportunities to get a big bonus? You can use the familiar tools, HOW HIGH and WHERE:

THE SLAM DECISIONS

1. HOW HIGH: DO WE HAVE SUFFICIENT COMBINED STRENGTH?
2. WHERE: DO WE HAVE **ANY** MAGIC FIT?

HOW HIGH: Do We Have Sufficient Combined Strength?

The earlier discussions of HOW HIGH were centered on the fact that experience has demonstrated that 26 combined points offer a reasonable play for a Game contract in Hearts or Spades or No Trump. For Slams, experience has shown that:

**33 OR MORE COMBINED POINTS OFFERS A
REASONABLE PLAY FOR A SMALL SLAM CONTRACT
37 OR MORE COMBINED POINTS OFFERS A
REASONABLE PLAY FOR A GRAND SLAM CONTRACT**

Taking Slam bidding into consideration, we modify the Key Question for HOW HIGH:

THE KEY QUESTIONS FOR HOW HIGH:

Do we have 26 combined points?
Do we have 33 combined points?
Do we have 37 combined points?

To decide HOW HIGH, the captain adds up the combined points. With less than 26 points, he wants to play in Part-Game. With 26 - 32 points, he wants to play in Game. With 33 - 36 points, he wants to play in a Small Slam contract. With 37 or more points, he wants to play in a Grand Slam contract.

Sometimes the captain will know the answer to HOW HIGH and sometimes he will need more information.

Here are some examples. Your partner opens the bidding One No Trump. HOW HIGH should you be with each of the following hands?

1) ♠ 6　　　　2) ♠ A K 8 4 3 2　　3) ♠ A Q 8 6 4 3
　♥ Q J 8 5 4 2　♥ A 8 5　　　　　♥ K 9 7
　♦ A K J 3　　　♦ J 3　　　　　　♦ 4
　♣ A 5　　　　　♣ 8 4　　　　　　♣ A J 6

1) HOW HIGH: Small Slam. You have 17 points and your partner is showing 16 to 18. You have at least 33 combined points (16 + 17) and could have 35 points (18 + 17).

2) HOW HIGH: Game. You have 14 points giving your side a combined total of between 30 points (16 + 14) and 32 points (18 + 14). This is enough for Game but not enough for Slam.

3) HOW HIGH: Maybe Slam. With 16 points you know the combined total is between 32 points (16 + 16) and 34 points (18 + 16). You may have enough combined strength for Slam but will need more information from opener. This is similar to the situation when you hold 8 or 9 points and partner opens One No Trump. You know there may be Game but need more information.

WHERE: Do We Have Any Magic Fit?

If you have any Magic Fit, play Slam in the Magic Fit. Otherwise, play Slam in No Trump. At the Slam level, you have to take the same number of tricks whether you play in a Minor suit, Major suit or No Trump. This is different from the Game level. You do not eliminate the possibility of playing in a Magic Fit in a Minor suit.

> PLAY SLAMS IN ANY AVAILABLE MAGIC FIT

For example, suppose partner opens the bidding One Heart and you have:

♠ A K 8 6
♥ A 9 5
♦ A Q 6 4
♣ K 5

Partner has at least 13 points to open the bidding and you have 20 points so there is sufficient combined strength for Slam. Before bidding a Slam, you need to concentrate on determining WHERE the partnership is going to play the hand.

With the above hand, it is possible that you can make a Slam in Spades, Hearts or Diamonds provided you can find a Magic Fit. It is also possible you could make a Slam in No Trump if you can't find a Magic Fit. With so many possibilities, your first task is to look for the appropriate denomination in which to play the contract. The first step is to apply responder's usual questions and bid a new suit at the one-level, One Spade. Perhaps opener will support your suit. Maybe opener will show that he also has a Diamond suit or he might rebid his Heart suit, informing you that there is a Magic Fit in Hearts. As captain, you can decide WHERE to play the Slam after you hear opener's rebid.

Bidding Slam When the Captain Knows HOW HIGH and WHERE

If the captain can count enough combined points for Slam **and** can find a Magic Fit, he can jump directly to the final contract.

For example, your partner opens the bidding One Heart and you hold:

♠ —
♥ A K 8 7 6 4
♦ A Q 8 6 5
♣ Q 4

HOW HIGH: Small Slam. Partner has at least 13 points and you have 21 dummy points...15 HCPs plus 5 for the Spade void and 1 for the doubleton Club... giving you a combined total of at least 34 points.

WHERE: Hearts. You have at least ten Hearts in the combined hands. Knowing both HOW HIGH and WHERE, you would respond Six Hearts.

Another example. Your partner opens the bidding One Club and you hold:

♠ A 9 8
♥ A
♦ A K 8 7
♣ A K 8 5 4

HOW HIGH: Grand Slam. Partner has at least 13 points and you have 25 dummy points...22 HCPs plus 3 for singleton Heart...giving you a combined total of at least 37 points. Note that responder can count dummy points when considering **Slam in a Minor suit** because the short suits will be valuable.

WHERE: Clubs. Since partner must have at least four Clubs, you have found a MAGIC FIT. Knowing both HOW HIGH and WHERE, you can bid Seven Clubs.

One more example. You are South and the auction starts off:

NORTH	EAST	SOUTH	WEST
(Partner)		(You)	
One Diamond	Pass	One Spade	Pass
Three Spades	Pass	?	

You hold:

♠ A Q 8 5 3
♥ 6
♦ A K 3
♣ Q 8 4 2

HOW HIGH: Small Slam. Partner has 17 - 18 points and you have 16. You have 33 or 34 combined points, enough for a Small Slam but not enough for a Grand Slam.

WHERE: Spades. Partner's raise has told you there is a Magic Fit. You would rebid Six Spades.

Bidding Slam When the Captain Knows HOW HIGH but not WHERE

When the captain has a strong hand but is not sure WHERE, he makes a forcing bid to get more information from partner. A new suit by responder at his second turn is marathon:

OPENER	RESPONDER		OPENER	RESPONDER
One Club	One Heart	or	One Diamond	One Spade
One Spade	**Two Diamonds**		One No Trump	**Two Hearts**

Any bid by responder is forcing if opener has made a marathon bid:

OPENER	RESPONDER		OPENER	RESPONDER
One Club	One Spade	or	Two Spades	**Three Clubs**
Two No Trump	**Three Spades**			

Here is an example of how responder goes about determining WHERE. You are South and the bidding starts:

NORTH	EAST	SOUTH	WEST
(Partner)		(You)	
One Diamond	Pass	One Spade	Pass
One No Trump	Pass	?	

You hold:

♠ A K Q 4 3
♥ A 6 5
♦ A 2
♣ K 5 4

HOW HIGH: Small Slam. Partner has 13 - 15 points and you have 21. You have at least 34 combined points, enough for a Small Slam.

WHERE: There might be a Magic Fit in Spades if partner has three of them. Otherwise, you want to play in No Trump. Bid Two Clubs. This is a marathon bid. If opener now bids Two Spades, showing you he has three Spades, bid Six Spades. If opener rebids Two Diamonds, showing he has a 5-card Diamond suit, bid Six No Trump because there is no Magic Fit.

Another example. You are South and the bidding starts:

NORTH (Partner)	EAST	SOUTH (You)	WEST
One Diamond	Pass	One Heart	Pass
Two No Trump	Pass	?	

You hold:

♠ 8 6 2
♥ A Q J 8 3
♦ A 8
♣ Q 4 3

HOW HIGH: Small Slam. Partner has 19 - 21 points and you have 14. You have between 33 and 35 combined points, enough for a Small Slam.

WHERE: There might be a Magic Fit in Hearts if partner has three of them. Otherwise, you want to play in No Trump. Bid Three Hearts. Opener's rebid was a marathon bid so it is not necessary for you to bid a new suit. If opener raises to Four Hearts, bid Six Hearts. If opener bid Three No Trump, there is no Magic Fit so bid Six No Trump.

Inviting Slam When the Captain Knows WHERE but not HOW HIGH

When the captain knows that there are at least 31 points and there may be 33 or more, he wants to make a bid that says "There may be Slam, partner". Since he would sign-off in Game if he wasn't interested in Slam, the captain can invite his partner to bid Slam by bidding beyond the Game level.

> ### BIDDING ONE LEVEL BEYOND GAME
> ### IS A SLAM INVITATION

For example, suppose your partner opens the bidding One Heart and you have:

- ♠ K 7 3
- ♥ A Q 8 4
- ♦ A 8 7 5
- ♣ A 3

HOW HIGH: Maybe Slam. You have 18 dummy points and partner has at least 13. If opener only has 13 or 14 points, there will not be enough combined strength for Slam. However, if opener has 15 or more points, there will be enough for Slam.

WHERE: Hearts. Partner's opening bid tells you that there is a Magic Fit. Bid Five Hearts. This tells partner that you know WHERE...Hearts. By bidding one level beyond Game, you are inviting partner to bid a Slam. As you will see in the next section, partner will bid on to Six Hearts if he has 15 or more points but will Pass with 13 or 14 points.

Another example. You are South and the bidding starts:

NORTH	EAST	SOUTH	WEST
(Partner)		(You)	
One Club	Pass	One Spade	Pass
Two Spades	Pass	?	

You hold:

- ♠ A Q 8 7 4
- ♥ A 10
- ♦ K Q
- ♣ Q 8 6 3

HOW HIGH: Maybe Slam. Opener has 13 - 16 points and you have 18. There are at least 31 combined points and may be as many as 34.

WHERE: Spades. Bid Five Spades. This invites opener to bid Six Spades if he has 15 or 16 points. Opener will Pass with 13 or 14 points.

Here is an example when partner opens the bidding One No Trump. You have:

- ♠ A 4 3
- ♥ K 7 2
- ♦ A K 8 4
- ♣ J 10 9

HOW HIGH: Maybe Slam. Opener has 16 - 18 points and you have 15. You have a combined total between 31 and 33 points.

WHERE: No Trump. There is unlikely to be a Magic Fit, so the contract should be played in No Trump. Bid one level beyond Game, Four No Trump. As you will see shortly, partner will bid Six No Trump if he has 18 points, otherwise he will Pass.

The following example shows how to invite Slam in a Minor suit. Suppose partner opens One Diamond and you have the following hand:

♠ 8 5 4
♥ A K 9
♦ A Q 8 5 4
♣ A 3

HOW HIGH: Maybe Slam. Partner has at least 13 points and you have 18. If partner has 15 or more points, there will be enough for Slam. Otherwise, you want to play in Game.

WHERE: Diamonds or No Trump. If you are going to play in Slam, you should play in the Magic Fit, Diamonds. If you are going to play in Game, you can play in No Trump. If partner opens a Minor suit and you have enough for Game (13 - 16 points) but no 4-card or longer suit other than partner's suit, you raise to Game...Three No Trump. To invite Slam, you bid one level beyond Game. Thus, you bid Four No Trump with the above hand. With 15 or more points, opener can bid Six Diamonds. With only 13 or 14 points, he can play in Game, passing Four No Trump if he prefers No Trump. He can bid Five Diamonds if he prefers to play in a trump suit.

Here is an example of inviting a Slam after making a marathon bid. You are South and the bidding goes:

NORTH (Partner)	EAST	SOUTH (You)	WEST
One Diamond	Pass	One Heart	Pass
One No Trump	Pass	Two Clubs	Pass
Two Hearts	Pass	?	

You have:

♠ 5 2
♥ A K J 9 7
♦ A Q 5
♣ K 9 3

HOW HIGH: Maybe Slam. You have 18 points and partner could have 15 points.

WHERE: Hearts. Using the marathon bid of Two Clubs, a new suit by responder, you have found a Magic Fit. Bid Five Hearts. This will invite partner to bid a Slam.

Here is an example showing how opener can invite a Slam. You open the bidding One Spade with the following hand and your partner raises to Four Spades:

♠ K Q 7 6 4
♥ A Q
♦ K J 6 3
♣ Q 2

HOW HIGH: Maybe Slam. Partner is showing 13 - 16 points and you have 18. There may be enough combined strength for Slam.

WHERE: Spades. Partner's bid shows 4-card or longer support. Bid Five Spades. As you will see next, partner will carry on to Six Spades with 15 or 16 points but Pass with only 13 or 14.

Responding to a Slam Invitation

If your partner makes a Slam invitation, he is saying that your side has at least 31 combined points if you have the minimum number of points you have shown by your bidding so far. If you have some "extra" points, there may be enough for Slam. Thus:

RESPONDING TO A SLAM INVITATION

- With 2 or more "extra" points, **accept** the invitation and bid a Small Slam in the agreed trump suit
- With 0 or 1 "extra" points, **reject** the invitation and settle for Game in the agreed trump suit

---

For example, suppose you open the bidding One Spade and your partner raises to Five Spades. What should you do with the following hand?

♠ K J 9 4 3
♥ A J
♦ K 8 7
♣ 6 5 2

With only 13 points, you have nothing "extra". You should Pass and reject partner's invitation.

On the other hand, suppose the auction went the same way and you held:

♠ A Q 8 6 5
♥ A K 7 5
♦ Q 4
♣ 7 3

You have 16 points...3 "extra" points. Accept partner's invitation and bid a Small Slam in the agreed trump suit, Six Spades.

Another example. You open the bidding One No Trump and your partner bids Four No Trump. What would you do with each of the following hands?

1) ♠ Q 8   2) ♠ K 9 6
   ♥ A J 7 4   ♥ A K 8
   ♦ K J 8 4   ♦ K Q 7 4
   ♣ K Q 7   ♣ Q J 10

1) PASS. You have shown 16 - 18 points with your opening bid of One No Trump. By bidding one level beyond Game, partner is inviting you to bid a Slam. With only 16 points, you have nothing extra, so Pass and reject the invitation.

2) SIX NO TRUMP. This time you have two "extra" points. Accept partner's invitation and bid a Small Slam in No Trump.

Summary

Bidding and making a Slam contract results in a large bonus. When considering bidding a Slam contract, you can use the familiar tools, HOW HIGH and WHERE:

THE SLAM DECISIONS	
HOW HIGH:	33 or more combined points are needed for a Small Slam
	37 or more combined points are needed for a Grand Slam
WHERE:	Play Slam in any Magic Fit, otherwise in No Trump

If you know HOW HIGH and WHERE, you can place the final contract.

If you know there are at least 31 points and may be 33 or more, you can **invite Slam by bidding one level beyond Game.** Partner will accept with two or more "extra" points. Otherwise, he will reject the invitation.

If you are not sure WHERE **make a marathon bid** to get more information from partner.

Exercises

1) You are South and the bidding proceeds:

NORTH (Partner)	EAST	SOUTH (You)	WEST
One Diamond	Pass	One Heart	Pass
Four Hearts	Pass	?	

What do you bid with each of the following hands?

a) ♠ 8 3
  ♥ K 7 3 2
  ♦ K 7 6 5
  ♣ Q J 3

b) ♠ K 3
  ♥ K J 7 6
  ♦ A 7
  ♣ Q 9 6 5 2

c) ♠ A 9 6
  ♥ K 9 5 4 2
  ♦ A 7 6
  ♣ A Q

d) ♠ A 6
  ♥ A Q 7 5
  ♦ 9 5 4 2
  ♣ Q 7 5

2) Your partner opens the bidding One No Trump. Ask yourself HOW HIGH and WHERE to determine your response with each of the following hands:

a) ♠ K 8 3
  ♥ J 3 2
  ♦ K 7 5
  ♣ K J 3 2

b) ♠ A Q 5
  ♥ A J 3
  ♦ K J 8 3
  ♣ 9 3 2

c) ♠ K Q J
  ♥ K Q 2
  ♦ K 10 9 7
  ♣ A 9 3

d) ♠ K 6
  ♥ K Q 5
  ♦ A J 10 3
  ♣ A K J 3

e) ♠ 8 3
  ♥ K J 7 6 3 2
  ♦ K 7 5
  ♣ A 2

f) ♠ A Q 9 8 6 5
  ♥ A J 3
  ♦ 3
  ♣ Q 3 2

g) ♠ Q J 8 7 4 3
  ♥ A
  ♦ K J 6 4
  ♣ A 3

h) ♠ —
  ♥ K Q 5
  ♦ J 10 3
  ♣ A K J 9 6 4 3

3) You open the bidding One Heart and your partner raises to Five Hearts. What do you bid next with the following hands?

a) ♠ A 8
  ♥ K Q J 9 6
  ♦ Q 8 6 3
  ♣ 9 3

b) ♠ K 6
  ♥ A Q 9 5 3 2
  ♦ A Q
  ♣ 5 4 3

For the Curious

Blackwood and Gerber

There are a couple of popular Slam bidding tools that you may encounter. They are difficult for the beginning or average player to use correctly and so we recommend that you avoid using them when first learning the game. Both conventions are designed to find out how many Aces the partnership has. This is to avoid getting to a Slam contract when the opponents can take the first one or two tricks.

The first is the *Blackwood Convention*, named after its inventor — Easley Blackwood of Indianapolis. This convention uses a bid of **Four No Trump** to ask "How many Aces do you have, partner?". The responses are artificial and show the number of Aces held:

Five Clubs:	No Aces (or all Four Aces)
Five Diamonds:	One Ace
Five Hearts:	Two Aces
Five Spades:	Three Aces

The basic mechanics are fairly simple, but there are many pitfalls for the casual player. For example, there is often confusion as to whether Four No Trump is meant as a natural bid (an invitation to Slam) or as the Blackwood Convention.

The second tool is the *Gerber Convention*, named after John Gerber of Houston. It uses a bid of **Four Clubs** to ask for Aces, in a similar fashion to Blackwood. Again, avoid using this convention until you are more familiar with the fundamentals of the game. The methods discussed in this chapter will provide you with everything you need to know to bid Slams successfully on most hands.

23

Pre-Emptive
Opening Bids

There are several advantages to interfering with the opponents' normal bidding sequence during an auction. Having insufficient bidding room on the Bidding Ladder to exchange information, they may:

- Reach the wrong final contract
- Allow you to play the contract when they could have made a contract of their own
- Bid too high in an effort to stop you from buying the contract

In addition, you may convey sufficient information to your partner, through the bids you make, to assist in defeating their contract.

There are some disadvantages to bidding in an effort to interfere with the opponents. They may:

- Double your contract and collect a penalty that is more than sufficient compensation for missing their own contract
- Use the information from your bidding to their advantage during the auction or the play of the hand

It is also possible that, by trying to interfere with the opponents' auction, you may interfere with your own orderly exchange of information and reach an inferior contract. Nonetheless, it is generally to your advantage to compete.

One of the best opportunities you have to interfere with the opponents is when you have an opportunity to open the bidding. While you use the one-level for opening bids with 13 to 21 points and the two-level for opening bids of 22 or more points, there is nothing to stop you from opening the bidding at the three-level or higher in a suit.

Opening bids at the three-level or higher in a suit are called *pre-emptive opening bids* or *pre-empts*. They are used to show hands **too weak** to open the bidding at the one-level (i.e. less than 13 points) and are a defensive action designed to interfere with the opponents' auction.

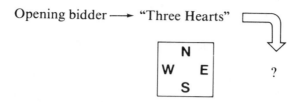

While it is easy to see that opening at the three-level takes a lot of bidding room away from the opponents, what type of hand would you have to have to open the auction at such a high level without the values for an opening bid?

The Requirements for a Pre-emptive Opening Bid

To open the bidding at the three-level or higher in a suit, you need a hand with the following characteristics:

REQUIREMENTS FOR A PRE-EMPTIVE OPENING BID
• **A GOOD SUIT:** At least 3 of the 5 highest cards in the suit
• **A LONG SUIT:** At least a 7-card suit.   — With a 7-card suit, open at the three-level   — With an 8-card suit, open at the four-level   — With a 9-card suit or longer, open at the Game level in your suit (Four Hearts, Four Spades, Five Clubs or Five Diamonds)
• **A WEAK HAND:** 9 - 12 points (not enough to open at the one-level)

The requirement of a good, long suit reduces the risk of a large penalty. If you are doubled and your contract is defeated, the requirement of a weak hand makes it likely that your opponents could have scored as much or more by playing the contract themselves.

Let's look at some examples:

You are the opening bidder. What would you bid with the following hands?

1) ♠ 9
   ♥ 7 6 3
   ♦ A Q J 9 7 6 4
   ♣ 5 4

2) ♠ K 8 7
   ♥ A K J 9 7 6 5
   ♦ 9
   ♣ 6 5

3) ♠ —
   ♥ K 8 7
   ♦ 10 3 2
   ♣ Q J 8 7 5 4 3

4) ♠ K Q J 7 6 4 3 2
   ♥ 4
   ♦ 8 6 5
   ♣ 10

5) ♠ —
   ♥ 5
   ♦ 8 6 5
   ♣ K Q J 8 6 5 4 3 2

6) ♠ Q J 10 8 7 4
   ♥ J 6 4
   ♦ K 7 3
   ♣ 10

1) THREE DIAMONDS. You have a 7-card suit with 3 of the top 5 cards and only 10 points. Open Three Diamonds.

2) ONE HEART. While you have a 7-card suit with 3 of the top 5 cards, you have 14 points... enough to open the bidding at the one-level. If you open with a pre-empt, you will mislead your partner as to the strength of your hand.

3) PASS. Here you have a 7-card suit and only 9 points. However, you only have 2 of the top 5 cards in your suit. With a weak suit, there is too much risk of suffering a large penalty if you are doubled. You should Pass.

4) FOUR SPADES. You have a good, long suit and only 10 points. With an 8-card suit, you open at the four-level, Four Spades.

5) FIVE CLUBS. Here you have 11 points and a good, long suit. With a 9-card suit, open at the Game level in your suit, Five Clubs.

6) PASS. You only have 9 points but you do not have a 7-card suit so you can't open the bidding with a pre-empt.

Responding to a Three-level Pre-emptive Opening Bid

What should you do if your partner opens the bidding at the three-level?

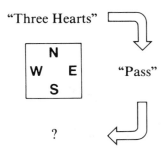

Responder can use his tools, **HOW HIGH** and **WHERE**, to help determine the final contract:

- **WHERE**   Opener is showing a GOOD, LONG suit (7-card suit), so you will usually play in his suit.
- **HOW HIGH**   Opener is showing a WEAK hand (9 - 12 points), so you will usually play in Part-Game.

You can assume that opener has about 10 points, and decide on your response accordingly:

RESPONDING TO A THREE-LEVEL PRE-EMPTIVE OPENING BID

0 - 15 points: Pass (STOP). Game is unlikely.

16 or more points: Raise partner's Major to Game (even with a singleton) (STOP)

                     Bid Four Hearts or Four Spades with a 7-card or longer suit (STOP)

                     Bid Three Hearts or Three Spades with a 5- or 6-card suit (GO)

                     Bid Three No Trump (STOP)

Let's look at some examples.

Your partner opens the bidding Three Diamonds. What would you respond with the following hands?

1) ♠ A J 8 7 3   2) ♠ A K J 8 7 3   3) ♠ A Q 3   4) ♠ A K J 8
    ♥ K 10 8 4   ♥ A K 10 3   ♥ K Q J 9 7 6 3   ♥ K J 8 7
    ♦ 8   ♦ 8 6   ♦ Q 3   ♦ 10 3 2
    ♣ K J 6   ♣ J   ♣ 9   ♣ A Q

1) PASS. You have 13 points. If partner opened the bidding at the one-level, you would get the partnership to Game. However, by opening at the three-level, partner has told you he has a weak hand with as few as 9 points. With less than 16 points, you Pass.

2) THREE SPADES. With 18 points, you have enough to respond. Since partner did not bid a Major, you can still look for a Magic Major Suit Fit when you have a 5- or 6-card Major of your own. Bid Three Spades. Partner will choose between raising your Major and bidding Three No Trump.

3) FOUR HEARTS. Here you have 17 points. With a 7-card Major suit of your own, bid Four Hearts. As long as partner has one or more Hearts, you'll be in a Magic Major Suit Fit.

4) THREE NO TRUMP. You have 18 points. Partner didn't bid a Major and you don't have a 5-card or longer Major of your own. Bid Three No Trump. You are the captain, so opener will accept your decision and Pass.

Responding to a Four-level or Higher Pre-emptive Opening Bid

Eight-card or longer suits are rare, so you won't often encounter a four-level or higher pre-empt.

- If partner opens at the Game level: Pass (STOP)
- If partner opens Four Clubs or Four Diamonds:
  — 0 - 15 points: Pass. Game is unlikely (STOP)
  — 16 or more points: Bid Four Hearts or Four Spades with a 7-card or longer suit (STOP)
  Raise to Five Clubs or Five Diamonds (STOP) (Three No Trump is no longer available)

Rebids by the Pre-emptive Opener

Opener has described his hand so responder is captain:

- If responder bids at the Game level: Pass
- If responder bids a new suit at the three-level:
  — Raise with 3-card support
  — Bid Three No Trump otherwise

For example, you open the bidding Three Diamonds and your partner responds Three Spades. What do you do with the following hands?

1) ♠ 10 7 3   2) ♠ 6
   ♥ 4   ♥ 10 3
   ♦ K Q 10 9 7 5 3 ♦ A K J 8 7 5 2
   ♣ J 6   ♣ 9 7 3

1) FOUR SPADES. With 3-card support, raise to Game... Four Spades.
2) THREE NO TRUMP. With only a singleton in partner's suit, you can't raise. Bid Three No Trump.

What to do if Your Opponent Pre-empts

What do you do when the opponent on your right opens the bidding at the three-level or higher? This bid is designed to create a problem for you and often does. Nonetheless, you can still use all your standard techniques for bidding in competition: the overcall and the take-out double. Because the bidding is already at the three-level, you will have to be a little more cautious.

BIDDING OVER AN OPPONENT'S PRE-EMPTIVE OPENING BID

0 - 15 points:	Pass. You do not have enough strength to start bidding at the three-level
16 - 21 points:	Overcall with a 5-card suit or longer ▼
	Double with support for the unbid suits **GO**
	Overcall Three No Trump with a stopper in the opponent's suit ▼
22 or more points:	Overcall in the opponent's suit (marathon bid) **GO** . Bidding the opponent's suit is called a *cue bid*.

Let's look at some examples.

Your right-hand opponent opens the bidding Three Diamonds. What would you do with the following hands?

1) ♠ K 9 3	2) ♠ A K J 8 6 3	3) ♠ K Q 6 4	4) ♠ K 10 2
♥ A 8	♥ 5 2	♥ A 10 8 5	♥ K J 2
♦ Q 7 5 2	♦ 6	♦ 3	♦ A Q
♣ K Q 4 3	♣ A Q 3 2	♣ A J 6 4	♣ A 10 5 3 2

5) ♠ A K 9
♥ A K J 8
♦ 7
♣ A K Q J 8

1) PASS. You only have 14 points, not enough to start competing at the three-level. The opponent's pre-empt has suceeded in making life difficult for you. If partner has a similar hand, you might miss a Game.

2) THREE SPADES. With 16 points and a 6-card suit, you have enough to overcall Three Spades.

3) DOUBLE. Here you have 17 dummy points and support for the unbid suits. You can make a take-out double and get partner to choose a suit.

4) THREE NO TRUMP. With 18 points, a balanced hand overcall in No Trump. This will land you in Game, but you must take some chances to compensate for the lost bidding room. Your right-hand opponent has shown a hand too weak to open the bidding at the one-level.

With luck partner will have enough of the missing points to enable you to make Game.

While a No Trump overcall at the one-level shows 16 - 18 points, at the three-level it can have a larger upper limit. For example, you would not have room to do much else if you had a balanced hand of 20 points.

5) FOUR DIAMONDS. With 26 points, you would have liked to open at the two-level, Two Clubs, to show a hand of 22 or more points. The opponent's pre-empt has removed this option. To tell partner that you have a hand strong enough to be in Game, even if he has nothing, bid the opponent's suit... Four Diamonds. The **cue bid** of the opponent's suit is a marathon bid. Partner cannot Pass until at least the Game level is reached. With this hand, you are interested in Slam if partner has a good hand.

Responding to Partner's Overcall
After a Pre-emptive Opening

The opponent's pre-empt has left you very little room to explore for the best contract but by using the familiar concepts...HOW HIGH and WHERE...you should be able to respond appropriately. Partner's overcall shows:

- A 5-card or longer suit
- 16 - 21 points

With 0 - 8 points, Game is unlikely as partner is more likely to have 16 or 17 points than 18 or more, so you should Pass. With 9 or more points, choose the best bid, planning to get to Game. If you can raise partner's Major, revalue your hand using dummy points.

RESPONSES AFTER PARTNER OVERCALLS
AN OPPONENT'S PRE-EMPT

0 - 8 points:	Pass.
9 or more points:	Raise partner's Major to Game with 3-card or longer support
	Bid a new suit at the three-level with a 4-card or longer suit
	Bid Three No Trump*

---

* You can choose this response even if you have a 4-card suit to show. There is not much bidding room available, so you will have to do some guessing.

Let's look at some examples.

Your left-hand opponent opens the bidding Three Clubs. Partner overcalls Three Hearts. What would you respond with the following hands?

1) ♠ K 10
   ♥ 9 7
   ♦ Q J 8 6 5
   ♣ 7 6 5 4

2) ♠ 8
   ♥ Q 8 6
   ♦ A 10 6 5 4
   ♣ J 8 5 4

3) ♠ K Q 9 7 6 4
   ♥ 8 5
   ♦ A J 9
   ♣ 10 3

4) ♠ A J 8 6
   ♥ 2
   ♦ K J 8 6 5
   ♣ Q J 3

1) PASS. You only have 7 points. Game is unlikely unless partner has 19 or more points. Pass to avoid getting the partnership too high when partner has only 16 or 17 points.

2) FOUR HEARTS. You have 3-card support for partner's Major so you can revalue using dummy points. In this case, you have 10 points...7 in high cards and 3 for the singleton Spade. Raise to Game, Four Hearts. Even if partner has a minimum hand for his overcall, you should have enough combined strength for Game.

3) THREE SPADES. With 12 points and only two cards in partner's suit, you can bid a new suit at the three-level, Three Spades. Partner may be able to support your suit and you will end up in Four Spades. If partner rebids Three No Trump or Four Hearts, you can Pass, having done your best to get to the right contract.

4) THREE NO TRUMP. Your choice is bidding Three Spades or Three No Trump. Three No Trump is probably best, but it would not be wrong if you chose Three Spades instead.

Responding to Partner's Double
After a Pre-emptive Opening

Since partner's double of a Part-Game contract is a Take-out Double, you can only Pass if partner doubled a Game-level pre-empt or you are very happy defending with your opponent's suit as trump. Otherwise, you must bid, even with no points. Keep in mind that partner's double of a pre-emptive opening bid shows:

- Support for the unbid suits
- 16 - 21 points

You would respond as follows:

> ### RESPONSES AFTER PARTNER DOUBLES
> ### AN OPPONENT'S PRE-EMPT
>
> 0 - 8 points: Bid a 4-card or longer unbid Major suit at the cheapest available level ▼
>
> Bid a 4-card or longer unbid Minor suit at the cheapest available level ▼
>
> 9 or more points: Bid Four Hearts or Four Spades with a 4-card or longer Major 🛑
>
> Bid Three No Trump 🛑

For example, your left-hand opponent opens the bidding Three Hearts. Partner doubles. What would you respond with the following hands?

1) ♠ 9 7 6 5
   ♥ 8 6
   ♦ 10 6 5 4
   ♣ J 4 3

2) ♠ K J 8 2
   ♥ 10 4
   ♦ J 9 7 6 3
   ♣ 5 4

3) ♠ A J 8 4
   ♥ 9
   ♦ 10 7 5
   ♣ A J 9 6 3

4) ♠ 10 4 2
   ♥ A 8
   ♦ Q 9 7
   ♣ K 10 6 5 4

5) ♠ 6 2
   ♥ Q J 9 7 6
   ♦ K 8 4
   ♣ 7 5 4

1) THREE SPADES. Even though you only have 1 point, you cannot Pass. Bid your 4-card Major at the cheapest available level, Three Spades.

2) THREE SPADES. This time you have 6 points. This is not enough to bid Game so bid your 4-card Major at the three-level, Three Spades. Even though you have a 5-card Diamond suit, you still prefer to bid a 4-card Major suit. First, this keeps the bidding at a lower level. Second, if partner has a very strong hand, he may be able to raise to Four Spades which should be an easier contract to make than Five Diamonds.

3) FOUR SPADES. Here you have 11 points. Since partner has at least 16 points, you want to be in Game. With a 4-card Major, bid Game in the Major, Four Spades. This is preferable to Game in your Minor suit, Five Clubs.

4) THREE NO TRUMP. With 10 points and no 4-card Major, bid Three No Trump. Again, this is preferable to Game in a Minor suit, Five Clubs.

5) PASS. On this hand, the opponent has bid your best suit. Pass and convert partner's take-out double into a penalty double. Your trump holding, combined with partner's 16 or more points, should be sufficient to defeat the contract.

Responding to Partner's Three No Trump Overcall

If partner overcalls Three No Trump after an opponent's pre-empt, Pass unless you have a 6-card or longer Major suit. Remember that partner did not have much room and could have an unbalanced hand.

For example, your left-hand opponent opens the bidding Three Hearts. Partner overcalls Three No Trump. What would you respond with the following hands?

1)	♠ K J 8 6 3	2)	♠ Q J 8 6 5 4
	♥ 10		♥ 8 7
	♦ 9 6 5		♦ Q 7 5 2
	♣ J 8 4 2		♣ J

1) PASS. Partner did not make a take-out double so it is unlikely that he is interested in playing in a Spade contract. The opponents have made things difficult for you. Pass and hope that Three No Trump is the best contract.

2) FOUR SPADES. Here you should show your 6-card Spade suit by bidding Four Spades. You'll have to hope that partner has at least two of them.

Responding to Partner's Cue Bid

If partner bids the opponent's suit, he is showing 22 or more points. This is a marathon bid, similar to the opening two-bid in a suit. You cannot Pass. Bid your longest suit, always preferring a Major suit, and continue bidding until Game is reached.

For example, your left-hand opponent opens the bidding Three Clubs and your partner cue bids Four Clubs. What do you respond with the following hands?

1)	♠ 6 5	2)	♠ 9 7 6 5 4	3)	♠ 10 4
	♥ K 9 7 6		♥ K Q 7 3		♥ J 10 6
	♦ J 8 4		♦ 10 7		♦ J 8 7 4 2
	♣ 10 7 4 3		♣ Q 8		♣ 9 6 3

1) FOUR HEARTS. Partner's cue bid forces you to bid. Bid your 4-card Major suit, Four Hearts.

2) FOUR SPADES. Here you have a choice of suits. Bid Four Spades, your longest suit.

3) FOUR DIAMONDS. With no 4-card Major, bid Four Diamonds. If partner rebids Four Hearts or Four Spades, you will Pass. You will also Pass if he raises your suit to Game, Five Diamonds.

We now shift our attention to another opportunity to use pre-emptive bids... when your opponents open the bidding.

Pre-emptive Jump Overcalls

What if your opponents open the bidding and you have a hand with a long suit but less than an opening bid? Since you are not strong enough to overcall, you can make a pre-emptive *jump overcall* to give partner some information and, at the same time, interfere with your opponents' auction. A pre-emptive jump overcall is similar to a pre-emptive opening bid. It shows:

REQUIREMENTS FOR A PRE-EMPTIVE JUMP OVERCALL

- A GOOD SUIT: At least 3 of the 5 highest cards in the suit
- A LONG SUIT: At least a 6-card suit.
  - With a 6-card suit, jump to the two-level*
  - With a 7-card suit, jump to the three-level
  - With an 8-card suit, jump to the four-level
  - With a 9-card suit or longer, jump to the Game level in your suit (Four Hearts, Four Spades, Five Clubs or Five Diamonds)
- A WEAK HAND: 9 - 12 points (not enough to overcall)

---

* Pass if you cannot **jump** to the two-level.

Here are some examples. What would you bid with the following hands if your right-hand opponent opens the bidding One Diamond?

	1)	2)	3)	4)
♠	A 7 3	8 7 3	4	J 9 2
♥	A K J 8 6 3	A K J 8 6 3	K Q J 10 8 7 6	K 9 7 6 5
♦	9 2	9 2	7 3	Q 10
♣	4 3	4 3	10 6 4	Q 7 4

1) ONE HEART. With a 6-card suit and 14 points, you can make a simple overcall at the one-level, One Heart.

2) TWO HEARTS. Here you have a 6-card suit with 3 of the top 5 cards and only 10 points. Jump to Two Hearts. This is a pre-emptive jump overcall.

3) THREE HEARTS. This time you have a 7-card suit, 4 of the top 5 cards and only 9 points. Jump to Three Hearts, the same bid you would make if you had a chance to open the bidding.

4) PASS. With no long suit and less than an opening bid, you should Pass. You don't have the ingredients for either a simple overcall or a jump overcall.

Summary

An opening bid in a suit at the three-level or higher is called a *pre-emptive opening bid*. The primary purpose of a pre-emptive opening bid is to take bidding space away from your opponents. It also gives partner a good description of your hand, in case your side can make something.

REQUIREMENTS FOR A PRE-EMPTIVE OPENING BID ▼

- **A GOOD SUIT:** At least 3 of the 5 highest cards in the suit
- **A LONG SUIT:** At least a 7-card suit.
  - With a 7-card suit, open at the three-level
  - With an 8-card suit, open at the four-level
  - With a 9-card suit or longer, open at the Game level in your suit (Four Hearts, Four Spades, Five Clubs or Five Diamonds)
- **A WEAK HAND:** 9 - 12 points (not enough to open at the one-level)

RESPONDING TO A THREE-LEVEL PRE-EMPTIVE OPENING BID

0 - 15 points:	Pass. Game is unlikely (STOP)
16 or more points:	Raise partner's Major to Game (even with a singleton) (STOP)
	Bid Four Hearts or Four Spades with a 7-card or longer suit (STOP)
	Bid Three Hearts or Three Spades with a 5- or 6-card suit (GO)
	Bid Three No Trump (STOP)

RESPONDING TO A FOUR-LEVEL PRE-EMPTIVE OPENING BID

- If partner opens Four Hearts or Four Spades: Pass
- If partner opens Four Clubs or Four Diamonds:
  —0-15 points: Pass. Game is unlikely.
  —16 or more points: Bid Four Hearts or Four Spade with a
     7-card or longer suit. Raise to Five Clubs or Five Diamonds.

REBIDS BY PRE-EMPTIVE OPENER

- If responder bids at the Game level: Pass.
- If responder bids a new suit at the three-level:
  —Raise with 3-card support.
  —Bid Three No Trump otherwise.

BIDDING OVER AN OPPONENT'S PRE-EMPTIVE OPENING BID

0 - 15 points:	Pass. You do not have enough strength to start bidding at the three-level
16 - 21 points:	Overcall with a 5-card suit or longer
	Double with support for the unbid suits
	Overcall Three No Trump with a stopper in the opponent's suit
22 or more points:	Cue bid the opponent's suit (Marathon bid)

RESPONSES AFTER PARTNER OVERCALLS AN OPPONENT'S PRE-EMPT

0 - 8 points:	Pass. Game is unlikely. Partner is more likely to have 16 or 17 points than 18 or more
9 or more points:	Raise partner's Major to Game with 3-card or longer support
	Bid a new suit at the three-level with a 4-card or longer suit
	Bid Three No Trump

```
┌─────────────────────────────────────────────────────────────┐
│              RESPONSES AFTER PARTNER DOUBLES                  │
│                  AN OPPONENT'S PRE-EMPT                       │
│                                                              │
│  0 - 8 points:         Bid a 4-card or longer unbid Major    │
│                        suit at the cheapest available level   │
│                                                              │
│                        Bid a 4-card or longer unbid Minor    │
│                        suit at the cheapest available level   │
│                                                              │
│  9 or more points:     Bid Four Hearts or Four Spades with   │
│                        a 4-card or longer Major              │
│                                                              │
│                        Bid Three No Trump                     │
└─────────────────────────────────────────────────────────────┘
```

If the opponents open the bidding, you can still take pre-emptive action by making a *pre-emptive jump overcall*.

```
┌─────────────────────────────────────────────────────────────┐
│              REQUIREMENTS FOR A PRE-EMPTIVE                   │
│                     JUMP OVERCALL                            │
│                                                              │
│   • A GOOD SUIT:     At least 3 of the 5 highest             │
│                      cards in the suit                       │
│   • A LONG SUIT:     At least a 6-card suit.                 │
│                      — With a 6-card suit, jump              │
│                         to the two-level                     │
│                      — With a 7-card suit, jump              │
│                         to the three-level                   │
│                      — With an 8-card suit,                  │
│                         jump to the four-level               │
│                      — With a 9-card suit or                 │
│                         longer, jump to the                  │
│                         Game level in your suit              │
│   • A WEAK HAND:     9 - 12 points (not enough to           │
│                      overcall)                               │
└─────────────────────────────────────────────────────────────┘
```

Exercises

1) You are the dealer. What would you bid with each of the following hands?

a) ♠ 3 2
   ♥ 6 3
   ♦ 9 2
   ♣ A Q J 9 5 4 3

b) ♠ 8 7 3
   ♥ J 9 7 5 4 3 2
   ♦ 9 2
   ♣ 3

c) ♠ 4
   ♥ K 4
   ♦ A Q J 9 8 7 3
   ♣ 7 6 4

d) ♠ 9 2
   ♥ K Q J 9 8 5 4 2
   ♦ 9 8
   ♣ 4

e) ♠ 7 3
   ♥ 6
   ♦ 9 7 3
   ♣ A K J 9 5 4 3

f) ♠ A K 3
   ♥ A K Q 5 4 3 2
   ♦ A 2
   ♣ 3

g) ♠ Q 6
   ♥ J
   ♦ A J 7 6 5 4 3
   ♣ 7 6 4

h) ♠ A K J 8 7 6 5 4
   ♥ 5 4 2
   ♦ 8
   ♣ 4

2) Your partner opens the bidding Three Spades. What would you respond with each of the following hands?

a) ♠ 7 3
   ♥ K J 9 6 3
   ♦ 9 2
   ♣ A K J 3

b) ♠ Q 3 2
   ♥ A 9 7 5
   ♦ 2
   ♣ A K 7 6 3

c) ♠ 4
   ♥ K 4
   ♦ 8 7 3
   ♣ A Q J 7 5 4 2

d) ♠ 2
   ♥ A K 8
   ♦ A Q 9 7 6 4
   ♣ J 10 4

3) The opponent on your right opens the bidding Three Hearts. What would you bid with each of the following hands?

a) ♠ 7 3
   ♥ 3
   ♦ A J 2
   ♣ A K J 8 7 5 3

b) ♠ A 8 7 5
   ♥ 7
   ♦ A K Q 2
   ♣ K 8 6 3

c) ♠ K 5
   ♥ A J 10
   ♦ A K Q 7 3
   ♣ Q 6 4

d) ♠ 9 2
   ♥ J 9 8 5
   ♦ A K Q 9
   ♣ K J 4

4) Your right hand opponent opens the bidding One Heart. What would you bid with each of the following hands?

a) ♠ A Q J 7 3
   ♥ 6 3
   ♦ 2
   ♣ A J 8 6 3

b) ♠ K Q J 10 9 3
   ♥ 8 6
   ♦ J 7 2
   ♣ 6 3

c) ♠ 4
   ♥ 9 4
   ♦ 8 7 3
   ♣ A Q J 7 5 4 2

d) ♠ Q 9 7 4 2
   ♥ K 8 4
   ♦ A 7 6 4
   ♣ 4

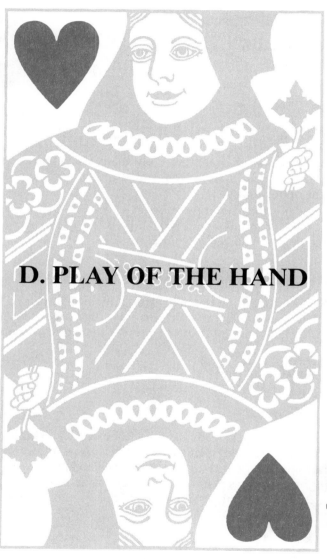

D. PLAY OF THE HAND

24

The Play of the Cards

When studying the play of the cards, keep two things in mind:

- Experience is the best teacher...especially when you add a dash of curiosity. You will increase your skill through playing whenever you get the opportunity.
- Be patient...the play of the cards can provide a lifetime of fascination. Understanding comes gradually so do not expect too much too soon from yourself or your partner.

Basic Ideas About Play

Declarer's objective during the play is to make his contract by taking at least the number of tricks for which his side contracted. The defenders' objective is to take enough tricks to prevent declarer from making his contract.

There are two kinds of tricks:

- Sure Tricks
- Building Tricks

Sure tricks are those tricks you can take without giving up the lead to your opponents. They are ready-made tricks such as Aces and can usually be taken at any time. *Building tricks* are those that you have to work a little to get. There are many ways to build tricks. Leaving considerations of trump suits aside for the moment, let's look at examples of both types of trick.

Sure Tricks

How do you know how many sure tricks you have in a suit? Here are some examples of counting sure tricks from a combined holding in a suit:

1)   DUMMY: 4 3
             DECLARER: A 2
               (You)

With this combination of cards in a suit, you can take only one trick, with the Ace. The opponents have the rest of the high cards with which to win the remaining tricks.

2) DUMMY: 6 5 3

    DECLARER: A K 2
    (You)

Here you can take two tricks, one with the Ace and one with the King.

3) DUMMY: 7 6 3

    DECLARER: A K Q
    (You)

With the Ace, King and Queen, you can take three sure tricks.

4) DUMMY: K 6 3

    DECLARER: A Q 7
    (You)

This is the same as the previous example except that one of the high cards, the King, is located in the dummy. It doesn't matter in which order you take the tricks. For example, you could take the Ace first, then play your Seven and win the trick with dummy's King, then lead dummy's remaining card and win the trick with the Queen in your hand. Or you could win the first trick with the Queen, the second trick with the Ace and the third trick with dummy's King.

5) DUMMY: K Q

    DECLARER: A 3
    (You)

In this case, you can take only two sure tricks even though you have the Ace, King and Queen. Why? When you play the Ace, you will have to also play the Queen from dummy since dummy has no small cards. Now you will have only the King left to take a second trick.

6) DUMMY: A K Q J 10

    DECLARER: 7 6 5
    (You)

Holding the Ace, King, Queen, Jack and Ten you will take five sure tricks.

7) DUMMY: Q 3

    DECLARER: A K 4
    (You)

Sometimes, as in this example, the way the cards are distributed between the two hands will affect the order in which you play the high cards. If you take your tricks with the Ace and King first, you will have to play your Queen on one of these tricks. This happens because the suit is not of equal length in both hands. Use the guideline:

TAKE YOUR TRICKS IN THE SHORT HAND FIRST

In the above example, win the trick with dummy's Queen first. Now you can lead dummy's Three back to your Ace and King to win two more tricks.

Entries

When you have a choice of winning a trick in dummy or in your own hand, there is sometimes an advantage to winning the trick in a particular hand. You may want to lead a suit starting from the dummy or you may want to have the lead in your own hand. Used in this way, sure tricks can represent *entries* from one hand to the other. The value of entries will be seen when we discuss planning the play.

Building Tricks by Promoting Cards

One of the ways to build tricks is through the *promotion* of cards. The basic idea is that a card is turned into a sure trick when all the higher-ranking cards in that suit have been played. Here are some examples.

1) DUMMY: 4 3 2
    DECLARER: K Q J
    (You)

Lead the King to force the opponents to play their Ace, if they want to win the trick. Now you have built two sure tricks by promoting the Queen and the Jack. They are now the highest-ranking cards remaining in the suit.

2) DUMMY: J 3
    DECLARER: K Q 2
    (You)

In this example, the high cards are not in the same hand. You can still promote two tricks by driving out the opponents' Ace, but because you don't have the same length in both hands, be careful of the order in which you play your high cards. Use the Jack first to drive out the Ace, following the principle of playing the high cards from the short hand first.

3)   DUMMY: 6 5 4

             DECLARER: Q J 10
             (You)

In this example, you are missing both the Ace and the King. You can still promote a trick with a little work. Lead your Queen to drive out the opponents' Ace or King. Next time you have an opportunity, lead the Jack to drive out the opponents' remaining high card. Now, because you have the Ten, you have built a trick in the suit.

4)   DUMMY: 5 4 3 2

             DECLARER: J 10 9 8
             (You)

This time you'll have to be very patient. The opponents have the Ace, King and Queen. Use your Jack to drive out one of their high cards, your Ten to drive out another and your Nine to drive out the remaining high card. Eventually, you will have established your Eight as the highest card remaining in the suit.

Building Tricks in Long Suits

Another way to build tricks is to use your long suits to *establish* extra tricks. Let's look at some examples of how this is done.

1)   DUMMY: 6 5 4 3

             DECLARER: A K 7 2
             (You)

Here you already have two sure tricks in the suit, the Ace and King. You also have eight cards in the suit which means that the opponents have only five between them (13 - 8 = 5). In most cases, the five outstanding cards will be divided between the opponents: three in one hand and two in the other. How does this help you? After you take tricks with the Ace and King there will only be one high card left in the opponents' hands. If you lead the suit again, playing little cards from both hands, you'll lose the trick to the opponents. However, when you next regain the lead, you will be able to take a trick with your remaining card because the opponents will have no cards left in the suit. In effect, you have promoted your little cards by getting rid of all the cards in the opponents' hands.

For this to work, the five cards held by the opponents will have to be divided three and two. You will be able to tell if this is the case. If both opponents follow suit when you play the Ace and King, you will know there is only one card outstanding. If either opponent discards when you are playing the Ace and King, you will know that the opponents' cards are not divided three and two so this method of building an extra trick won't work.

2)   DUMMY: 7 5 4 3

            DECLARER: A 8 4 2
            (You)

Here you have one sure trick, the Ace, but again you have eight cards in the suit. If the five outstanding cards are divided three and two, you can still build a second trick in the suit. Take a trick with the Ace and then give the opponents a trick. When you next have a chance to lead, lead the suit again and give the opponents another trick. When you have an opportunity to lead the suit for the fourth time, the opponents will have no cards left in that suit and so you will win a second trick.

3)   DUMMY: 7 5 4 3

            DECLARER: 9 8 6 2
            (You)

At first glance, this suit might seem useless as a source of tricks since you have no high cards. You do, however, have some length. Be patient...after you have led the suit three times you should have a trick...as long as the opponents' cards are distributed three and two.

4)   DUMMY: 5 4 3

            DECLARER: A K 7 6 2
            (You)

Again you have eight cards in the suit and the opponents have only five. This time you have an opportunity to build two additional tricks in the suit. If the five outstanding cards are divided three and two, there will be only one card outstanding after you take the first two tricks with the Ace and King. You can lead the suit a third time to drive out the opponents' remaining card. Next time you have the lead, you will have two cards remaining in the suit, each of which will win a trick when you play it.

Even if the outstanding cards are divided four and one, you can still build one additional trick. After taking the Ace and King, you will have to give up two tricks to the opponent who started with four cards but eventually your fifth card in the suit will become a winning trick.

5)   DUMMY: K 4

            DECLARER: A 7 6 5 2
            (You)

This is similar to the preceding example except that you only have seven cards between the combined hands. There are six cards outstanding in the opponents' hands (13 - 7 = 6). There are still good possibilities for building extra tricks. Win the first trick with dummy's King and then lead dummy's Four to your Ace. Now watch what happens when you lead the suit a third time. If the six outstanding cards are divided three and three, both the opponents' remaining high cards will fall together when they win this trick. This means that your remaining two cards will both be built into sure tricks.

If, as is more likely, one opponent started with four cards in the suit and the other with only two, you will have to give up another trick and end up with only one extra trick. However, that is better than just having the two sure tricks you started with. If one opponent has five or all six of the outstanding cards, you will have to settle for your original two sure tricks.

Note that it is important to win the first trick in the short hand. If you win the first trick with your Ace and then lead a little card to dummy's King, you will be unable to immediately lead the suit a third time. You want to end up in the long hand.

6)   DUMMY: K 7 5 2
        DECLARER: A 4 3
          (You)

You have seven cards in the suit, leaving six in the opponents' hands. You can try and build an extra trick by taking your two sure tricks and leading the suit a third time. If the outstanding cards are divided three and three, you will establish dummy's final card in the suit as a winner. Of course, if either opponent has four or more of the outstanding cards, this will not work.

When considering building tricks through length, it is useful to have an idea how the outstanding cards in the suit will be divided in the opponents' hands. As a general guideline: **if the opponents have an odd number of cards, they will divide evenly; if the opponents have an even number of cards, they will divide unevenly**.

NUMBER OF OUTSTANDING CARDS	MOST LIKELY DISTRIBUTION
3	2 - 1
4	3 - 1
5	3 - 2
6	4 - 2
7	4 - 3
8	5 - 3

Building Tricks by Trapping the Opponents' High Cards — The Finesse

Another way to build tricks is by *trapping* the opponents' high cards. For this to work, you need the proper technique and some luck. Here are some examples.

1)   DUMMY: K 5

         DECLARER: 4 2
         (You)

If you lead the King, the opponents will play the Ace and you will lose the trick. Since you don't have the Queen, you will end up taking no tricks in the suit. There is a chance, however, to win a trick with your King.

Instead of leading the King, you can lead a small card from your hand **toward** the King and give yourself a 50% chance of winning a trick. When you lead the Two from your hand first, the opponent on your left must play before you have to choose a card from the dummy. If your left-hand opponent has the Ace and plays it, you can play your Five from dummy and save the King to take a trick later. If your left-hand opponent has the Ace but doesn't play it, you can play dummy's King on this trick. This will win the trick since your right-hand opponent does not have a higher card. This kind of play is called a *finesse*. In a finesse, you almost always lead **toward** your high card(s).

What if your right-hand opponent has the Ace? Then, when you lead your Two and try to take a trick with your King, your right-hand opponent will play the Ace and you will lose the trick. This is why there is only a 50% chance of winning a trick with your King. Half the time your left-hand opponent will have the Ace...the other half of the time your right-hand opponent will have the Ace. Still, a 50% chance is better than none.

2)   DUMMY: 5 4 2

         DECLARER: K Q 3
         (You)

With both the King and Queen, you can build one trick through promotion. You could lead the King or Queen and drive out the opponents' Ace, establishing your remaining high card as a trick. But you can give yourself an opportunity to win two tricks by leading **toward** your high cards. Lead a small card from the dummy. If your right-hand opponent has the Ace and plays it, you can play your little card from your hand and have two sure tricks for later, the King and the Queen. If your right-hand opponent doesn't play his Ace, you can play the King or Queen and win the trick. Now the situation is similar to the first example. You can go back to the dummy using another suit and lead toward your remaining high card. Again your right-hand opponent has to play first. Of course, if your left-hand opponent has the Ace, he will be able to put it on your King or Queen and keep you to one trick.

3) DUMMY: A Q
 DECLARER: 4 3
 (You)

In this example you have the Ace and Queen but you are missing the King. If you play the Ace and then lead the Queen, your opponents will win the second trick with their King. How can you give yourself a chance to win two tricks with your Ace and Queen? Lead the Three from your hand toward the dummy. Your left-hand opponent plays before you choose the card to play from dummy. If he has the King and plays it, you can win the trick with your Ace and the Queen is now established as a second trick. If your left-hand opponent has the King and doesn't play it, playing a small card instead, you can win the trick by playing the Queen from dummy and will still have the Ace left to win a second trick.

Of course, if your right-hand opponent started with the King, he will be able to win the trick when you play dummy's Queen and keep you to one trick. Still, since your left-hand opponent will have the King half of the time, you will profit in the long run by leading toward this combination rather than taking just one sure trick with the Ace.

4) DUMMY: A Q J
 DECLARER: 7 3 2
 (You)

Here you could take two tricks by leading the Ace and then leading the Queen to force out the opponents' King and build your Jack as a second trick. However, you might be able to take three tricks if you lead toward your high cards twice. Lead the Two from your hand and, if your left-hand opponent plays a little card, **finesse** dummy's Jack. If your right-hand opponent doesn't have the King, the Jack will win the trick. Now come back to your hand using another suit and lead another small card toward the dummy. By making your left-hand opponent play before you do, you will get three tricks any time he has the King. Of course, if your right-hand opponent has the King, you will only get the two sure tricks you started with.

5) DUMMY: A 7 5
 DECLARER: Q J 10
 (You)

How about this combination of cards? You could build one extra trick by playing the Ace then leading the Queen or Jack to drive out the King. This gives you two tricks. Is there any way to win three tricks?

Suppose you lead the Queen **from your hand toward** the Ace in dummy. If your left-hand opponent has the King and doesn't play it, you can play a small card from dummy and your Queen will win the trick. If he plays the King, you will play the Ace. You have trapped his King.

If your right-hand opponent has the King, the finesse will not work. When you lead the Queen and play a little card from dummy, your right-hand opponent will win with King and keep you to two tricks. However, playing the cards in this way does give you a 50% chance of getting three tricks.

6)	DUMMY:	A 7 5
	DECLARER:	Q 3 2
	(You)	

This situation may look similar to the previous example. But look what happens if you lead the Queen toward dummy's Ace. If your left-hand opponent has the King, he can play it on your Queen and make you take the Ace to win the trick. Now you have nothing left but small cards. If your right-hand opponent has the King, he will capture your Queen with it and you will still only take one trick in the suit.

What is the difference between this example and the previous one? In the previous example, you had the Queen, the Jack and the Ten. You could afford to have your left-hand opponent play the King when you led the Queen because this would promote tricks for your side. In this example, you cannot afford to have your left-hand opponent *cover* your Queen with his King because that would promote tricks for the opponents, not you.

Instead, you should win the first trick with the Ace and then lead **toward** your Queen. If your right-hand opponent has the King, he will have to play before you do and you will be able to win a trick with your Queen. Of course, if your left-hand opponent has the King, this will not work. But, as you have seen, leading the Queen first would not work either.

As a general guideline in these situations:

> LEAD A HIGH CARD IF YOU CAN AFFORD TO HAVE
> THE OPPONENT COVER IT WITH A HIGHER CARD.
> OTHERWISE, LEAD TOWARD YOUR HIGH CARD.

Building Tricks by Trumping Losers

The techniques discussed so far work very well in No Trump contracts. They will also work in trump contracts but, if you are playing in a trump contract, there is the danger that the opponents will be able to take tricks by trumping your high cards. You will find out what to do about this danger in the next chapter. For now, we will look at how you can take extra tricks by **trumping your losers**. A *loser* is a trick that the opponents might take. For example, suppose Spades are the trump suit and this is your combined holding in Spades and Hearts:

DUMMY: ♠ 8 7 6
                ♥ 6 3

DECLARER: ♠ A K Q J 10
(You)   ♥ 4 2

In the Heart suit, you have two losers. The opponents can win the first two Heart tricks. If they try and take any more Heart tricks, you can win the trick by trumping. That is the advantage of playing in a trump contract.

Notice that you have **five** sure Spade tricks in the above example. Sometimes it is possible to build extra tricks using the trump suit. Suppose we change the example slightly:

DUMMY: ♠ 8 7 6
                ♥ 3

DECLARER: ♠ A K Q J 10
(You)   ♥ 4 2

You still have two potential Heart losers in your hand. However, because dummy has only one Heart, the opponents can only take one trick in the suit. If they lead the suit a second time, you can trump with one of dummy's Spades. Notice that you will now win **six** Spade tricks: you win one trick with dummy's trump and still have five sure Spade tricks.

> ### YOU CAN BUILD EXTRA TRICKS BY TRUMPING
> ### LOSERS WITH DUMMY'S TRUMPS

Why do we emphasize trumping losers with dummy's trumps and not with declarer's trumps? Let's modify the above example again:

DUMMY: ♠ 8 7 6
                ♥ 6 3

DECLARER: ♠ A K Q J 10
(You)   ♥ 2

Again the opponents can only take one Heart trick. If they try and take a second trick you can trump with one of your Spades. But you will win only **five** Spade tricks: you used one of your trumps and have four remaining sure tricks.

The key to building extra tricks using trumps is to trump in the hand with the shorter trump suit. This will usually be dummy. In general, **avoid going out of your way to trump in the long hand** as it will not gain you any extra tricks. Of course, in the last example, you had to trump to prevent the opponents from winning two Heart tricks.

Here are some more examples of trumping losers. In each case, Spades are the trump suit.

1) DUMMY: ♠ J 7 6
                      ♥ 4

    DECLARER: ♠ A K Q 10 9
    (You)   ♥ A 3

You have a potential loser in the Heart suit. If you take your five sure tricks in Spades and then your Ace of Hearts, you will end up with six tricks. If instead you first take a trick with the Heart Ace, dummy will now have a void (no cards remaining in the suit). You can now lead your Heart loser and put one of dummy's trumps on it. By doing this, you will end up winning seven tricks. It is important that you trump your loser in dummy **before** you take all your sure tricks in Spades, otherwise dummy will have no Spades left with which to trump your loser.

2) DUMMY: ♠ 8 7 6
                      ♥ 6 3

    DECLARER: ♠ A K Q J 10
    (You)   ♥ 5 4 2

With three potential Heart losers, you can eliminate one of them with a little work. You will have to give two Heart tricks to your opponents, but then dummy will be void and you can lead your remaining loser and make an extra trick by trumping it with one of dummy's Spades.

Summary

The objective during the play is to take tricks. There are two types of tricks:

- *sure tricks* which you can take without giving up the lead to your opponents
- *building tricks* which may be developed with a little work by:
  — *promoting* cards
  — *establishing* long suits
  — *finessing*…trapping opponents' high cards
  — *trumping* losers

When building tricks, keep the following in mind:

- Take your tricks in the short hand first
- Lead a high card if you can afford to have the opponent put a higher card on it. Otherwise lead toward your high card.
- Trump losers in the hand with short trumps, usually the dummy. Don't go out of your way to trump in the long hand.

Exercises

1) How many sure tricks do you have in the following suit combinations?

DUMMY:	a) K Q 8	b) A 9 8 3	c) A Q	d) 5 4 2
DECLARER: (You)	A 8 2	K 4	K J	A K Q J 7 3

2) What is the maximum number of tricks you could take with the following suits? How would you play them to try and take the maximum number of tricks?

DUMMY:	a) K J 8	b) K 2	c) J 10 9 4 3	d) A 5 4 2
DECLARER: (You)	Q 7 3	Q J 10 9 3	Q 6 2	7 6 5 4

DUMMY:	e) 7 5 3	f) 9 7 4	g) K 6 3	h) 5 4 2
DECLARER: (You)	A 8 6 5 2	10 8 6 5 3 2	5 4 2	A Q 6 3

25

Planning the Play

Suppose you open the bidding One No Trump and everyone says Pass. Now you are declarer in a contract of One No Trump. West, your left-hand opponent, leads the Queen of Spades and your partner puts his hand down as dummy:

DUMMY:

♠ K 7 5 2
♥ Q 2
♦ 6 5 4
♣ 7 6 4 3

♠ Q
(Opening Lead)

```
      N
   W     E
      S
```

DECLARER:
(You)

♠ A 4 3
♥ A K 3
♦ K Q J
♣ 9 8 5 2

How do you, as declarer, go about playing the hand to make the contract? Playing a bridge hand is no different than any other undertaking. You must make a plan. Declarer's Four Questions will guide you in planning the play:

DECLARER'S FOUR QUESTIONS

1. HOW MANY TRICKS DO I NEED?
2. HOW MANY SURE TRICKS DO I HAVE?
3. HOW CAN I BUILD EXTRA TRICKS?
4. HOW DO I PUT IT ALL TOGETHER?

Question One

> **1. HOW MANY TRICKS DO I NEED?**

Finding the answer is straightforward:

- Add 6 tricks (book) to the level of your contract

For example, if your contract is Three No Trump, you need 6 + 3 = 9 tricks. If your contract is Four Hearts, you need 6 + 4 = 10 tricks. In the sample hand above, your contract is One No Trump and you need 6 + 1 = 7 tricks.

Question Two

Having established your objective, it's time to examine how close you are to achieving it.

> **2. HOW MANY SURE TRICKS DO I HAVE?**

Look at the combined holding in each suit and then add together the number of sure tricks in each suit to come up with the total number of sure tricks.

Let's add up the sure tricks in the sample hand:

DUMMY:
- ♠ K 7 5 2
- ♥ Q 2
- ♦ 6 5 4
- ♣ 7 6 4 3

DECLARER:
(You)
- ♠ A 4 3
- ♥ A K 3
- ♦ K Q J
- ♣ 9 8 5 2

You have two Spade tricks...the Ace and the King...and you have three Heart tricks...the Ace, King and Queen. Even though you have the King, Queen and Jack of Diamonds, you do not yet have any **sure tricks** in that suit...the opponents have the Ace. Similarly, you do not have any sure tricks in the Club suit...the opponents have the Ace, King, Queen, Jack and Ten. Adding up your sure tricks you have a total of five, two in Spades and three in Hearts.

You have five sure tricks; should you take them right away? No! First you must look at the objective you established with Question One...to win seven tricks to make your contract of One No Trump. If you have enough tricks to reach your objective, then take them and make your contract. However, in the majority of cases, you will not have enough sure tricks ...there will be work to do to build tricks. If this is the case, you should generally not take your sure tricks as that will not help you to reach your objective. It may instead help the opponents achieve their objective, which is to take enough tricks to defeat the contract.

In the example hand above, if you immediately take the Queen, King and Ace of Hearts, you will have taken three tricks but, at the same time, you will have established any remaining Hearts in the opponents' hands as sure tricks. Instead, you should hold on to these sure tricks for now and move on to the next question.

Question Three

The third question is used to determine how you can close the gap between the number of tricks you need (Question One) and the number of sure tricks you have (Question Two):

> 3. HOW CAN I BUILD EXTRA TRICKS?

Look at each combined suit and see if any of the basic methods of building extra tricks can be used:

- Promoting cards
- Establishing long suits
- Trapping opponents' high cards
- Trumping losers

Which of these methods can be used in the example hand?

DUMMY:	♠ K 7 5 2
	♥ Q 2
	♦ 6 5 4
	♣ 7 6 4 3

```
        N
     W     E
        S
```

DECLARER:	♠ A 4 3
(You)	♥ A K 3
	♦ K Q J
	♣ 9 8 5 2

When you examine each suit combination in turn, you see that there are three possibilities for building extra tricks. In the Spade suit, you could take your two sure tricks and then lead the suit a third time. If the outstanding cards are divided three and three, you will be able to establish dummy's fourth Spade as an additional trick. In Hearts you are already counting on your three sure tricks... there is no possibility for more. In the Diamond suit, you could use the King to drive out the opponents' Ace and thereby promote the Queen and Jack. In the Club suit, there is the possibility of establishing a trick from your length by leading the suit three times. No suit offers the possibility of trapping an opponent's high card and of course you cannot trump losers because you are playing in No Trump.

Having looked at the possible ways you could build extra tricks, it is time to move on to the final question.

Question Four

Question Four links together all the information gathered from the first three questions and puts it into a plan for playing the hand:

> **4. HOW DO I PUT IT ALL TOGETHER?**

From Questions One and Two you know you need to build two extra tricks in order to make your contract. From Question Three you know what ways are available to build the extra tricks. Question Four requires that you choose the way that gives you the best chance of building the necessary extra tricks. Let's see how this works with the sample hand.

DUMMY:
♠ K 7 5 2
♥ Q 2
♦ 6 5 4
♣ 7 6 4 3

♠ Q
(Opening Lead)

DECLARER:
(You)
♠ A 4 3
♥ A K 3
♦ K Q J
♣ 9 8 5 2

In answering the fourth question, you choose the approach that offers the best chance of success. Building an extra trick in the Spade suit will only work if the opponents' cards are divided three and three... not too likely.

Besides, that will only develop one trick. Likewise, the Club suit will only provide one additional trick and requires that the opponents' cards be divided three and two. The Diamond suit represents the best choice. It can provide both the extra tricks needed and is certain to succeed since it doesn't depend on a favorable distribution of the opponents' cards.

After reaching this conclusion, you make your plan. Your left-hand opponent has led the Queen of Spades. You can win this trick with the Ace and set about building the extra tricks needed by leading Diamonds. Once you have driven out the opponents' Ace, you will have built enough tricks to make your contract. When you next regain the lead, you will be able to take your second Spade trick, your three sure Heart tricks and your two established Diamond tricks, for a total of seven tricks.

There is nothing to worry about when you let the opponents win a trick with their Ace of Diamonds. If they lead Spades, you have the King left to win the trick. If they lead Hearts, you have the three top tricks in that suit. If they lead Diamonds, you have your two established tricks. If they lead Clubs, there are only five cards outstanding. They could only take five tricks if all of them were in one hand. Even so, this would not be enough to defeat your contract. More likely, if the Clubs are divided three and two and they take their three tricks, they will establish an extra Club trick for you!

Another Example in No Trump

Here's another example of the use of Declarer's Four Questions. This time you are in a contract of Three No Trump.

DUMMY: ♠ 7 5 2
              ♥ 8 3
              ♦ K 9 2
              ♣ A K 6 4 3

♦ Q   ┌─ N ─┐
(Opening Lead) │ W   E │
              └─ S ─┘
DECLARER: ♠ A K 4 3
(You)   ♥ A Q 4
              ♦ A 7 3
              ♣ 8 5 2

Question One: HOW MANY TRICKS DO I NEED?

- Three No Trump = 6 + 3 = 9 tricks

Question Two: HOW MANY SURE TRICKS DO I HAVE?

- Spades: 2 - the Ace and King
- Hearts: 1 - the Ace
- Diamonds: 2 - the Ace and King
- Clubs: 2 - the Ace and King
- A total of 7 tricks

Question Three: HOW CAN I BUILD EXTRA TRICKS?

- Spades: By playing the Ace and King and then giving the opponents a trick, the fourth Spade will become established as a trick if the opponents' Spades are divided three and three.
- Hearts: By leading from dummy and finessing the Queen you may get an extra trick by trapping your right-hand opponent's King.
- Diamonds: There is no way to build any extra tricks.
- Clubs: By playing the Ace and King and then giving the opponents a trick, two extra tricks will be built if the outstanding Clubs are divided three and two.

Question Four: HOW DO I PUT IT ALL TOGETHER?

- Two extra tricks must be built. Both the Heart suit and the Spade suit can only provide one extra trick. You would have to be successful in building an extra trick in both cases in order to get the two tricks needed. The Club suit seems to offer the best possibility for providing both extra tricks.
- Since the opponent has lead the Queen of Diamonds, you should win a Diamond trick and immediately start to build your extra tricks in the Club suit. Be careful! If you win the first Diamond trick with dummy's King, after you have built the two extra Club tricks, you will have no way to get to dummy to lead them! Win the first trick with your Ace. You will then be able to use dummy's King as an **entry** to the dummy to take your two Club tricks.

Answering the fourth question is not always easy because you may have a number of choices. If you are in doubt, here are some guidelines:

> ## GUIDELINES FOR PLAYING NO TRUMP CONTRACTS
> - Take your tricks when you have enough to make your contract
> - Build the tricks you need for your contract before taking your sure tricks
> - Find the longest combined suit and play it first
> - Watch your entries to be sure that you can get to the hand from which you want to lead to the next trick

Play in a Trump Contract

When you are playing in a trump contract, you can still use Declarer's Four Questions to guide you. Here is an example.

You open the bidding One Heart, your partner raises you to Four Hearts and this is followed by three Passes. Your left-hand opponent leads the King of Diamonds and your partner puts his hand down as dummy:

DUMMY:
- ♠ 6 3 2
- ♥ K Q J 2
- ♦ 9 7 4
- ♣ A K 4

♦ K
(Opening Lead)

	N	
W		E
	S	

DECLARER:
(You)
- ♠ A 7
- ♥ A 10 9 7 6
- ♦ A 8 3
- ♣ Q 7 2

Question One: HOW MANY TRICKS DO I NEED?

- Four Hearts = 6 + 4 = 10 tricks

Question Two: HOW MANY SURE TRICKS DO I HAVE?

- Spades: 1 - the Ace
- Hearts: 5 - the Ace, King, Queen, Jack and Ten
- Diamonds: 1 - the Ace
- Clubs: 3 - the Ace, King and Queen
- Total: 10

Question Three: HOW CAN I BUILD EXTRA TRICKS?

- In this hand you do not need any extra tricks, you already have ten sure tricks.

Question Four: HOW DO I PUT IT ALL TOGETHER?

- This hand looks straight-forward as you already have the ten sure tricks you need to make your contract. But be careful. Playing with a trump suit is a double-edged sword. If you win the first trick with the Ace of Diamonds and immediately try to take your sure Club tricks, there is some possibility that one of your opponents has only one or two Clubs and will be able to win one of the tricks by playing a trump to it. Then you would no longer have ten tricks.
- How can you avoid this? Play the trump suit first until the opponents no longer have any left. It will then be safe to take your Club tricks. This process of exhausting the opponents of their trumps is called *drawing trumps*.
- In this hand, you win the first trick with your Ace of Diamonds and immediately start taking some of your Heart tricks. You have nine Hearts so the opponents have four (13 - 9 = 4). You need to play Hearts until all four of the missing trumps have appeared. This may happen after two tricks if each opponent started with two trumps, or may take three or four tricks if one opponent started with three or four trumps. After drawing trumps, you can safely take your remaining sure tricks and make your contract.

Drawing Trump

The decision as to whether or not to draw the opponents' trumps is an important one in the play of a suit contract. You want to draw the opponents' trumps whenever possible so that they will not be able to trump any of your winning tricks. On the other hand, you want to keep sufficient trumps in the combined hands to trump losers and to stop the opponents from taking winning tricks in other suits.

Let's look at another example. You open the bidding One Spade, your partner raises you to Two Spades and this is followed by three Passes. Your left-hand opponent leads the King of Diamonds and your partner puts his hand down as dummy:

DUMMY:

- ♠ J 10 5 2
- ♥ 7 2
- ♦ 9 7 4
- ♣ A 8 4 3

♦ K
(Opening Lead)

```
      N
  W       E
      S
```

DECLARER:
(You)

- ♠ K Q 9 8 7
- ♥ A 6 4
- ♦ 6 5 3
- ♣ K 2

Question One: HOW MANY TRICKS DO I NEED?

- Two Spades = 6 + 2 = 8 tricks

Question Two: HOW MANY SURE TRICKS DO I HAVE?

- Spades: 0 - the opponents have the Ace
- Hearts: 1 - the Ace
- Diamonds: 0 - the opponents have all the high cards
- Clubs: 2 - the Ace and King
- Total: 3

Question Three: HOW CAN I BUILD EXTRA TRICKS?

- Spades: By playing the King of Spades to drive out the opponents' Ace, you can promote your remaining Spades to winners. This will build four tricks for your side.
- Hearts: Since dummy has only two Hearts, you could take the Ace, give one trick to the opponents and then be able to trump the remaining loser in dummy. This will give you one extra trick.
- Diamonds: There is no way to build any extra tricks.
- Clubs: There is no way to build extra tricks.

Question Four: HOW DO I PUT IT ALL TOGETHER?

- You need 8 tricks to make your contract and only have 3 sure tricks. There is work to be done. As you saw in the answer to Question Three, it is possible to get the extra tricks: four in the Spade suit and one by trumping a Heart. You will need to do both to make your contract.
- After the opponents take the first three Diamond tricks, suppose they lead a Heart and you win a trick with your Ace. Now, play a

Spade to drive out the opponents' Ace of Spades and promote your remaining cards in the suit. When you have the lead again, you should draw the remaining trumps. You should do this before trying to take tricks with your Club suit to avoid the possibility of an opponent putting a little trump on one of your Club tricks.

- Eventually, you will need to trump one of your Hearts with a Spade in dummy. So be careful to play only enough Spades to draw the opponents' trumps. You have nine Spades so they have four (13 - 9 = 4). If they each have two, you only need to play the suit twice. If one opponent has three and the other has one, you will need to play the suit three times to draw the trump.

- What if one opponent has all four trumps? Now you must be careful. If you play Spades four times to draw all the trumps, you will not have a Spade left in dummy with which to trump your Heart. Can you do anything about this? Yes. You can trump your Heart in dummy **before** drawing all the trumps. You will know that one opponent has all four if the other opponent has none when you drive out their Ace. Now you should stop drawing trumps and work on trumping your Heart in dummy. You will have to give up a Heart trick to your opponents, then dummy will be void. After trumping your remaining Heart in dummy, you can go back to drawing trumps.

This last example shows the importance of planning your play. It is one of the major fascinations of the game. Here are some guidelines to help you when playing in a suit contract:

GUIDELINES FOR PLAYING SUIT CONTRACTS

- Check to see if you need to trump a loser in dummy before drawing trumps
- Draw trumps until the opponents have no more
- Build the tricks you need for your contract before taking your sure tricks
- Do not make a special effort to trump tricks in your hand

Summary

When you are playing in a contract, ask yourself the following questions:

Question One: HOW MANY TRICKS DO I NEED?

- Add six to the level of your contract

Question Two: HOW MANY SURE TRICKS DO I HAVE?

- Add together the number of sure tricks in each suit

Question Three: HOW CAN I BUILD EXTRA TRICKS?

- By promoting cards
- By length
- By leading toward high cards
- By trumping losers (if playing in a trump contract)

Question Four: HOW DO I PUT IT ALL TOGETHER?

- Choose from among your alternatives the safest and surest way of building the extra tricks needed to fulfill your contract.

Here are some additional guidelines to help you plan your play:

GUIDELINES FOR PLAYING NO TRUMP CONTRACTS

- Take your tricks when you have enough to make your contract
- Build the tricks you need for your contract before taking your sure tricks
- Find the longest combined suit and play it first
- Watch your *entries* to be sure that you can get to the hand from which you want to lead to the next trick

---

GUIDELINES FOR PLAYING SUIT CONTRACTS

- Check to see if you need to trump a loser in dummy before *drawing trumps*
- Draw trumps until the opponents have no more
- Build the tricks you need for your contract before taking your sure tricks
- Do not make a special effort to trump tricks in your hand

Exercises

1) How many tricks do you need in the following contracts:

a) One No Trump?   b) Two No Trump?   c) Three No Trump?

d) Six No Trump?   e) Two Clubs?   f) Four Spades?

g) Six Hearts?   h) Seven Spades?

2) You are in a contract of One No Trump. Use Declarer's Four Questions to determine how you would play the following hand:

DUMMY:
♠ 6 5 2
♥ A 3 2
♦ 9 7 4
♣ K 6 4 3

♠ 7
(Opening Lead)

N
W   E
S

DECLARER:
(You)
♠ A K 4
♥ 8 6 4
♦ A Q 3
♣ A 8 5 2

3) You are in a contract of Three No Trump. Use Declarer's Four Questions to determine how you would play the following hand:

DUMMY:
♠ 6 5 2
♥ A 3 2
♦ K 4
♣ Q J 10 7 3

♥ Q
(Opening Lead)

N
W   E
S

DECLARER:
(You)
♠ A 9 7 4
♥ K 6 4
♦ A Q 7 3
♣ K 8

4) You are in a contract of Two Hearts. Use Declarer's Four Questions to determine how you would play the following hand:

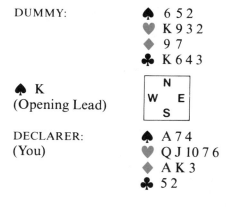

DUMMY:
♠ 6 5 2
♥ K 9 3 2
♦ 9 7
♣ K 6 4 3

♠ K
(Opening Lead)

N
W   E
S

DECLARER:
(You)
♠ A 7 4
♥ Q J 10 7 6
♦ A K 3
♣ 5 2

5) You are in a contract of Four Spades. Use Declarer's Four Questions to determine how you would play the following hand:

DUMMY:

♠ 7 6 5 2
♥ K Q
♦ 8 7 6 2
♣ A K 3

♦ K
(Opening Lead)

```
    N
  W   E
    S
```

DECLARER:
(You)

♠ Q J 10 8 4 3
♥ A 7 6
♦ A 9
♣ 7 2

26

The Defenders

The opponents win the auction and have the contract. What happens now? The defender on declarer's left leads. Then the dummy is put down and declarer plays the hand. During the play, the defenders' objective will be to try and take enough tricks to defeat the contract.

Ideally, each defender should go through a series of questions to determine the best plan. They are basically the same as Declarer's Four Questions:

- How many tricks do we need?
- How many sure tricks do we have?
- How can we build extra tricks?
- How can we put it all together?

Answering these questions is not as straight-forward as it is for declarer because it is "we" rather than "I". Declarer has the advantage of being able to see the strengths and weaknesses in the combined holdings in each suit. If he is missing an Ace, he knows that one of the opponents has it. Neither defender is in a similar position. If one defender doesn't have the Ace in a suit, and can't see it in the dummy, he doesn't necessarily know whether his partner has it or declarer has it. When choosing the opening lead, the defender does not even get a chance to look at what dummy holds.

There is compensation. The defenders choose the suit for the opening lead, perhaps taking or building enough tricks to defeat the contract before declarer has a chance to build his own tricks. There are guidelines which each defender can follow when uncertain what to do. We will look at two aspects of defensive play:

- Opening leads
- General guidelines

The Opening Lead

To decide what to lead against a contract, you need to answer two questions:

1. Which suit should I lead?
2. Which card should I lead?

The choice of suit to lead and the choice of which card to lead in that suit will depend on whether you are defending a No Trump contract or a suit contract.

Let's look at each case in turn.

Opening Leads Against No Trump Contracts

The first question is:

---

1. WHICH SUIT SHOULD I LEAD?

Usually your longest **combined** suit will be your best source of tricks. This suit will have the potential for building the most tricks. The contract is No Trump and, if you can build tricks in a long suit, you can take them without the possibility of declarer trumping your winning tricks.

What is the longest suit in your combined hands? If your partner has opened the bidding or overcalled in a suit, you will know what his longest suit is and, unless you have a clearly better choice, you should lead his suit. If partner has not bid, you will have to pick the longest suit in your hand and hope that it is the longest suit in the combined hands.

If you have a choice between two or more equally long suits, pick the stronger suit, the one with the most high cards. The stronger your suit, the less help you will need from your partner to establish tricks in the suit.

CHOOSING THE SUIT TO LEAD
AGAINST A NO TRUMP CONTRACT

- If partner has bid a suit, lead that suit.
- Otherwise, lead your longest suit. With two equally long suits, lead the stronger suit.

The second question is:

---

2. WHICH CARD SHOULD I LEAD?

If you are leading partner's suit, lead as follows:

LEADING PARTNER'S SUIT AGAINST NO TRUMP

- Top of a doubleton (K 4, 7 3)
- Top of touching high cards (K Q 7, J 10 4)
- Low from three or more cards (K 7 3, Q 9 5, 8 6 3, K 8 6 5)

What if partner has not bid a suit and you are leading your suit? In general:

LEADING YOUR SUIT AGAINST NO TRUMP

- Lead the top of touching high cards
- Otherwise, lead low

Here is an example of leading the top of touching high cards:

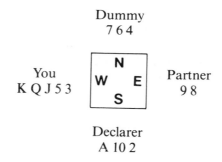

Dummy
7 6 4

You
K Q J 5 3

Partner
9 8

Declarer
A 10 2

If you lead a low card, declarer will be able to win the trick with his Ten and still have the Ace left to win a second trick. If you lead one of your high cards instead, this will drive out the Ace. When you later regain the lead, you can take two tricks with your promoted high cards and, since declarer will have no cards left in the suit, take two more tricks with your remaining little cards. By leading one of your high cards, you keep declarer to one trick in the suit.

Let's look at some more examples. What card would you lead from the following suits if you were defending against a No Trump contract?

1) A Q 7 2   2) K J 6 4 3   3) J 8 7 6 5 3   4) Q J 10 7

5) K J 10 6 4   6) A K Q 4 3   7) A 6   8) J 7 3

1) Since your high cards are not touching, you should lead low, the Two.

2) Here you should lead low, the Three. Some players lead "fourth best" and would lead the Four. This is discussed in For The Curious.

3) With this 6-card suit you would lead low, the three, or fourth-best, the Six.

4) With touching high cards, you lead the top one, the Queen.

5) Lead the top of your **touching** high cards, the Jack.

6) With three touching high cards, start with the top card, the Ace. With luck, by the time you take tricks with the Ace, King and Queen, the opponents will no longer have any cards left in the suit and you can take two more tricks.

7) If you are going to lead this suit, lead the Ace, top of a doubleton. Presumably, you will only be leading this suit if your partner has bid it.

8) If you are leading a 3-card suit with no touching high cards, lead low, the Three. Again, you will probably only be leading a 3-card suit if partner has bid it.

Leads After the First Trick

Suppose your partner leads a Spade against a No Trump contract. Declarer wins the trick and leads a Diamond. You win the trick. What suit should you lead now? You should **lead (return) partner's suit**, hoping to take or build tricks in that suit. If you and your partner both try to build tricks in different suits, you will be working at cross-purposes. You need to cooperate to defeat declarer's contract.

> **LEAD BACK THE SUIT LED BY YOUR PARTNER UNLESS YOU HAVE A CLEARLY BETTER ALTERNATIVE**

Opening Leads Against Suit Contracts

To decide what to lead against a suit contract, you need to answer the same two questions as when leading against a No Trump contract. The first question is:

> **1. WHICH SUIT SHOULD I LEAD?**

If partner has bid a suit, lead that suit unless you have a clearly better alternative. Partner will have some length and, with luck, strength in the suit that he bid.

If partner has not bid a suit, your choice of suit is not as clear cut. Unlike when defending against No Trump contracts, it may do no good to build small cards into tricks by leading your longest suit. When you try to take your winning tricks, declarer may be able to trump them with his trump suit. Instead, it is more important to build tricks by promoting high cards. For example, if you have the King and Queen in a suit, you can lead the King to drive out the Ace and promote your Queen into a trick.

What suit should you lead if you have no suit containing touching high cards? You might try leading a suit, other than the trump suit, in which you only have one or two little cards. If you can make yourself void in a suit, you can perhaps trump in later on. Partner may be able to win a trick and lead the suit back. You will then be able to play a trump on one of declarer's winning tricks and win it for your side instead.

If partner didn't bid and you have no touching high cards or short suit (other than trumps), lead an *unbid suit*. An unbid suit is one that the opponents have not bid. If the opponents have bid a suit, it is likely that they, rather than partner, have most or all of the remaining high cards in the suit.

**CHOOSING THE SUIT TO LEAD AGAINST
A TRUMP CONTRACT**

- If partner has bid a suit, lead that suit.

Otherwise:
  — lead a suit in which you have a high card sequence
  — lead a short suit (other than the trump suit)
  — lead an unbid suit

The second question is:

---

2. WHICH CARD SHOULD I LEAD?

If you are leading partner's suit, you can choose the same card that you would lead against a No Trump contract:

LEADING PARTNER'S SUIT AGAINST A SUIT CONTRACT

- Top of a doubleton (K 4, 7 3)
- Top of touching high cards (K Q 7, J 10 4)
- Low from three or more cards (K 7 3, Q 9 5, 8 6 3, K 8 6 5)

If you are leading your own suit, you also choose the same card that you would lead against a No Trump contract:

LEADING YOUR SUIT AGAINST SUIT CONTRACTS

- Lead the top of touching high cards (K Q J 3, A K 7 5 4 2)
- Otherwise, lead low (K 8 5 4 3, Q 9 7 2)

Here are some examples of choosing the appropriate card to lead. What card would you lead from the following suits if you were defending against a suit contract?

1) A K 7 2   2) K Q 6 3   3) K 7 5 3 2   4) Q 9 7

5) K J 10 6 4   6) 6 5 3   7) K 6

1) Lead the top of your touching high cards, the Ace.
2) Again, with touching high cards, lead the top card, the King. If the opponents have the Ace, you will drive it out and establish your Queen as a trick. If partner has the Ace, he will let you take the trick with your King. You can then continue to take more tricks in the suit.
3) Since you don't have touching high cards, lead low, the Two, or Three if you want to lead fourth best.
4) With three cards lacking touching high cards, lead low, the Seven.
5) Here you have touching high cards. Lead the Jack.
6) From three cards, lead low, the Three.
7) Lead the King, top of a doubleton. If partner has the Ace or Queen, you want to play the high cards from the short hand first.

General Guidelines

There are several guidelines that are often quoted to assist when defending a hand:

- Second player to a trick plays low
- Third player to a trick plays high
- Cover an honor with an honor

These sayings are certainly useful but it is important to remember that they are guidelines, not rules. Let's look at where they come from.

Second Hand Low

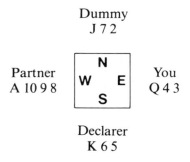

Dummy
J 7 2

Partner
A 10 9 8

You
Q 4 3

Declarer
K 6 5

Suppose declarer leads the Two from dummy. You are the second player to the trick. There is no need to play your Queen to drive out declarer's King. Declarer is not likely to play one of his little cards anyway and, if he does, your partner will be able to win the trick since he gets to play last. You should play "second hand low" and put your Three on the trick. If declarer plays his King, your partner can win the trick with the Ace. You will still have the Queen left to win the second trick in the suit. If you play your Queen, declarer will play his King to drive out your partner's Ace. Then declarer will have built dummy's Jack as a trick.

Third Hand High

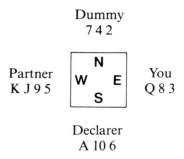

Dummy
7 4 2

Partner
K J 9 5

You
Q 8 3

Declarer
A 10 6

Suppose your partner leads the Five and declarer plays the Two from dummy. You are the third player to the trick. You have the last opportunity to play to the trick for your side. In this situation, you should play "third hand high" and put your Queen on the trick. You are attempting to win the trick for your side.

Even if you can't win the trick, as in this example, you will drive out a high card, the Ace, from declarer. This will establish your partner's King and Jack as tricks which can be taken later. If you had played the Three or the

Eight, declarer would win the Ten and still have the Ace left to win a second trick. Don't get carried away! Only play as high a card as is necessary to win the trick.

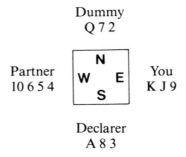

Dummy
Q 7 2

Partner
10 6 5 4

You
K J 9

Declarer
A 8 3

If your partner leads the Four and dummy plays the Two (declarer often uses the "second hand low" guideline also), you don't need to play your highest card, the King. Since you can see the Queen in dummy, you can play your Jack. This will win the trick if partner has the Ace. If declarer has the Ace, he will win the trick but you still have your King in case declarer tries to take a trick by leading toward dummy's Queen. If instead you play the King, declarer will win the Ace and have the Queen for a second trick.

Cover an Honor With an Honor

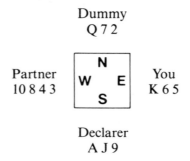

Dummy
Q 7 2

Partner
10 8 4 3

You
K 6 5

Declarer
A J 9

Suppose declarer attempts to finesse by leading the Queen from the dummy. If you do not put your King on this trick, declarer will be able to play a small card and win the trick since partner does not have a higher card. Declarer can then lead the suit again and trap your King, winning all three tricks in the suit. Instead, you should "cover an honor with an honor" and play your King. (An *honor* is one of the top five cards in the suit: the Ace, King, Queen, Jack or Ten.)   To win the trick, declarer will have to play the Ace. Declarer has promoted his Jack into a trick but that is only two tricks. On the third trick, partner's Ten will win. It has been promoted to the highest card remaining in the suit.

You should only cover when you see an opportunity to promote (build) a trick for your side. If dummy had the Jack and the Ten in the above example, it would not help you to cover, since you would only promote the opponent's cards.

The general principles will often help, but use them carefully.

Summary

To decide what to lead against a contract, you need to answer two questions:

Question One: WHICH SUIT SHOULD I LEAD?

CHOOSING THE SUIT TO LEAD AGAINST A NO TRUMP CONTRACT

- If partner has bid a suit, lead that suit.
- Otherwise, lead your longest suit. With two equally long suits, lead the stronger suit.

CHOOSING THE SUIT TO LEAD AGAINST A TRUMP CONTRACT

- If partner has bid a suit, lead that suit.
- Otherwise:
  —Lead a suit in which you have touching high cards
  —Lead a short suit (other than the trump suit)
  —Lead an unbid suit

Question Two: WHICH CARD SHOULD I LEAD?

LEADING PARTNER'S SUIT

- Lead the top of a doubleton (A 4, K 3)
- Lead the top of touching high cards (Q J 7, K J 10)
- Lead low from three or more cards when you lack touching high cards (Q 9 3, K J 5, Q 7 6 4, 7 6 3)

> ### LEADING YOUR SUIT
> - Lead the top of touching high cards (K Q J 3, A K 7 5 4 2)
> - Otherwise, lead low (K J 8 4 3, Q 9 7 2)

During the defense of the hand, if you are uncertain which card to play, you can use the following:

> ### DEFENSIVE GUIDELINES
> - Second player to a trick plays low
> - Third player to a trick plays high
> - Cover an honor with an honor

Exercises

1) What card do you lead from the following suit holdings against a No Trump contract?

   a) A 8 6 4 3   b) K Q J 4 3   c) Q J 9 3   d) 9 7 5 4 2

   e) K 4 3   f) J 3   g) A K Q 3   h) A Q J 7 4

2) What card do you lead from the following suit holdings against a suit contract?

   a) A K 6   b) Q 7 6 4 3   c) 7 3   d) K J 7 2

   e) Q 6 5 3   f) K Q J 8   g) 8 5 3   h) J 8 2

3) What would you lead from the following hands against a contract of One No Trump? What would you lead against a contract of Two Spades?

   a) ♠ 6 3   b) ♠ 7 5
      ♥ Q 8 6 5 3   ♥ A K 4
      ♦ K Q J   ♦ J 6 4 3
      ♣ A 8 4   ♣ Q 10 7 3

4) You are East. What card should you play if declarer leads the indicated card from dummy?

   a) Dummy   b) Dummy   c) Dummy
      8 7 3   Q 7 3   Q J 10
      ☐ You   ☐ You   ☐ You
        K 9 5 2   K 9 5 2   K 9 5 2

For the Curious

Leading Against Suit Contracts When You Have the Ace

Suppose you decide to lead a Spade holding the AQ432 in the suit. If the contract is No Trump, you lead low. You would not be surprised to lose one or even two tricks before your suit was established. There is little concern about not getting a trick with your ace, because there are no trumps. You could probably take your Ace later in the hand, as you try to 'run' your spade suit.

The situation is very different if the opponents are playing with a trump suit. The concern is not with establishing tricks for your small cards, but for getting your tricks in a suit before they can trump. For this reason, you should **lead your Ace**.

IF YOU LEAD A SUIT VERSUS A TRUMP CONTRACT IN WHICH YOU HAVE THE ACE, LEAD THE ACE... NOT LOW.

There is another idea that is useful to keep in mind. Much of the art of Bridge is getting **extra** tricks. One way to do this, as we have seen, is by trapping your opponent's High Cards. The way to do this is to make them play before you. If your Right-Hand Opponent has the King, leading your Ace will build a trick for his King.   You will probably never get a trick with your Queen, because they would likely be able to trump the third lead of Spades. If you wait for someone else... partner or an opponent... to play spades, you could trap Declarer's King. As a rule then, **avoid leading an Ace "unsupported" by the King against a Trump contract**.

Popular Defensive Signals

We have seen how valuable it is for partners to communicate with each other in the bidding of a hand to reach to best contract. The defenders also need to work together to defeat Declarer's contract. Some ways that we have seen that they can help each other are leading the suit partner bid, returning partner's suit, and not putting an Ace on partner's King.

The Defenders can also communicate with each other using Defensive Signals. You have learned several defensive signals already: Leading the highest of touching honors, leading the highest card of a doubleton, and leading low from three or more cards. These signals can help partners work together to win extra tricks.

There are several other popular defensive signals which you may encounter. We do not recommend them for beginners because they are difficult to use properly. However, by all means try them after playing for a while if you wish.

The first defensive signal is to **lead the fourth highest card when you are leading low**. (If you have only 3 cards, lead low...the closest to fourth highest.) This convention is called *Fourth Best Leads*. It will do no harm to play this convention, but it will not help your partner unless he understands a lot of intermediate and advanced concepts about defence and the "rule of eleven" to apply when he thinks you are leading fourth highest. The rule of eleven is beyond the scope of basic bridge and will not be discussed here.

There is a very useful convention called Attitude Signals. If your partner leads a suit, and you can afford to play a low one, you can signal your 'attitude' toward the lead as follows:

Playing **a low card is discouraging** and says "please don't lead this suit any more."

Playing **a high card is encouraging** saying "please keep leading this suit."

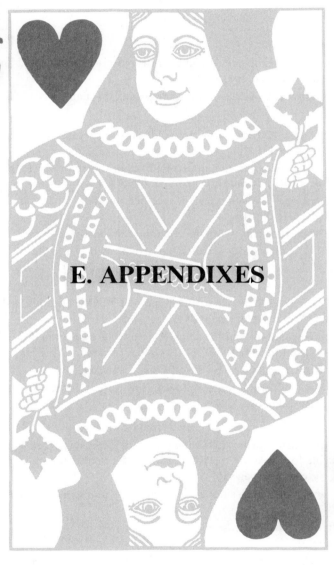

E. APPENDIXES

Appendix 1: Glossary of Terms

ABOVE THE LINE The top half of a Rubber Bridge score sheet where bonuses and penalties are recorded. (page 32)

AUCTION The process of determining the contract through a series of bids. (page 7)

BALANCED HAND A hand with no voids, no singletons and at most one doubleton. (page 17)

BELOW THE LINE The bottom half of a Rubber Bridge score sheet where points for contracts bid and made are recorded. (page 32)

BID An undertaking to win at least a specified number of tricks in a specified denomination. (page 8)

BIDDING The various bids which make up the auction. (page 7)

BIDDING LADDER The order in which bids can be made. (page 9)

BIDDING MESSAGE Whether a bid is marathon, forcing, invitational or a sign-off. (page 59)

BLACKWOOD CONVENTION An artificial bid of Four No Trump to ask partner how many Aces he holds. (page 241)

BONUS Points scored for making a Part-Game, a Game, a Slam or defeating the opponents' contract. (page 27)

BOOK The first six tricks won by the offensive team. (page 7)

BUILDING TRICKS Turning potential tricks into sure tricks through the way in which the cards are played. (page 258)

CALL Any bid, double, redouble or pass. (page 147)

CAPTAIN The partner who knows the most about the combined hands and is responsible for directing the partnership to its final contract. Responder is usually the captain. (page 36)

COMPETITION When both sides are bidding to try and name the final contract. (page 147)

COMBINED HANDS The cards making up both hands belonging to one partnership. (page 36)

CONTRACT The undertaking by declarer's side to win at least a specific number of tricks in a specific denomination as determined by the final bid in the auction. (page 9)

CONVENTION A bid which conveys a meaning other than would normally be attributed to it. (page 209)

COVER (AN HONOR) Playing a higher-ranking card than the previously played card on a trick. (page 290)

CUE BID A bid of a suit bid by the opponents. It is forcing to the Game level (marathon bid). (pages 190, 247)

CUT (THE CARDS) To draw a random card from a face down pack of cards; to divide the deck into approximately two halves and place the bottom half on top. (page 2)

DEAL The distribution of the cards to the four players. (page 4)

DEALER The player who distributes the cards. The dealer has the first opportunity to open the bidding. (page 4)

DECLARER The player for the side that won the contract who first bid the denomination named in the final contract. (page 11)

DEFEAT Stop declarer from making the contract. (page 9)

DEFENSE The side that did not win the contract. (page 9)

DENOMINATION The suit or No Trump specified in a bid. (page 8)

DESCRIBER The opening bidder. (page 37)

DISCARD(ING) Play to a trick of a card of a different suit, not trump, than the suit led. (page 5)

DISCOURAGING BID A bid that discourages partner from bidding again. (page 115)

DISTRIBUTION The number of cards held in each suit by a particular player; the number of cards held in a particular suit by a partnership. (page 18)

DOUBLE A bid that increases the bonus for making or defeating a contract. (page 144)

DOUBLETON A holding of two cards in a suit. (page 17)

DRAWING TRUMP Playing the trump suit until the opponents have none left. (page 277)

DUMMY Declarer's partner; the hand that is placed face up on the table after the opening lead. (page 11)

DUMMY POINTS A method of hand valuation used when planning to support partner's Major suit. (page 66)

ENTRY A card that provides a means of winning a trick in a particular hand. (page 260)

ESTABLISH Set up sure tricks by driving out winning cards in the opponents' hands. (page 261)

FINESSE A method of building extra tricks by trapping an opponent's high card(s). (page 264)

FOLLOW SUIT Play a card in the suit that is led. (page 5)

FORCING (BID) A bid that compels partner to continue to bid (i.e. partner cannot Pass). (page 56)

FOUR QUESTIONS In several common situations a player asks himself four questions, in order, which indicate what action he should take. (page 65)

FOURTH BEST LEADS A player, lacking touching honours, leads his fourth highest card. (page 294)

GAME A total trick score of 100 or more points. (page 27)

GAME CONTRACT A contract which has a trick score value of 100 or more points. (page 27)

GAME RAISE A raise of partner's suit to the Game level. The Game level when raising a Minor suit is Three No Trump. (page 106)

GERBER An artificial bid of Four Clubs to ask partner how many Aces he holds. (page 241)

GIVING PREFERENCE Choosing one of partner's suits. (page 128)

GONE DOWN (or DOWN) Been defeated in a contract. (page 29)

GRAND SLAM A contract to take all thirteen tricks. (page 30)

HAND The cards held by one of the players: a deal of bridge. (page 4)

HAND VALUATION The method of determining the value of a particular hand during the auction. Usually a combination of high card strength and suit length or shortness. (page 15)

HCPs High Card Points; the value of the high cards in a hand. (page 16)

HIGH CARD One of the top four cards in a suit: Ace, King, Queen or Jack. (page 15)

HIGH CARD POINTS The value of the high cards in a hand: Ace - 4; King - 3; Queen - 2; Jack - 1. (page 16)

HIGHER-RANKING SUIT A suit that ranks higher on the Bidding Ladder than another suit: Spades are highest; Hearts are second; Diamonds are third; Clubs are the lowest-ranking suit. (page 2)

HONOR (CARD) An Ace, King, Queen, Jack or Ten. (page 290)

HOW HIGH The level at which the contract should be played. (page 37)

INVITATIONAL (BID) A bid that invites partner to bid again. (page 54)

JUMP OVERCALL A suit overcall at a level one higher than necessary. This is usually played as a pre-emptive bid. (page 252)

JUMP RAISE A raise of partner's suit skipping a level. (page 106)

JUMP SHIFT A Rebid by opener in a new suit at a level one higher than necessary. Such a bid is forcing to the Game level or higher (marathon bid). (page 78)

LANGUAGE OF BIDDING The exchange of information by partners through the bids which they make. (page 34)

LEAD(ING) The first card played to a trick. (page 5)

LEFT HAND OPPONENT The opponent on a player's left. (page 149)

LENGTH POINTS The value of long suits in a hand: 5-card suit - one; 6-card suit - two; 7-card suit - three; 8-card suit - four. (page 16)

LEVEL The number of tricks the partnership contracts to take when it makes a bid. It includes an assumed six tricks (Book). (page 8)

LINE The horizontal line on a Rubber Bridge score sheet dividing the bonuses from the trick scores. (page 32)

LONG(EST) SUIT The suit containing the most cards in a given hand. (page 18)

LOSER A trick which might be lost to the opponents. (page 267)

LOWER-RANKING SUIT A suit which is lower on the Bidding Ladder than another suit. (page 2)

MAGIC FIT A suit in which the partnership has eight or more combined cards. (page 41)

MAGIC MAJOR SUIT FIT A Major suit in which the partnership has eight or more combined cards. (page 42)

MAJOR (SUIT) Spades or Hearts. (pages 25, 27)

MAKE (A CONTRACT) Succeed in taking enough tricks to fulfill the contract. (page 9)

MARATHON BID A bid that is forcing to Game. Neither partner can Pass until the Game level (at least) is reached. (page 61)

MINOR (SUIT) Diamonds or Clubs. (pages 25, 27)

NEW SUIT A suit which has not previously been bid by the partnership during the auction. (page 119)

NO TRUMP A contract with no trump suit. The highest card played in the suit led always wins the trick. (page 7)

OFFENSE The partnership which wins the contract. (page 9)

OLD SUIT A suit that has already been bid by the partnership during the auction. (page 115)

ONE OF A SUIT An opening suit bid at the one-level. (page 18)

ONE-LEVEL The lowest level at which the auction can start. It represents seven tricks. (page 7)

OPEN THE BIDDING Make the first bid in the auction. (page 7)

OPENER The player who makes the first bid in an auction. (page 7)

OPENER'S REBID The opening bidder's second bid. (page 80)

OPENING BID The first bid made during an auction. (page 7)

OPENING BIDDER The player who makes the first bid in an auction. (page 7)

OPENING LEAD The card led to the first trick. The player on declarer's left leads first. (page 11)

OVERCALL Make a bid after the opponents have opened the bidding. (page 147)

OVERTRICK A trick won by declarer's side in excess of the contract. (page 29)

PARTNERSHIP The two players seated opposite each other at the table. (page 2)

PART-GAME A contract with a trick score worth less than 100 points. (page 28)

PART-SCORE Part-Game. (page 28)

PASS A call specifying that a player does not want, at that turn, to bid. (page 7)

PASSED OUT A deal in which no one Makes a bid. (page 35)

PENALTY The bonus awarded to the defending side for defeating a contract. (page 27)

PENALTY DOUBLE A Double with the intention of increasing the penalty bonus for defeating the opponents' contract. (page 145)

PLAY The part of the game following the auction during which the declarer tries to make the contract. (page 4)

POINTS Points are awarded on a score sheet for bidding and making contracts and for defeating the opponents' contracts. (page 26)

POINT COUNT A method of hand valuation which assigns points for the high cards held and the distribution. (page 16)

PRE-EMPTIVE BID A bid made to interfere with the opponents' auction. It is usually made with a long suit and weak hand. (page 242)

PROMOTION The increase in the trick-taking potential of a card in a suit as the higher-ranking cards are played. (page 260)

RANK OF CARDS The cards in each suit are ranked in order during the play: the Ace is the highest, then the King, Queen, Jack, Ten...down to the Two. (page 2)

RANK OF SUITS The suits are ranked in order during the bidding: Spades are highest, then Hearts, Diamonds and Clubs. No Trump ranks higher than Spades. (page 2)

RAISE Supporting partner's suit by bidding that suit at a higher level. (page 65)

REBID A second bid by opener or responder. (page 80)

REDOUBLE A bid that increases the scoring value of tricks and penalties after an opposing Double. Also used as an artificial bid. (page 146)

RESPOND Make a bid, other than Pass, when partner has previously made a bid. (page 35)

RESPONDER The partner of the opening bidder; the partner of the overcaller or take-out doubler. (page 35)

RESPONDER'S REBID Responder's second bid. (page 113)

RIGHT HAND OPPONENT The opponent on a player's right. (page 148)

ROUND A series of four hands, one dealt by each player. This is the unit used in *Joy of Bridge* scoring. (page 26)

RUBBER A Bridge match. For Rubber Bridge it is the unit in scoring denoting the winning of two Games by one side. (page 32)

RUFF(ING) Playing a trump on a trick when you are void in the suit led. (page 7)

SCORE SHEET The paper on which points are recorded. Points won or lost are recorded on a score sheet which has a vertical line dividing the sheet into a WE side and a THEY side. (page 26)

SCORING A GAME Making a Game contract. (page 27)

SET (THE CONTRACT) Defeat the contract. (page 9)

SHAPE The number of cards held in each suit by a particular player. (page 16)

SIGN-OFF (BID) A bid that asks partner to Pass. (page 53)

SINGLE RAISE A raise to the next available level. (page 106)

SINGLETON Holding of one card in a suit. (page 17)

SLAM A contract to take twelve or thirteen tricks. (page 231)

SMALL SLAM A contract to take twelve tricks. (page 30)

STAYMAN CONVENTION An artificial response of Two Clubs to an opening bid of One Trump, asking opener to bid a 4-card Major suit. (page 209)

STRENGTH The point count value of a hand. (page 16)

STRONG TWO-BID An opening bid at the two-level in a suit. (page 217)

SUITS The four groups of cards in the deck, each having a characteristic symbol: Spades, Hearts, Diamonds and Clubs. (page 4)

SUPPORT The number of cards held in a suit that partner has bid. (page 65)

SURE TRICK A trick which can be taken without giving up the lead to the opponents. (page 258)

TAKE-OUT DOUBLE A Double of a Part-Game contract which requests partner to bid an unbid suit. (page 171)

TRAPPING A technique for building tricks through making an opponent play his card before you select your card. (page 264)

TRICK The standard unit of play consisting of four cards, one contributed by each player in clockwise rotation, beginning with the lead. (page 4)

TRICK SCORE The points scored for contracts bid and made. Does not include overtricks. (page 27)

TRUMP SUIT The suit, if any, named in the contract. (page 7)

TRUMPING Playing a trump on a trick when void in the suit led. (page 7)

UNBID SUIT A suit that has not been bid by either side during the auction. (page 287)

UNDERTRICK Each trick by which declarer's side fails to fulfill the contract. (page 30)

VALUATION The method of determining the value of a particular hand during the auction. Usually a combination of values for high cards held and length. (page 15)

VOID A holding of zero cards in a suit. (page 17)

VULNERABILITY The status of the hand during a round of bridge which affects the size of the bonuses scored for making or defeating contracts. Bonuses and penalties are higher when declarer is vulnerable. (page 28)

WHERE The denomination in which the contract should be played. (page 38)

Appendix 2: Answers to Exercises

Chapter 1

1) The players drawing the QUEEN OF HEARTS AND TEN OF HEARTS are one partnership. The players drawing the TEN OF CLUBS AND FOUR OF DIAMONDS are the other partnership. The player drawing the QUEEN OF HEARTS would be the dealer.

2) The ACE OF SPADES is the highest-ranking card in the deck. The TWO OF CLUBS is the lowest-ranking card.

3) The maximum number of tricks that you and your partner can win is THIRTEEN.

4) EAST won the trick by playing the highest-ranking Diamond, the Ace, and will lead to the next trick.

5) SOUTH won the trick with the Jack of Hearts and will lead to the next trick.

6) SOUTH wins the trick by playing a higher trump than East.

7) You are contracting to try and win EIGHT tricks when you make a bid of Two Spades...six (Book) plus two. To make Two Spades the final contract, the other three players would all have to say PASS.

8) You will need to take FOUR tricks to defeat a contract of Four Hearts.

9) You would have to bid FOUR HEARTS to suggest Hearts as trumps if the previous bid was Three Spades (Hearts are lower-ranking than Spades).

10) The opponent on your LEFT will make the opening lead. Your PARTNER will be the dummy. You will need to take NINE tricks (6 + 3) to make your contract.

Chapter 2

1a) PASS...you only have 9 points, not enough to open the bidding.

1b) ONE NO TRUMP...you have a balanced hand with 16 points.

1c) ONE SPADE...with 15 points, open your longest suit.

1d) ONE HEART...with 13 points and two 5-card suits open the higher-ranking.

1e) ONE CLUB...with 14 points and two 4-card suits, open the lower-ranking.

1f) ONE DIAMOND...with an unbalanced hand of 16 points open the middle-ranking of three 4-card suits.

1g) ONE NO TRUMP...you have 17 points and a balanced hand.

1h) ONE HEART...with 15 points open the higher-ranking of your 6-card suits.

1i) ONE HEART...with 19 points open the lower-ranking of your two 4-card suits.

1j) ONE DIAMOND...with 13 points open the middle-ranking of three 4-card suits.

Chapter 3

1) Your trick score is 120 POINTS. Your bonus is 300 POINTS for making a Game.

2) Since the opponents dealt the first hand, your side will deal the second hand, making YOUR SIDE VULNERABLE. The opponents get a trick score of 120 points for bidding and making Four Hearts. They get 300 points as their not vulnerable bonus for making a Game, giving them a total of 420 POINTS.

3) For making Two Diamonds, you get a trick score of 40 POINTS. Your bonus is 50 POINTS for making a Part-Game.

4) It is the fourth hand and both sides are vulnerable. Your bonus is 100 points because the opponents went down one trick.

5)

	WE	THEY	
Your trick score for making Four Spades	120	120	Their trick score for making Four Hearts
Your not vulnerable Game bonus	300	300	Their not vulnerable Game bonus
Your trick score for making Two Diamonds	40		
Your Part-Game bonus	50		
Your bonus for one vulnerable undertrick	100		
	610	420	

You have won the round by a score of 610 to 420.

6) You must bid FOUR SPADES to score enough points for Game (4 x 30 = 120). You might want to bid higher to try and get a bonus for bidding and making a SLAM contract. The danger is that you might get too high and be DEFEATED in your contract. You would then not even get the points for Game.

7) Playing in THREE NO TRUMP would be preferable since you would score 100 points, enough for Game. *You would then get a Game bonus.* Making Three Clubs would only score 60 points plus a bonus of 50 points for Part-Game.

8) You would need to take at least SIX tricks to defeat the opponents' contract of Two Spades. If you did, you would receive a bonus of 100 POINTS.

9) You would get a trick score of 60 points plus 50 points for the Part-Game bonus and 30 points for the overtrick, for a total of 140 POINTS. If you only

303

took seven tricks, the opponents would get 50 points for defeating your not vulnerable contract.

10) You would have taken TEN TRICKS to make Four Hearts. The opponents would have taken THREE TRICKS. You would get a trick score of 120 points and 500 points for your vulnerable Game bonus, giving you a total of 620 POINTS.

Chapter 4

1) YOU are both responder and captain when your partner opens the bidding One No Trump.

2a) You have 5 points. You have a combined total of between 21 points (16 + 5) and 23 points (18 + 5). You should play in PART-GAME.

2b) You have 12 points. Your combined total is between 28 points (16 + 12) and 30 points (18 + 12). You should play in GAME.

2c) You have 7 points. Your combined total is between 23 points (16 + 7) and 25 points (18 + 7). You should play in PART-GAME.

2d) You have 11 points giving you a combined total of between 27 points (16 + 11) and 29 points (18 + 11). You should play in GAME.

3) You have 4 points. The minimum number of combined points is 17 (13 + 4). The maximum number of combined points is 25 (21 + 4). The final contract should be played in PART-GAME.

4) There are at least EIGHT Hearts in the combined hands (4 + 4). The contract should be played in the MAGIC MAJOR SUIT FIT...HEARTS. You have 13 high card points and partner has at least 13 to open the bidding. The final contract should be played in GAME.

5) You need at least FOUR Spades to be certain there is a MAGIC MAJOR SUIT FIT.

6) You must hold SIX Hearts to be certain that there is a MAGIC MAJOR SUIT FIT (partner could have as few as two).

7) With 26 or more combined points, you should play in Game. With no MAGIC MAJOR SUIT FIT, you should play in THREE NO TRUMP.

Chapter 5

1a) TWO NO TRUMP...with 9 points there maybe Game.

1b) TWO HEARTS...with 4 points play in Part-Game in your 5-card Heart suit.

1c) THREE SPADES...with 13 points and a 5-card Major suit, get partner to choose between Four Spades and Three No Trump.

1d) FOUR HEARTS...with 13 points and a 6-card Major suit, bid Game.

1e) THREE NO TRUMP...with 11 points and no likely MAGIC MAJOR SUIT FIT, play Game in No Trump.

1f) THREE SPADES...with 11 points and a 5-card Major suit, get partner to choose between Four Spades and Three No Trump.

1g) FOUR SPADES...with 11 points and a 6-card Major suit, bid Game.

1h) TWO SPADES...with 6 points play Part-Game by bidding the higher- ranking of your two 5-card suits.

1i) THREE NO TRUMP...with 12 points and no likely MAGIC MAJOR SUIT FIT, play Game in No Trump.

1j) PASS...with 7 points play Part-Game. Note that you don't bid Two Clubs even though you have a 6-card suit.

Chapter 6

1) Opening one bids are INVITATIONAL. Since opener may have anywhere from 13 - 21 points, partner is only INVITED to respond. If responder has no points, he can Pass and play in Part-Game.

2) Two Diamonds, Two Hearts, Two Spades, Three No Trump, Four Hearts and Four Spades are all SIGN-OFF responses.

3) TWO NO TRUMP is the invitational response to a One No Trump opening bid.

4) Three Hearts and Three Spades are forcing responses to a One No Trump opening bid because opener MUST BID AGAIN (either Four of the Major suit or Three No Trump).

5) PASS because partner's response is a SIGN-OFF bid.

6) PASS because you only have 16 POINTS and partner is only inviting you to bid Game if you have 18 points.

7) Bid THREE NO TRUMP because you have 18 POINTS, enough to accept responder's invitation.

8) With 13 points, bid FOUR HEARTS. Partner will PASS because this is a SIGN-OFF response.

9) PASS because partner has made a SIGN-OFF response.

10) Bid FOUR SPADES. Partner is asking you to choose between Four Spades and Three No Trump. Since partner is showing a 5-card Spade suit, you would choose Four Spades with 3-CARD SUPPORT (5 + 3 = 8). If partner had bid Three Hearts, you would bid THREE NO TRUMP because you only have two Hearts.

Chapter 7

1) TWO HEARTS...with 4-card support for partner's Major and 8 dummy points, raise to the two-level.

2) PASS...with a weak hand (4 points) you do not have enough to bid.

3) ONE SPADE...with 8 points you can bid a new suit at the one-level.

4) ONE NO TRUMP...with 9 points you have a minimum hand, not enough to bid a new suit at the two-level.

5) TWO DIAMONDS...with 17 points you have enough to bid a new suit at the two-level.

6) ONE HEART...with a choice of two 4-card suits, bid the lower-ranking.

7) TWO CLUBS...with 14 points and no suit to bid at the one-level you can bid a new suit at the two-level.

8) TWO DIAMONDS...with 8 points, no suit to bid at the one-level and support for partner's Minor you can raise to the two-level.

9) THREE DIAMONDS...with 11 points you have enough to raise opener's Minor to the three-level.

10) THREE NO TRUMP...with 15 points and no other suit to bid, raise to Game.

Chapter 8

1a) ONE SPADE...you still have room to bid a new suit at the one-level.

1b) ONE NO TRUMP...with no suit left to bid at the one-level and a balanced hand of 14 points rebid No Trump at the cheapest level.

1c) TWO CLUBS...with an unbalanced hand, no second suit and 13 points rebid your suit at the two-level.

1d) TWO DIAMONDS...with four card support for partner's Minor and only 13 points raised to the cheapest level.

2a) TWO HEARTS...with support for partner's Major and 15 points, raise to the two-level.

2b) ONE SPADE...you still have room to bid a new suit at the one-level.

2c) TWO CLUBS...with only 13 points you do not have a strong enough hand to bid a higher-ranking suit at the two-level.

2d) THREE CLUBS...with 17 points you have enough to jump in your own suit.

3a) THREE SPADES...with support for partner's Major you can revalue your hand to 17 dummy points, enough to raise to the three-level.

3b) TWO CLUBS...with 15 points, no support for partner's Major and an unbalanced hand you can bid your second suit at the two-level.

3c) FOUR HEARTS...with a maximum hand of 19 points jump to Game in your suit.

3d) THREE DIAMONDS...with 20 points you "jump shift" in your second suit.

4a) PASS...with a minimum balanced hand of 14 points play No Trump at the cheapest level.

4b) TWO SPADES...with 18 points you have enough to bid a higher-ranking suit at the two-level.

4c) TWO CLUBS...with 13 points you can bid a lower-ranking suit at the two-level.

4d) THREE NO TRUMP...with 20 points you have enough to jump to Game in No Trump.

5a) FOUR SPADES...with support for partner's Major and 20 dummy points you have enough to raise to Game.

5b) TWO CLUBS...with 14 points you can bid your second suit at the two-level.

5c) TWO NO TRUMP...with a balanced hand of 20 points you jump rebid in No Trump.

5d) THREE CLUBS...with a maximum hand of 20 points you "jump shift" in your second suit.

Chapter 9

1a) THREE HEARTS...with support for partner's Major and 15 dummy points, raise one level.

1b) TWO NO TRUMP...with a balanced hand of 14 points rebid No Trump at the cheapest level.

1c) TWO SPADES...with only 14 points you are not strong enough to bid a new suit at the three-level so rebid your first suit.

1d) FOUR HEARTS...with support for partner's Major and 18 dummy points, raise partner with a jump.

2a) TWO HEARTS...with 14 points you can bid a lower-ranking suit at the two-level.

2b) THREE NO TRUMP...with a balanced hand of 20 points rebid No Trump with a jump.

2c) TWO SPADES...with 14 points you do not have enough to bid a new suit at the three-level so rebid your first suit.

2d) THREE CLUBS...with 18 points you have enough to bid your second suit at the three-level.

3a) TWO NO TRUMP...with a balanced hand of 14 points rebid No Trump at the cheapest level.

3b) THREE CLUBS...with 15 points and 4-card support for responder's Minor you can raise to the three-level.

3c) TWO SPADES...with a medium hand of 18 points you have enough to bid a higher-ranking suit at the two-level.

3d) FOUR HEARTS...with a maximum hand of 20 points you can jump to Game.

4a) TWO NO TRUMP...with a minimum balanced hand of 14 points rebid No Trump at the cheapest level.

4b) TWO DIAMONDS...with a minimum unbalanced hand of 13 points you can rebid your suit at the two-level.

4c) THREE DIAMONDS...with a medium hand of 18 points, rebid your suit with a jump.

4d) THREE NO TRUMP...with a maximum balanced hand of 19 points, rebid No Trump with a jump.

4e) TWO DIAMONDS...with a minimum hand of 14 points you are not strong enough to bid a higher-ranking suit at the two-level.

4f) THREE CLUBS...with 14 points and support for partner's Minor, raise to the three-level.

4g) FOUR CLUBS...with 17 points and support for partner's Minor you can jump raise to the four-level.

4h) TWO SPADES...with 18 points you have enough to bid a higher-ranking suit at the two-level.

Chapter 10

1a) FOUR SPADES...with a maximum hand of 21 points you have enough for Game.

1b) PASS...with a minimum hand of 13 points settle for Part-Game.

1c) THREE SPADES...with a medium hand of 17 points make a try for Game.

2a) FOUR HEARTS...with 15 points there is enough combined strength for Game.

2b) PASS...with only 13 points, stop in Part-Game.

2c) FOUR HEARTS...with 18 points there is enough for Game but not enough to consider a Slam.

3a) PASS...with 14 points settle for Game.

3b) SIX SPADES...with a maximum hand of 21 points there should be enough combined strength to make a Slam.

3c) FIVE SPADES...with 18 points there is enough strength to try for Slam.

4a) THREE CLUBS...with 18 points you have enough to raise to the three-level.

4b) PASS...with a minimum hand of 14 points stop in Part-Game.

4c) THREE NO TRUMP...with a maximum hand of 20 points you have enough for Game.

5a) PASS...with a minimum hand of 13 points settle for Part-Game.

5b) THREE NO TRUMP...with 19 points you have enough for Game but not for Slam.

5c) THREE NO TRUMP...with 16 points you should have enough for Game.

Chapter 11

1a) PASS...with 6 points stop in Part-Game.

1b) THREE HEARTS...with 11 points you have enough to try for Game.

1c) FOUR HEARTS...with 15 points you have enough for Game.

1d) PASS...with 7 points settle for Part-Game.

2a) TWO SPADES...with 10 dummmy points there may be Game if opener has a medium hand.

2b) THREE SPADES...with 12 dummy points you have enough to bid an old suit at the three-level.

2c) FOUR SPADES...with 16 dummy points there are enough for Game.

3a) PASS...with a minimum hand of 9 points settle for Part-Game.

3b) TWO SPADES...with 7 points settle for Part-Game, an old suit at the two-level.

3c) TWO NO TRUMP...with 12 points you have enough to try for Game.

3d) TWO CLUBS...with 15 points but uncertain WHERE to play, bid a new suit.

4a) TWO SPADES...with 8 points give preference to partner's suit at the two-level.

4b) PASS...with 8 points settle for Part-Game in opener's second suit.

4c) TWO SPADES...with 9 points give preference to opener's first suit which will be as long or longer than his second suit.

4d) PASS...with 6 points settle for a Part-Game in opener's second suit.

5a) THREE NO TRUMP...with 15 points and no MAGIC MAJOR SUIT FIT play Game in No Trump.

5b) THREE HEARTS...with 12 points you can bid an old suit at the three-level.

5c) PASS...with 7 points settle for Part-Game in opener's suit.

5d) THREE CLUBS...with 15 points but uncertain WHERE to play, bid a new suit.

Chapter 12

1a) PASS...with only 6 points settle for Part-Game.

1b) FOUR HEARTS...with 11 points you have enough to accept opener's invitation.

1c) FOUR HEARTS...with 13 points you have enough for Game but not enough for Slam.

1d) PASS...with 8 points you are right on the borderline. If opener has only 17 points you will not have enough combined strength for Four Hearts. It would not be unreasonable to bid Four Hearts, opener may have 18 points.

2a) PASS...with 7 dummy points settle for Part-Game.

2b) FOUR HEARTS...with 9 points you have enough for Game and partner is showing an unbalanced hand with long Hearts.

2c) THREE NO TRUMP...with 10 points you have enough for Game and No Trump looks preferable to playing in Hearts.

2d) THREE NO TRUMP...with 13 points Game again looks better in No Trump.

3a) THREE NO TRUMP...opener's bid is marathon and you have enough information to bid Game.

3b) THREE SPADES...you must bid again so make the most descriptive bid.

3c) FOUR HEARTS...the '5-4' inference tells you opener has at least five Hearts so you can bid the appropriate Game.

3d) THREE SPADES...this is more descriptive than bidding Three No Trump.

4a) PASS...with only 7 points you do not have enough to bid Game.

4b) THREE NO TRUMP...with 10 points you have enough for Game but do not have enough support to play in partner's suit.

4c) FOUR SPADES...9 points is enough for Game and 2-card support is sufficient for a suit in which partner has jumped.

4d) PASS...with 8 points you are right on the borderline between passing and carrying on to Game. Bidding Four Spades will work well if partner has 18 points, but not if he has only 17 points.

5a) THREE NO TRUMP...opener's rebid is marathon and there is no MAGIC MAJOR SUIT FIT.

5b) FOUR HEARTS...opener has a balanced hand so must have at least two Hearts.

5c) THREE HEARTS...this will ask opener to choose between Four Hearts or Three No Trump.

5d) THREE NO TRUMP...there is no MAGIC MAJOR SUIT FIT so bid Game in No Trump.

Chapter 13

1) The opponents would get a bonus of 100 POINTS for defeating your contract two tricks (50 + 50).

2) They get a bonus of 300 POINTS (100 + 100 + 100) for defeating you.

3) You receive 300 POINTS (100 + 200) for defeating their doubled contract by two tricks.

4) The opponents get 500 POINTS (200 + 300) for defeating your doubled contract.

5)

	WE	THEY
Your trick score for making Two Hearts doubled (2 x 60)	120	
Your bonus for the 'insult of being doubled'	50	
Your bonus for a not vulnerable Game	300	
Your score for the overtrick	100	

Note that the double has given you enough trick score for Game.

Chapter 14

1a) ONE SPADE...with 14 points overcall your 5-card suit.

1b) PASS...although you have 13 points, you do not have a 5-card suit.

1c) TWO CLUBS...with 14 points you have enough to overcall your 5-card suit.

1d) ONE NO TRUMP...with a balanced hand of 17 points an overcall in No Trump is preferable to bidding your 5-card Club suit.

1e) ONE HEART...with two 5-card suits bid the higher-ranking.

1f) PASS...do not overcall in the opponent's suit.

1g) PASS...with only 11 points you do not have enough to overcall.

1h) PASS...you do not have a 5-card suit.

2a) TWO HEARTS...with 14 points and a 6-card suit you have enough to overcall.

2b) PASS...even though you have 15 points you do not have a 5-card suit other than one bid by the opponents.

2c) THREE CLUBS...with 18 points you should overcall with your 6-card suit even though you will be at the three-level.

Chapter 15

1a) PASS...after revaluing with dummy points you only have 5 points.

1b) TWO HEARTS...with 8 dummy points and 3-card support you have enough to raise to the two-level.

1c) THREE HEARTS...with 11 dummy points raise to the three-level.

1d) FOUR HEARTS...with 15 dummy points raise to Game.

1e) PASS...with 4 points you do not have enough to bid.

1f) ONE SPADE...with 8 points you can bid a new suit at the one-level.

1g) ONE NO TRUMP...with 10 points you do not have enough to bid a new suit at the two-level.

1h) TWO CLUBS...with 14 points and only two cards in partner's suit, bid a new suit.

1i) TWO CLUBS...with 12 points you have enough to bid a new suit at the two-level.

1j) ONE SPADE...without support, bid a new suit at the one-level if you can.

2a) PASS...with 5 points settle for Part-Game.

2b) TWO DIAMONDS...with 6 points sign-off in your 6-card suit.

2c) THREE SPADES...with 13 points and a 5-card suit have opener choose between Four Spades and Three No Trump.

2d) THREE NO TRUMP...with 11 points and no MAGIC MAJOR SUIT FIT, bid Game in No Trump.

Chapter 16

1a) PASS...with only 6 points you do not have enough to bid after a two-level overcall.

1b) THREE HEARTS...with 11 dummy points you have enough to raise to the three-level.

1c) FOUR HEARTS...with 13 dummy points you have enough to raise to Game.

1d) FOUR HEARTS...with 14 dummy points, raise to Game.

2a) PASS...you only have 6 points, not enough to raise to the three-level.

2b) TWO DIAMONDS...with 11 points you have enough to bid a new suit at the two-level.

2c) TWO HEARTS...with 16 points you can bid a new suit at the two-level.

2d) TWO HEARTS...bid the higher-ranking of two 5-card suits.

2e) THREE CLUBS...with 11 points and 4-card support, raise to the three-level.

2f) THREE NO TRUMP...with 14 points and no 4-card or longer suit other than partner's Minor, bid Game in No Trump.

Chapter 17

1a) Partner's Double is for TAKE-OUT.

1b) Partner's Double is for TAKE-OUT (showing support for Spades and Diamonds).

1c) Partner's Double is for PENALTY because you have already bid a suit.

1d) Partner's Double is for PENALTY because it is a double of a Game contract.

2a) PASS...with only 11 dummy points you do not have enough to overcall or make a take-out Double.

2b) DOUBLE...you have 16 dummy points and support for the unbid suits.

2c) ONE SPADE...with 15 points and a 5-card suit, the overcall is preferable to a take-out Double because you do not have support for Hearts.

2d) ONE NO TRUMP...with a balanced hand, 18 points and stoppers in the opponent's suit, overcall No Trump.

2e) PASS...although you have 13 points, you have no 5-card suit and you don't have support for Hearts.

2f) DOUBLE...you only have 10 HCPs but you can count 5 dummy points for your Diamond void, giving you enough to make a take-out Double.

2g) PASS...your only 5-card suit is the one bid by the opponents so you can't overcall.

Chapter 18

1a) ONE SPADE...you can't pass so bid your 4-card Major suit.

1b) TWO HEARTS...with 11 points you have enough to jump in your 4-card Major.

1c) FOUR SPADES...with 13 points you can jump to Game in your 5-card suit.

1d) ONE DIAMOND...with no 4-card Major suit, bid your best Minor suit at the cheapest possible level.

1e) ONE NO TRUMP...with 8 points and no 4-card suit other than the opponent's suit, bid No Trump at the cheapest available level.

1f) TWO NO TRUMP...with 12 points and no 4-card suit other than the opponent's suit you can jump in No Trump.

1g) THREE NO TRUMP...with 14 points and no MAGIC MAJOR SUIT FIT, bid Game in No Trump.

1h) ONE SPADE...with two 5-card suits, bid the higher-ranking.

1i) TWO DIAMONDS ...with 11 points you have enough to jump in your Minor suit.

2a) PASS...with 16 dummy points you do not have enough to bid again when partner has only 0 - 10 points.

2b) TWO HEARTS...with 17 dummy points you have enough to raise to the two-level.

2c) THREE HEARTS...with 20 dummy points, raise to the three-level.

2d) PASS...you only have 15 dummy points.

2e) THREE HEARTS...you have 21 dummy points, enough to try for Game even though partner may have nothing.

Chapter 19

1a) ONE SPADE...the opponent's bid has not stopped you from bidding a new suit at the one-level.

1b) ONE NO TRUMP...with 10 points you can make your normal response.

1c) TWO DIAMONDS...with 7 points and 5-card support for partner's Minor you can raise to the two-level.

1d) TWO CLUBS...with 14 points you have enough to bid a new suit at the two-level.

2a) FOUR HEARTS...with 14 dummy points you can raise to Game.

2b) TWO SPADES...with 12 points you have enough to bid a new suit at the two-level.

2c) TWO NO TRUMP...with 12 points you must say something and bidding No Trump is the most descriptive bid.

2d) DOUBLE...it doesn't look like the opponents can make their contract so you can make a penalty Double.

3a) PASS...the opponent's Double has no effect on your response.

3b) ONE HEART...with two 4-card suits, bid the lower-ranking.

3c) TWO CLUBS...with 8 points and support for partner's Minor suit, raise to the two-level.

3d) THREE NO TRUMP...with 14 points and no 4-card suit other than partner's

Minor, bid Game in No Trump.

4a) PASS...with only 9 points and less than 3-card support for partner, you have no convenient bid.

4b) THREE SPADES...with 11 dummy points you have enough to raise to the three-level.

4c) FOUR SPADES...with 15 dummy points you have enough to bid Game.

4d) THREE SPADES...with 12 points and 3-card support, raise to the three-level.

5a) PASS...right-hand opponent's bid means you no longer have to bid.

5b) TWO HEARTS...with 7 points you have enough to compete by bidding your longer Major suit at the cheapest available level.

5c) THREE SPADES...with 11 points you have enough to jump in your 4-card Major suit.

5d) THREE DIAMONDS...with 12 points, jump in your Minor suit.

Chapter 20

1a) TWO SPADES...bid your 4-card Major suit.

1b) TWO HEARTS...bid your 4-card Major suit.

1c) TWO HEARTS...with two 4-card Majors, bid the lower-ranking first.

1d) TWO DIAMONDS...make the conventional response to show no 4-card Major suit.

2a) PASS...with 5 points and no 5-card suit, settle for the best Part-Game.

2b) TWO SPADES...with 6 points, sign-off in your 5-card suit.

2c) TWO NO TRUMP...with 8 points, make an invitational raise.

2d) TWO CLUBS...with 10 points and interest in Game in a Major suit, use the Stayman Convention to find out if opener has a 4-card Spade suit.

2e) TWO CLUBS...with 8 points you have enough to try for Game and look for a MAGIC MAJOR SUIT FIT using the Stayman Convention.

2f) TWO CLUBS...with 9 points and interest in finding a MAGIC MAJOR SUIT FIT start off with the Stayman Convention.

2g) THREE NO TRUMP...with no interest in the Majors and 10 points, bid Game in No Trump.

2h) THREE SPADES...with 10 points bid your 5-card Major suit at the three-level to ask opener to choose between Four Spades and Three No Trump.

2i) FOUR HEARTS...with 11 points and a 6-card Major suit, bid Game.

2j) TWO CLUBS...with 8 points and interest in both Majors, start with the Stayman Convention.

2k) TWO CLUBS...with 8 points and interest in playing in a Major suit, use the Stayman Convention.

Chapter 21

1a) TWO NO TRUMP...you have a balanced hand with 23 points.

1b) TWO SPADES...with two 5-card suits and 27 points, open the higher-ranking suit at the two-level.

1c) TWO CLUBS...with an unbalanced hand of 25 points open your longest suit at the two-level.

1d) THREE NO TRUMP...you have 26 points and a balanced hand.

1e) ONE SPADE...with 21 points you do not have enough to open at the two-level.

1f) TWO DIAMONDS...open your longest suit at the two-level with an unbalanced hand of 23 points.

1g) TWO DIAMONDS...with 23 points open at the two-level with the middle-ranking of three 4-card suits.

1h) ONE CLUB...with 20 points open your longest suit.

2a) TWO NO TRUMP...with only 2 points make the conventional response to show a weak hand.

2b) THREE HEARTS...with 8 dummy points, raise partner to the three-level.

2c) THREE CLUBS...with 9 points you can bid a new suit.

2d) THREE HEARTS...with 9 points and 3-card support for partner's Major, raise to the three-level.

2e) TWO NO TRUMP...with only 5 points, respond conventionally to show a weak hand.

2f) THREE DIAMONDS...with 10 points and two 5-card suits, bid the higher-ranking.

2g) THREE HEARTS...you have 8 dummy points, enough to raise.

2h) THREE CLUBS...with 12 points, bid a new suit.

3a) THREE CLUBS...with 4 points, use the Stayman Convention to find out if there is a MAGIC MAJOR SUIT FIT.

3b) THREE HEARTS...with 6 points, bid your 5-card Major suit and ask opener to choose between Four Hearts and Three No Trump.

3c) PASS...with no points you don't have to respond to a Two No Trump opening.

3d) THREE NO TRUMP...with 6 points and no likely MAGIC MAJOR SUIT FIT, bid Game in No Trump.

Chapter 22

1a) PASS...even though partner has 19 - 21 points, you only have 9 points.

1b) SIX HEARTS...with 14 points, there is enough combined strength for a Small Slam even if partner only has 19 points.

1c) SEVEN HEARTS...with 18 points, there is enough for a Grand Slam since partner has at least 19 points.

1d) FIVE HEARTS...with 12 points, invite partner to Slam. Partner will only bid Six Hearts if he has 21 points, two "extra" points.

2a) THREE NO TRUMP...you have 11 points and no MAGIC MAJOR SUIT FIT.

2b) FOUR NO TRUMP...with 15 points you have enough to invite Slam. If partner has 18, two "extra" points, he will bid six. With no MAGIC MAJOR SUIT FIT, No Trump looks to be the appropriate denomination.

2c) SIX NO TRUMP...with 18 points, there will be a Slam even if partner has only 16 points.

2d) SEVEN NO TRUMP...with 21 points, bid a Grand Slam since there are at least 37 combined points.

2e) FOUR HEARTS...you have 13 points, enough for Game, and you know there is a MAGIC MAJOR SUIT FIT.

2f) FIVE SPADES...with 15 points, you can invite Slam by bidding one level beyond Game. Partner will bid Six Hearts if he has 18 points.

2g) SIX SPADES...with 17 points, you can bid Slam in the MAGIC FIT.

2h) SIX CLUBS...you have 17 points, enough for Slam. When deciding WHERE, any MAGIC FIT is satisfactory at the Slam level.

3a) PASS...with 13 points you have nothing extra so reject partner's invitation.

3b) SIX HEARTS...you have 17 points, four more than you needed to open the bidding. Accept partner's invitation to bid a Slam.

Chapter 23

1a) THREE CLUBS...with a 7-card suit, three of the top five cards and only 10 points, you have the right hand to make a pre-emptive opening bid.

1b) PASS...with only one of the top 5 cards in your suit and 4 points you cannot open at the three-level.

1c) ONE DIAMOND...with 13 points make a normal opening bid at the one-level.

1d) FOUR HEARTS...with an 8-card suit and only 10 points, open at the four-level.

1e) THREE CLUBS...another perfect hand for a pre-emptive opening.

1f) TWO HEARTS...with an unbalanced hand of 23 points, open at the two-level.

1g) PASS...with only 11 points and lacking three of the top five cards in your suit, you should not open with a pre-empt.

1h) FOUR SPADES...open at the four-level with an 8-card suit and only 12 points.

2a) PASS...with only 13 points you do not have enough to bid after partner opens with a pre-empt.

2b) FOUR SPADES...you have 16 dummy points, enough to raise to Game.

2c) PASS...with 13 points, you don't have enough to respond to partner's bid.

2d) FOUR SPADES...with 16 points you can raise to Game, even with a singleton.

3a) FOUR CLUBS...with 16 points you are strong enough to overcall your long suit.

3b) DOUBLE...with 19 dummy points and support for the unbid suits, make a take-out Double.

3c) THREE NO TRUMP...with 20 points bidding Game in No Trump looks like a better bid than overcalling your 5-card suit at the four-level.

3d) PASS...with only 14 points and no support for Spades, you have no convenient bid.

4a) ONE SPADE...with 14 points and two 5-card suits, overcall the higher-ranking.

4b) TWO SPADES...with a good 6-card suit and only 9 points, you can make a pre-emptive jump overcall.

4c) THREE CLUBS...with a 7-card suit, three of the top five cards and only 10 points, make a pre-emptive jump overcall.

4d) PASS...with only a 5-card suit and 10 points you are not strong enough to bid.

Chapter 24

1a) You have THREE sure tricks, the Ace, King and Queen.

1b) You have TWO sure tricks, the Ace and the King.

1c) You only have TWO sure tricks because you have to play two high cards on each trick.

1d) You have SIX sure tricks. After taking tricks with your four high cards, the opponents will not have any cards left in the suit so you can take two tricks with your small cards.

2a) You can take TWO tricks. Lead your King (or Queen or Jack) to drive out the opponents' Ace and PROMOTE your Queen and Jack into sure tricks.

2b) You can take FOUR tricks. Lead the King to drive out the Ace and promote your remaining cards. Lead the high card from the SHORT HAND FIRST.

2c) Here you should get THREE tricks. Lead the Queen to drive out the Ace (or King) and later lead the Jack to drive out the remaining high card. This will PROMOTE your Ten and Nine as sure tricks. In addition, you can hope that the opponents have no cards left after you have played the suit four times so that your remaining card will be a trick built from LENGTH.

2d) You can hope for TWO tricks. Play the Ace, a sure trick, and then lead the suit two more times, giving the tricks to the opponents. If the five missing cards (13 - 8 = 5) are divided three and two, your will eventually build a trick from LENGTH.

2e) Again you have eight cards and so the opponents have only five. If the opponents cards are divided three and two, you can win THREE tricks by leading the suit at every opportunity. You will win the Ace and two additional tricks by LENGTH. If the opponents cards are divided four and one, you will only be able to build one extra trick.

2f) You might be able to build FOUR tricks. You have nine cards and the opponents have four (13 - 9 = 4). If you lead the suit twice and the opponents cards are divided two and two, your remaining cards will be built into tricks by LENGTH. If the opponents cards are divided three and one, you can only build three extra tricks. If they are divided four and nothing, you can can still get two extra tricks.

2g) Here you only have a chance for ONE trick. You can try to trap your left-hand opponent's Ace by leading TOWARD your King.

2h) You might get as many as THREE tricks from this combination. Lead from dummy TOWARD your Queen and try to trap your right-hand opponent's King. If the finesse is successful, you will have two tricks instead of one. Also, if the opponents cards are divided three and three, you can build a third trick by LENGTH.

Chapter 25

1a) You need SEVEN tricks in One No Trump.

1b) You need EIGHT tricks in Two No Trump.

1c) You need NINE tricks in Three No Trump.

1d) You need TWELVE tricks in Six No Trump.

1e) You need EIGHT tricks in Two Clubs.

1f) You need TEN tricks in Four Spades.

1g) You need TWELVE tricks in Six Hearts.

1h) You need THIRTEEN tricks in Seven Spades.

2) How many tricks do I need? SEVEN in One No Trump.

How many sure tricks do I have? SIX: the Ace and King of Spades, the Ace of Hearts, the Ace of Diamonds and the Ace and King of Clubs. How can I build extra tricks? There are two possibilities: in Diamonds you can build an extra trick if you can trap the King by leading toward your Ace and Queen (FINESSE); in Clubs you can build an extra trick through LENGTH by playing the suit three times and hoping the opponents' five cards (13 - 8 = 5) are divided three and two.

How do I put it all together? Win the first trick with the King (or Ace) of Spades and try to build an extra trick in Clubs. Play the Ace, then the King, then a third Club and watch to see if the opponents' Clubs are divided three and two. If they are, you can win whichever suit the opponents lead next and take your established Club trick along with your other sure tricks. If one opponent has four or five Clubs (you will find out when you take your Ace and King), you can try your second chance to build a trick. Use your Ace of Hearts to get to dummy (entry) and lead a Diamond toward your hand to try and trap your right-hand opponent's King.

3) How many tricks do I need? NINE in Three No Trump.

How many sure tricks do I have? SIX: the Ace of Spades, the Ace and King of Hearts, the Ace, King and Queen of Diamonds.

How can I build extra tricks? There are two possibilities: you have seven Spades so the opponents have six (13 - 7 = 6) and you can hope they are divided three and three; in Clubs you can PROMOTE your Queen, Jack and Ten into tricks by driving out the opponents' Ace with your King (you might get an additional trick from length).

How do I put it all together? Playing the Spade suit will only build one trick and you will have to be lucky...the opponents' cards will have to be divided three and three. Instead, build the three tricks you need in Clubs. Lead the King (short hand first) and continue leading the suit until the Ace is driven out. You will promote the three tricks you need. You can then take your remaining sure tricks. Be careful when taking your Diamond tricks to win the first trick with the King...short hand first. If neither opponent has more than four Clubs, you will get an extra trick from your fifth Club...it will be established by length.

4) How many tricks do I need? EIGHT in Two Hearts.

How many sure tricks do I have? THREE: the Ace of Spades and the Ace and King of Diamonds.

How can I build extra tricks? In Hearts you can PROMOTE four tricks by driving out the opponents' Ace. In Diamonds you can get one extra trick by TRUMPING your losing Diamond with one of dummy's trumps. In Clubs, you can try for an extra trick by leading TOWARD your King, hoping to trap your left-hand opponent's Ace.

How do I put it all together? You should win the first trick with your Ace of Spades and lead Hearts to drive out the opponents' Ace. You want to DRAW TRUMPS before taking your sure tricks. However, you must be careful not to take four trump tricks right away. You need to ruff your Diamond loser in dummy. This will give you the eight tricks you need to make the contract. You can try for an extra trick (overtrick) by leading toward dummy's King of Clubs when you get an opportunity.

5) How many tricks do I need? You need TEN tricks in a contract of Four Spades.

How many sure tricks do I have? SIX: the King, Queen and Ace of Hearts, the Ace of Diamonds and the Ace and King of Clubs.

How can I build extra tricks? In Spades, you can drive out the opponents' Ace and King to PROMOTE four tricks. There are no other possibilities for extra tricks. Note that it would not do you any good to trump dummy's little Club with one of your trumps, you still only get four Spade tricks.

How do I put it all together? With six sure tricks and needing only four more, you can make your contract just by DRAWING TRUMP. The opponents will only get three tricks, the Ace and King of Spades and a Diamond trick. Do not be afraid to lead trumps when you are missing the top high cards.

Chapter 26

1a) Lead the THREE, low from your long suit.

1b) Lead the KING, top of touching high cards.

1c) Lead the QUEEN, top of touching high cards.

1d) Lead low from your long suit, the TWO.

1e) Lead low from three or more cards, the THREE.

1f) Lead the JACK, top of a doubleton.

1g) Lead the top of your touching high cards, the ACE.

1h) Lead the QUEEN, top of touching high cards.

2a) Lead the ACE, top of touching high cards.

2b) Lead low from three or more cards not headed by touching high cards, the THREE.

2c) Lead the SEVEN, top of a doubleton.

2d) With four cards and no touching high cards, lead low, the TWO.

2e) Lead low, the THREE.

2f) Lead the KING, top of touching high cards.

2g) Lead the THREE, low from three or more cards not headed by touching high cards.

2h) Lead the TWO, low from three cards not headed by touching high cards.

3a) Lead the THREE OF HEARTS, low from your longest suit against a No Trump contract. Lead the KING OF DIAMONDS, top of touching high cards, against a suit contract.

3b) Lead the THREE OF CLUBS against a No Trump contract, low from the stronger of your two long suits. Lead the ACE OF HEARTS, top of touching high cards, against the suit contract of Two Spades.

4a) Play the TWO, second hand low.

4b) Play the KING, cover an honor with an honor.

4c) Play the TWO. You should not cover an honor if you can see that there is nothing to be promoted for your side.

Appendix 3: Scoring Summary

Trick Score

No Trump	40 for the first trick 30 for each additional trick
Spades or Hearts	30 points per trick
Diamonds or Clubs	20 points per trick
Doubled contracts	Twice the undoubled trick score
Redoubled contracts	Four times the undoubled trick score

Bonus Levels

Part-Game	Any contract with trick score less than 100 points
Game	Any contract with trick score 100 points or more: Five Diamonds or Five Clubs Four Spades or Four Hearts Three No Trump
Small Slam	Any twelve-trick contract
Grand Slam	Any thirteen-trick contract

Bonus Points

	Vulnerable	*Not Vulnerable*
Part-Game	50 points	50 points
Game	500 points	300 points
Small Slam	750 points	500 points
Grand Slam	1500 points	1000 points
Doubled or Redoubled Contract made (insult bonus)	50 points	50 points

Overtricks

Undoubled	trick score	trick score
Doubled	200 per overtrick	100 per overtrick
Redoubled	400 per overtrick	200 per overtrick

Penalties

Undoubled	100 per undertrick	50 per undertrick
Doubled	200 for the first undertrick	100 for the first undertrick
	300 for each trick after that	200 for each trick after that

| Redoubled | 400 for the first undertrick | 200 for the first undertrick |
| | 600 for each trick after that | 400 for each trick after that |

Adding up the Score

Part-Game	Trick Score + Part-Game Bonus
Game	Trick Score + Game Bonus
Small Slam	Trick Score + Game Bonus + Small Slam Bonus
Grand Slam	Trick Score + Game Bonus + Grand Slam Bonus
Doubled or Redoubled Contract	Doubled (Redoubled) Trick Score + appropriate Bonus(es) + Insult Bonus (50 points)

Overtricks, if there are any, are added to the appropriate score above.

Examples:

1) Six Heart Contract, Not Vulnerable. Declarer takes all 13 tricks.

Trick Score	180
Not Vulnerable Game Bonus	300
Not Vulnerable Small Slam Bonus	500
Overtrick Bonus	+ 30
Total Score	1010

2) Seven Club Contract, Vulnerable. Declarer takes all 13 tricks.

Trick Score	140
Vulnerable Game Bonus	500
Vulnerable Grand Slam Bonus	+1500
Total Score	2140

3) Two Club Contract, Doubled, Not Vulnerable. Declarer takes 9 tricks.

Doubled Trick Score	80
Part-Game Bonus	50
Insult Bonus	50
Doubled Overtrick, Not Vulnerable	+ 100
Total Score	280

4) One No Trump Contract, Redoubled, Vulnerable. Declarer takes 5 tricks.

First Redoubled Undertrick, Vulnerable	400
Additional Redoubled Undertrick	+ 600
Total Score	1000

Vulnerability

First Deal of a Round	Neither Side Vulnerable
Second Deal of a Round	Dealer's Side Vulnerable
Third Deal of a Round	Dealer's Side Vulnerable
Fourth (final) deal of a Round	Both Sides Vulnerable